REAL QUESTIONS, REAL ANSWERS ABOUT SEX

DR. LOUIS & MELISSA McBURNEY

REAL QUESTIONS, REAL ANSWERS ABOUT SEX

THE COMPLETE GUIDE TO INTIMACY AS GOD INTENDED

ZONDERVAN™

GRAND RAPIDS, MICHIGAN 49530 USA

ZONDERVAN™

Real Questions, Real Answers about Sex
Copyright © 2005 by Christianity Today International

Requests for information should be addressed to:
Zondervan, *Grand Rapids, Michigan 49530*

Library of Congress Cataloging-in-Publication Data

McBurney, Louis.
    Real questions, real answers about sex: the complete guide to intimacy as God
intended / Louis and Melissa McBurney.
      p. cm.
    Includes bibliographical references and index.
    ISBN 0-310-25658-5 (softcover)
    1. Sex instruction.   2. Sex in marriage.   3. Sex—Religious aspects—Christianity.
4. Sex in marriage—Religious aspects—Christianity.   I. McBurney, Melissa.   II. Title.
HQ31.M134 2005
306.7'08827—dc22

2004018196

Interior design by Michelle Espinoza

Printed in the United States of America

04 05 06 07 08 09 10 /❖ DCI/ 10 9 8 7 6 5 4 3 2 1

To Red and Minnie, Robert and Louise.
You taught us love and commitment. We miss you.

TABLE OF CONTENTS

PART ONE: SEX GOD'S WAY

PART TWO: PREPARING FOR THE FIRST TIME

◦ PART THREE: SEX AND OUR BODIES ◦

⤳ PART FOUR: ⤳
MAKING MARITAL ADJUSTMENTS

to Ejaculate? • Failure to Reach Vaginal Orgasm • Why Doesn't She Have Vaginal Orgasms? • Four Ways to Approach a Problem with Sex • How to Confront a Problem • Talk about It

12. SEX AND HEALTH: When the Problem Is Physical 170

Physical Turnoffs to Sex • Is He Too Disabled to Make Love? • Why Won't He Wash First? • Lynn and Bart: PMS Killed Their Sex Life • Why His Equipment Fails • Wesley and Jan: When Erections Fail • Five Ways to Handle Impotence • Will Antiseizure Medication Forever Dim Desire? • Should I Get Off Prozac? • When the System Fails • How Viagra Works • Weight Issues • Talk about It • Am I Gaining Weight to Avoid Love? • Why Won't She Lose Weight? • How Can I Love Him When He's Fat?

PART FIVE: SEX AND THE REST OF LIFE

13. SEX AND OTHERS: The Influence of Family 187
and Friends on Lovemaking

Talk about It • Bobbie's Parent Tapes • Messages in the Womb • How Parents Model Sex • What Parents Expect • Our Conflicting Values • Talk about It • Scrambled Signals from Childhood • Two Ways to Decode Distortions • In-Law Interference • The Mark of Siblings • Friends and Your Sex Life • Can Grief Shut Down Sex? • A Guide for Whom to Confide In • Why Don't I Want Him on Top of Me? • Talk about It

14. SEX AND RAISING CHILDREN: 200
Loving with Interruptions

Three Reasons to Have Kids • How Can We Have Kids If He Never Wants Sex? • Why Hasn't He Touched Me Since the Miscarriage? • The Oops Pregnancy • What Should We Do about Infertility? • Her Changing Body: Is She Still Sexy? • Can We Have Sex during Pregnancy? • After the Baby Comes: A Time to Adjust • Aren't Moms Desirable? • How Can I Feel Sexy with Stretch Marks? • Preschoolers, Fatigue, and Lovemaking • Surviving Adolescence • Should We Hide Lovemaking from the Kids? • Has Being a Mom Killed My Desire? • Talk about It • Nudity in the Home • Should the Kids See Us Naked? • Will I Ever Have Enough Energy for Sex? • How Can We Make Love without Feeling Rushed?

PART SIX: SEXUAL SINS AND SECRETS

ILLUSTRATIONS

Acknowledgments

In 1995, we began writing "Real Sex" columns for *Marriage Partnership*, a publication of Christianity Today International, to respond to readers' questions about sex issues. We thank the editors who guided us through that eye-opening experience: Annette LaPlaca, Elizabeth Newenhuyse, Caryn Rivadeneira, Ginger Kolbaba, Kevin Miller, and Ron Lee.

In 2002, we met with Phyllis Ten Elshof, editor of CTI Resources. She proposed a book that would build on the work we had done in "Real Sex" columns. *Real Questions, Real Answers about Sex* is the result of that endeavor. We thank Phyllis for her encouragement, creativity, and hard work.

Thanks also to our editors at Zondervan who saw the potential in this book and pushed it to completion: Cindy Lambert, Lori Vanden Bosch, and Dirk Buursma.

We're also grateful for the teaching and training we received at Baylor Medical College, at the psychiatric section of Mayo Clinic, from numerous workshop leaders at professional conferences, as well as for the advice from our friends Joe McIlhaney and Alan Nelson. We also thank thousands of clients who came to Marble Retreat, where we've worked as therapists for the past thirty years. They have contributed to the illustrations we've used in this book. However, each story represents the real-life experiences of hundreds of retreat guests so that individual identities are protected.

Finally, we thank the board of directors, staff, and donors of Marble Retreat who have worked with us in this rewarding ministry.

A Letter from the Editor of *Marriage Partnership*

Dear Reader,

I remember when I first met Dr. Louis McBurney. I was impressed by how easy it was to talk to this Mayo Clinic–trained psychiatrist. His laid-back nature put me right at ease. He was wise, godly, and trustworthy. *What a great combination for someone writing about sex*, I thought.

But what really struck me was when Dr. McBurney said, "My wife, Melissa, and I love to read those questions you and your staff create for us to answer." That took me by surprise—since the McBurneys have been our "Real Sex" columnists for almost ten years. I naturally assumed they knew the truth.

"You think we make up those questions?" I asked him.

"Don't you?"

"You give us way too much credit," I said. "No, those are real questions from real people!"

The lines around Louis's eyes shifted ever so slightly. He was putting me on!

Marriage Partnership magazine receives hundreds of letters each week from married Christian men and women who desperately want to know the truth about sex but have no place to go for answers. Let's face it, being Christian doesn't mean we automatically know everything about sex once we say, "I do." We're not going to hear answers to our questions about sex from the pulpit (when was the last time you heard a sermon on premature ejaculation or a low libido?). Many times we can't comfortably approach a family member with our questions either ("Mom, when you were too tired for sex with Dad, what did you do?") or even a friend ("Sarah, you say all your husband ever thinks about is sex—but my husband is exactly the opposite! Do you have any advice?").

Where can a Christian couple go for wisdom and help? The secular media? Hollywood? They can hardly provide you with the right role models on which to base your sexual knowledge.

But readers can and do come to *Marriage Partnership* with any question, knowing they will be treated with respect. Most important, they will receive biblically based, truthful answers to their questions.

Our "Real Sex" columns, from which we took questions for this book, ranks consistently as one of our readers' top picks. Much of that has to do with the McBurneys.

Louis and Melissa enjoy life and each other. They are genuine, honest, and incredibly insightful. If you have a question, they have an answer—and it's one you can trust. They've helped thousands of couples through *Marriage Partnership* and also through Marble Retreat, an organization they founded in 1974 to help ministry couples who are in crisis.

Throughout the pages of this book, I think you'll find the answers you need to your real-life questions. May you be blessed in this journey to discover the intimacy God intended for you and your mate.

Ginger Kolbaba, managing editor,
Marriage Partnership (www.marriagepartnership.com)

FOREWORD

"Penis." "Vagina." "Penis." "Vagina." I (Les) couldn't believe these words were coming out of my mouth. One after the other, like an old-fashioned record stuck in one place. "Penis." "Vagina." I just kept saying them. Actually, I was being instructed to say them by a no-nonsense graduate professor while I was standing before a group of twenty Ph.D. students, all of whom were strangers. It was the first day of a course on human sexuality. With no introduction, the professor wrote her name on the board, turned to the class of psychologists-in-training, and said, "Sexuality makes most people uncomfortable, and you can't be a good psychologist if you get nervous talking about sex. It's time to get real."

With those words, I could sense every student squirming uncomfortably, like sixth-graders in a sex-education class. "Dr. Parrott, let's start with you," she said looking at her class roster. *Start with me and do what?* I wondered. *Anybody but me! Why start with me?* I wanted to run from the room, or crawl under my chair at the very least. I wanted to escape. "Come to the front of the class," she said. My heart began to race, my face turned red, and beads of sweat instantly formed on my forehead.

"How are you feeling?" the professor asked.

"Fine," I stuttered. "Just fine, thanks."

"Good," she said while looking at the other students. "That's very good. What I want you to do is maintain eye contact with Dr. Stewart over here and say the words *penis* and *vagina*."

There was nervous laughter and an air of disbelief throughout the classroom. Surely this was a joke, we all thought. But it wasn't. One by one, the professor had every student stand before the group and make eye contact with each individual in the room while saying (apparently) her two favorite words. What a relief to be first and get it over with. After my turn, I went back to my seat, mopped the sweat from my brow, and tried to recuperate while every other student endured the same uncomfortable exercise.

The whole thing took more than thirty minutes. And looking back on it (as I recounted in our book *Relationships*), the time was actually well spent. The professor was right: If you're going to be a good psychotherapist, you've got to get over the normal anxiety we humans have when it comes to talking frankly about sex. You've got to get real.

And that's exactly what Dr. Louis and Melissa McBurney do in this straightforward book. I doubt either of them had to endure such a strange classroom exercise, but they certainly learned the same lesson long ago. The McBurneys never shy away from the truth. They don't skirt uncomfortable issues. They don't tiptoe on the truth. They calmly cut to the bone and say it like it is. That's why we were thrilled to learn they were writing this book. We have admired the McBurneys' work, as well as their relationship, for years. Tucked away in their corner of Colorado, they've done more good for more couples across North America than anyone will ever know. Having heard it all and seen it all, they write this book from atop a literal mountain of experience. Not only are they clinically astute and biblically sound, however, Louis and Melissa are uncommonly down-to-earth.

After years of working with countless couples and writing memorable columns and penetrating articles on the subject of sex, it's high time the McBurneys dispensed their expert knowledge in an easy-to-use guide like this. What a resource! The title says it perfectly: *Real Questions, Real Answers about Sex*. How refreshing to hear specialists peel away the cloudy clichés and smoky gibber-jabber to reveal honest answers to candid questions. This book is a treasure trove for everyone—regardless of comfort level or knowledge base—who is interested in knowing the honest-to-goodness truth about sex.

Drs. Les and Leslie Parrott,
Seattle Pacific University, authors of *Love Talk*

PART ONE:
SEX GOD'S WAY

GET REAL:

What We Need to Know about Sex

In our sexually explicit society, it seems almost inconceivable that anyone could be uninformed about sex. Yet we run into that problem all the time.

In the thousand-plus couples we've counseled in the past twenty-five years at Marble Retreat in Marble, Colorado, we have found a disturbing number of struggles in the area of sexuality. Indeed, 46 percent of those surveyed in our work indicated problems with sex.

Most married adults have a basic knowledge of the anatomy and physiology of the reproductive system, but that's about as far as their knowledge goes. Wives and husbands know they react differently to sexual drive and stimulation and that their sex drives vary, but they don't understand the intricacies of their two very different systems.

For example, most women don't realize testosterone creates a physiological drive in their husbands that demands expression every few days. Without that kind of hormonal insistence, women have less physical drive for sexual release. Rather, what they crave is the relational closeness that leads to sexual intimacy.

Likewise, many husbands assume their wives will get aroused and reach climax as quickly as they do. But most women are only in the early arousal stage when their husbands achieve orgasm. So a wife feels cheated when her husband falls asleep just when she's getting interested. And a husband feels inadequate as a lover because he has failed to bring his wife to orgasm.

Lack of knowledge about technique is only one kind of ignorance.

Another has to do with expectations. Where did you get your ideas about a "normal" sex life? Probably by picking it up here and there—from movies, romance novels, a college roommate, or a sex manual. But did you ever talk about those expectations, ideas, and beliefs with your spouse?

For many couples, sexual expression has narrow boundaries. They think intercourse should take place only in bed, in the dark, under a sheet. A couple can certainly find intense pleasure and oneness with this routine, but a few variations could substantially improve the experience for a lifetime.

That's what we'd like to do for you in this book—take the covers off the whole subject of sex. We'll explore different areas of sexuality together, answer questions, and help you and your spouse move toward a healthier, more robust appreciation for each other as sexual beings created to pleasure and enjoy each other.

MARY AND BILL: WHAT THEY WISH THEY'D KNOWN

Mary and Bill had been married for twenty-one years. They were leaders in church staff positions, and their moral principles were beyond reproach. They were committed to fidelity.

The problem was that Mary had never experienced an orgasm. She had sex with her husband only because it was her duty. Bill had always been troubled by his wife's lack of enthusiasm in lovemaking, but he had no idea she had never had an orgasm.

During counseling, we explored this couple's sexual history. Bill and Mary were astonished by the discoveries they began to make about each other. Bill found that Mary secretly wondered what was missing in their lovemaking and was eager to explore her own sexual responses. Mary learned that Bill was not an oversexed pervert; rather, he had a normal male libido and normal male ignorance about a female's sexual needs.

For years, fearfulness and embarrassment had kept this couple from talking openly about sex. Once they opened up, guilt and disappointment gave way to hope—and a sense of fun—about how this part of their relationship could be improved.

WHY WE NEED SEX

For physical relief. It all starts in the body juices! Our hormones affect the sexual drive center in our brains. That center stimulates the production of seminal fluid, vaginal and penile secretions, and genital pheromones. These are the basic ingredients of the mating instinct that drives procreation. In men, the production and accumulation of seminal fluid demands release through ejaculation. This relief of vague pelvic pressure *will* occur—whether through nocturnal emissions, masturbation, or intercourse.

Some women experience heaviness deep in their pelvis when they are in need of sexual release. It feels something like the onset of a period, but not quite. They aren't always aware of the connection between that sensation and sexual need. More often, women are driven by the need for sexual intimacy. We've heard some wives express it this way: "I wasn't aware that I needed sexual release, but after my orgasm I sensed a wonderful peace and calm."

For true bonding. Sexual intercourse is so much more than coupling. We like to think of this union in the same way that Paul did in his letter to the Ephesians. He said that becoming one flesh in sexual intercourse is a profound mystery—like the spiritual union of Christ and the church.

WHAT'S SO GREAT ABOUT SEX?

The union of man and woman in sex is profoundly beautiful because it offers the following:

A way out of isolation. No other experience allows us to

dissolve individual walls and blend with another person so completely. We join with each other not only physically but also with the kind of erotic exhaustion that brings us to collapse in each other's embrace.

True intimacy. Within a faithful marriage, sex offers the gratification of being in a unique relationship. Within this relationship, sexual intimacy is absolutely private. No one else can be joined with us when we are so vulnerable. The way we look, the way we feel, the smells of our bodies, the rhythm of our pelvic thrusts—all are private and reserved only for us.

Deep affirmation. We can be praised for our appearance. We can be complimented on our clothes. We can be thrilled when someone flirts with us. But only my marriage partner sees me naked and vulnerable in asking for sexual union. There's nothing quite like hearing "You're a fantastic lover" to affirm one's adequacy as a sexual person.

Sex in a Relationship

Great sex doesn't just happen. It begins with a good relationship. The important elements in any relationship include:

- Courtesy
- Mutual respect
- Emotional sensitivity
- Knowing how and when to apologize
- Accepting differences
- Resolving conflict

Q & A

Are There Rules for Married Sex?

Is there a uniquely Christian way to make love? I mean, should married Christian couples limit their sexual expression based on certain biblical rules? If so, what are those rules? Are they relationship rules or physical rules—or both?

Louis: Lovemaking between a Christian married couple should be the most passionate, erotic, playful, and satisfying expression of sexuality known to humankind. Our sexuality is a powerful gift of the Creator. We're free in Christ to delight in our physical being. When we follow God's guidelines about relational faithfulness, loving-kindness, and mutual submissiveness, the resulting sex is free from guilt and doubt.

So is there a Christian way to make love? Yes, but only in the sense of showing mutual respect for each other and physically expressing the desire to celebrate the oneness of marriage. In my opinion, the Bible contains no specific rules or guidelines for lovemaking between husband and wife. I've heard interpretations of Song of Songs that suggest positions for intercourse, the delights of oral sex, and the proper use of perfumes. However, I personally see those poetic passages not as instructions but as expressions of erotic images reflecting God's approval of marital sex.

WHAT'S OK AND WHAT'S NOT

Wondering about oral sex, initiation of sexual activity, positions for intercourse, and mutual masturbation? We find no scriptural injunction against any of these sexual behaviors.

Paul's admonition in 1 Corinthians not to withhold sex except by mutual consent provides some guidance. It acknowledges the legitimacy of sexual desire yet reinforces the principle that all sexual practices within marriage should be agreeable to both husband and wife.

When it comes to sex, most married Christians do what works for them. If they have discovered something that brings satisfaction, pleasure, closeness, and climax, they most likely will continue that practice. However, some are plagued with guilt because they wonder if what they're doing is sinful.

Wouldn't it be nice to have a list of sexual practices categorized as either sinful or OK? Is there such a list? Would everyone agree with the list? Is there a solution to this dilemma?

We'd love to offer something that could forever settle niggling doubts about sexual practices. But that's not possible. Different communities of Christians have different understandings about sexual practices that are based on a few general biblical principles. No list would be acceptable to all Christians. Still, we do want to provide some guidelines that will help you enjoy the gift of your sexuality to the fullest—which is what we believe God wants for each of his children. So read on.

THE BIBLE ON SEX

We doubt that God is surprised by the intensity of our sexual desire. Enjoying sex with passion and pleasure seems to fit with his creative nature. However, God's Word does establish some boundaries to protect and enhance the maximum enjoyment of sex.

We think these prohibitions are like the safety rules we give a child along with a new bicycle to help him enjoy the ride without being run over by a car. The rules allow us to enjoy sex without being wrecked by unsafe or unwise practices.

WHAT SCRIPTURE FORBIDS

Adultery—having sex with someone other than your spouse. In the Sermon on the Mount, Jesus deepens the importance of marital faithfulness by extending the concept of infidelity to include lustful thoughts as well as the act of intercourse. Purifying our minds and hearts is an important principle for safeguarding the delights of intimacy.

Fornication—premarital sexual intercourse. Though most people in our culture accept fornication as normal and irresistible, the Bible forbids it—and rightly so. We have seen the pain and suffering experienced by many couples who indulged in early promiscuity. The sexual freedom of our time isn't free; it carries some pretty heavy costs.

Bestiality—sexual relations with animals. (See Leviticus 18:23.)

Incest—sexual relations with a close relative, such as one's mother, sister, granddaughter, aunt, daughter-in-law, wife's sister, etc. (See Leviticus 18:6–18.)

Homosexuality—sexual relations with a person of the same gender. (See Leviticus 18:22; Romans 1:21–32; 1 Corinthians 6:12–20; 1 Thessalonians 4:1–8.)

THE UNMENTIONABLES

Many sexual practices for married couples are not mentioned at all in Scripture. We can find no explicit reference, for example, to Internet pornography, vibrators, or sexually explicit videos. Since we aren't likely to find Scripture that directly addresses those practices, the best we can do is apply the principles God has given us to the cultural setting we're living in. Here's what we find:

The urges for these practices are not new. Humans are not much different today than we've been since creation. We have the same hormones, the same capacity for lust and fantasy, and the same relational needs that drive men and women to seek sexual pleasure and intimacy. As Ecclesiastes 1:9 says, "There is nothing new under the sun."

They are highly addictive. Achieving sexual release within the marriage relationship can be replaced with various stimuli that are essentially fantasy based. We have seen men deeply hooked on Internet pornography or cybersex relationships. People who indulge in them become compulsively driven toward pornographic stimulation and masturbatory release of sexual tension. We have seen women equally hooked on romance novels or chat rooms for sexual release. All of these toys bypass the relational dimension of sexuality.

They may interfere with real sex. Someone who is addicted to sex toys such as vibrators or pornography participates in marital sex, if at all, only mechanically. Even then, the marital act is marred by fantasies that provide sexual stimulation. That robs marriage of the most crucial part of intimacy—the blend of relational and sexual connectedness.

They can destroy relationships. Pornographic films, photography, or Internet sites can provide sexual excitement and arousal, but that form of stimulation will eventually erode a couple's enjoyment of each other. Pornographic images may also create a basic sense of dissatisfaction with one's spouse, since most people don't look as beautiful or sexy as porn actors and models. The pornography industry is based on illusions, and those lies can lead to sexual dissatisfaction as well as the death of your relationship.

God wants you to have a faithful marital relationship that includes intimate sex. So as you develop your sexual relationship, you can count on God's help to move together in the direction he desires toward increased oneness. If your sexual desire is driven by selfishness or other sin, however, you're on your own. God isn't going to help you move in the wrong direction.

EIGHT THINGS THE BIBLE STRESSES

The Bible is explicit about our sexuality. Yes, there are restrictions, but there are also abundant references to the delights and enjoyment of sexual union. Some areas it stresses:

Male-female union. God created our sexual differences and blessed our desire to be one with a member of the opposite gender. Genesis 1:27–28 tells us, "So God created man in his own image, in the image of God he created him; male and female he created them. God blessed them and said to them, 'Be fruitful and increase in number.'"

Procreation within marriage. The Bible is serious about sex within marriage. Genesis 2:24 says, "For this reason a man will leave his father and mother and be united to his wife, and they will become one flesh." The importance of propagation through family is stressed in genealogy passages such as Genesis 5; Genesis 12:1–3; Genesis 21:1–5; Matthew 1:1–17; and Luke 3:23–38. Jesus reinforced the principle of "becoming one flesh" and added that what God has joined together, no man (or woman) should separate.

Romance. Some of the best love stories of all time are in the Bible: Abraham and Sarah, Isaac and Rebekah, Jacob and Rachel, Boaz and Ruth. Song of Songs is especially vivid in describing the delights of sexual love.

Boundaries. Moses recorded God's guidelines for sex in commands such as "You shall not commit adultery" (Exodus 20:14). Levitical laws (Leviticus 18–20) were more explicit: Do not have sexual relations with your mother, sister, son's daughter, father's sister, brother's wife, and so on. Jesus saved from death the woman who was caught in adultery, but he told her to sin no more. In Matthew 5:28, he went to the heart of adultery, saying, "Anyone who looks at a woman lustfully has already committed adultery with her in his heart." The point is, if we step outside the bounds of marital faithfulness in our sexual thoughts, fantasies, or behavior, we open ourselves to relational, physical, and spiritual damage.

Dangers. The Bible is explicit about the perils of sex outside of marriage. Proverbs 5:3–5 warns, "The lips of an adulteress drip honey, and her speech is smoother than oil; but in the end she is bitter as gall, sharp as a double-edged sword. Her feet go down to death; her steps lead straight to the grave." Proverbs 6:27–29 restates the caution about sexual infidelity, adding: "Can a man scoop fire into his lap without his clothes being burned? . . . So is he who sleeps with another man's wife; no one who touches her will go unpunished." In his letter to Roman Christians, Paul names specific sexual sins (sexual impurity, shameful lusts, unnatural relations), all of which erode one's relationship with others and our Creator God.

Pleasure. Song of Songs is devoted to the pleasure of lovemaking. Consider this from verses 10 and 11 of chapter 4: "How much more pleasing is your love than wine, and the fragrance of your perfume than any spice! Your lips drop sweetness as the honeycomb, my bride; milk and honey are under your tongue."

A profound mystery. Proverbs 30:18 has an intriguing note on this aspect of sex: "There are three things that are too amazing for me, four that I do not understand: the way of an eagle in the sky, the way of a snake on a rock, the way of a ship on the high seas, and the way of a man with a maiden."

A spiritual picture. Paul also talks about the sexual union as a profound mystery, and adds that it is a picture of Christ's spiritual union with his church. In Ephesians 5:31–32 Paul wrote, "'A man will leave his father and mother and be united to his wife, and the two will become one flesh.' This is a profound mystery—but I am talking about Christ and the church."

SIX INGREDIENTS OF LASTING INTIMACY

Commitment. Sexual pleasure is most satisfying within the context of a long-term, committed relationship. Knowing another person on an intimate level enhances the physical pleasure of sexual stimulation. Of course, sexual pleasure can occur outside of traditional marriage, but experience shows that it is not as likely to be maintained over time.

Maturity through life changes. Couples in long-term marriages adapt as they confront various life changes. Some of these stages, such as pregnancy, childbirth, midlife transition, and aging, are predictable. Others such as illness, loss, and economic pressures may blindside us. Most of these events affect sexual drive or response. However, even problems such as erectile dysfunction or chronic illness can provide opportunities for committed couples to discover ways to pleasure each other besides intercourse. Relationships that are held together primarily by sexual gratification are less likely to achieve this kind of intimacy.

Relationship. Arousal, genital union, and orgasm can be achieved with very little relational encounter. However, the most likely results of such brief physical encounters are mistrust, fear of failure, and disappointment. It takes time in a committed relationship to master skills for intimacy. Rather than allowing life's stresses to diminish physical pleasure and increase tension, a couple can discover the joy of overcoming barriers. Husband and wife can learn how to express negative feelings and settle conflict in a way that restores sexual desire and fulfillment. Doing both relational and sexual work provides long-term satisfaction and a legacy for generations.

Trust. Women tend to be modest about their bodies, while men tend to be modest about their souls. Men may struggle to reveal thoughts and feelings. Add to that the realization that men need visual stimulation for sex and women need emotional stimulation for sex, and understand why there can be difficulty. The common denominator in most impasses is fear. Men fear inadequacy, and women fear rejection. Only within an atmosphere of acceptance, love, and trust can fears be relieved.

Safety. The consequences of ignoring boundaries for sexual expression surround us: HIV, syphilis, gonorrhea, genital warts, hepatitis, herpes, and dozens of other sexually transmitted diseases. Believing the "safe sex" myth is pure foolishness. By contrast, as Proverbs 18:22 suggests, "He who finds a wife finds what is good and receives favor from the Lord."

Solid sexual identity. Sex is a deep part of our entire being, not just a reproductive function. We are created male and female with differences written in every molecule of our DNA. Becoming comfortable with one's maleness makes a man a better son, husband, lover, and father. Embracing one's femaleness empowers a woman to celebrate being daughter, wife, lover, and mother. It's a lovely dance of distinctions.

PART TWO:
PREPARING FOR
THE FIRST TIME

2

Your Sexual History:

How Much Do You Share?

Many couples come to marriage today as nonvirgins. Whether their virginity was stolen through abuse or date rape, lost as a rite of passage in our permissive culture, or given away in a passionate romance, the effect can be disastrous. Some problems that can occur:

Unrealistic memories of the past. If your experience with a previous partner was pleasurable, you may have idealized memories of it. Often first loves were fueled by adventure, romance, and the thrill of stepping over the edge. They were free from the stresses of bills and babies and other aspects of marital relationships.

Memories of that time make great fantasies, but that's all they are. Furthermore, they're dangerous to replay. Your marriage partner is doomed to fail if expected to compete with old romance tapes. You can celebrate the warm excitement of a first love, but then let it go. Remind yourself that the person of that time is probably very different today, largely due to age, maturity, and reality. Furthermore, lots of red-hot romances—even yours—would have cooled off in the stress of everyday relationship.

On the other hand, if your premarital experience was negative—you suffered the horror of a date rape or sexual abuse—those memories may have forced you to build barriers to all sex. Even if the painful experience was not forced, pain or disgust may rob you of marital delights.

Don't despair. Ask the Lord for help in cleansing those painful pictures from your mind. Only he can offer you peace in this. You and your spouse can also begin building positive new memories together.

Jealousy. Jealousy—even of a partner prior to marriage—is a normal response to any threat to the exclusive bond of marriage. But it can drive a wedge between a husband and wife that's totally out of proportion to the actual breach of commitment.

In the case of premarital sex, you and your mate probably hadn't yet made a commitment to each other. You might not even know the person he or she was involved with. Still the idea that your mate gave up his or her virginity to another may prompt painful images and jealousy.

Fear. After learning that your spouse had sex with someone prior to you, you may fear that the other person was better at lovemaking. You may fear that you still aren't good enough to keep your partner faithful within marriage.

Do not hold on to fear. Tell your spouse about the struggle you're having with fearful thoughts. Ask for reassurance that he or she is committed to you and your exclusive relationship.

Guilt. Consider how your own premarital sexual relations have affected your self-concept and self-acceptance. Very frequently guilt and self-loathing dominate the picture. Your sin does not disqualify you from grace. The formula is simple: confess your sins, repent of them, and choose not to continue in your sin. Then ask forgiveness from God, from others, and from yourself. Once that's done, you need to look at yourself through God's eyes. The Bible says that God remembers your sin no more. So you too need to put your sin behind you.

Change. God's redemptive grace empowers you to change your behavior. People who have been sexually promiscuous often believe the sexual act is the closest they'll ever come to being loved. How sad. Having intercourse is only a part of real love. You deserve more than a quick high. You were made for lifelong intimacy. God designed sex to be like the spiritual union we have with God through Christ. Every aspect of our being gets included: our emotions, our spirits, our intellect, our dreams, our pain, our sorrow, and our bodies.

WHAT TO SAY ABOUT THE PAST

John and Vicki decided on their honeymoon that they wanted their relationship to be built on total honesty. That included complete descriptions of their premarital sexual experiences. Each was reasonably sure the other was not a virgin, so neither was surprised to learn that each had had two previous sexual partners.

After sharing their stories, John and Vicki, who had gone to college together, recognized each other's former lovers. Images and questions began to haunt them. John had a hard time with picturing Vicki engaging in oral sex with one of his fraternity brothers. He began resenting Vicki for doing that.

In contrast, Sue and Matt *never* asked each other about premarital relationships. Both assumed each had not been sexually intimate before the wedding. Years later, Matt discovered by accident that Sue had had a baby out of wedlock when she was age sixteen. The baby had been placed for adoption years before Sue and Matt began dating.

Neither couple handled their sexual pasts well. John and Vicki told each other too much; Matt and Sue shared too little. Both couples struggled to rebuild trust in their marriage. But things could have been different.

When considering what to tell each other, ask yourself:

What's the point? You may want total honesty with your spouse. That may be a compelling reason to reveal any secrets you have. But if you're baring your soul in retaliation for some hurt you've experienced or to ease your guilt or to get it off your chest, tell a friend or counselor instead of your spouse or spouse-to-be. While we don't have a hard-and-fast rule for couples about what to share about premarital relationships, we do advise against going into detail about what happened.

Does your loved one want to know? Many husbands and wives don't want to know more than they already do. Your spouse may know about your past, accept you anyway, and see no value in hearing details. Details only create negative images that put up a barrier between the two of you. Discuss whether it's important to each of you to have complete disclosure.

Is this something your mate must know? If you have a sexually transmitted disease, you must let your prospective mate know about it. It is unfair to expose anyone to a communicable disease without warning him or her of the danger. If you're deeply in love, it may be a problem you choose to fight together. That should be an informed decision, though, not a surprising discovery after the honeymoon.

Most sexually transmitted diseases can be effectively treated or at least controlled, but only if they're diagnosed. These include gonorrhea, syphilis, chlamydia, human papillomavirus, lymphogranuloma venereum, granuloma inguinale, and chancroid. Others may be controlled symptomatically, but cannot be cured (hepatitis B and genital herpes), and some are resistant to known treatment (HIV/AIDS).

Did that list scare you? It should. Many of these infections are epidemic in sexually promiscuous individuals—meaning anyone who has had more than one partner. Condoms and spermicides give some protection, but they are not totally effective.

If you or your marriage partner has symptoms (discharge from genital areas, itching, sores, warts, swelling, redness, or pain), see a doctor immediately. In most cases, if one of you is infected, the other will be too—even if you don't have symptoms. Both of you should be treated simultaneously so that you don't pass the organism back and forth. Some infections are painful

Talk about It

You spent months—even years—getting to know each other. But how much do you really know about each other's past? What have you said to each other about past relationships? In what ways was that information helpful? In what ways was it hurtful? What would you still like to know? What must you know? What boundaries could you set to prevent past relationships from intruding on your marriage?

or irritating. Some cause infertility, and several can cause death (HPV, syphilis, hepatitis, and HIV).

Q & A

What about Women from the Past?

I know my husband was sexually intimate with other women before we married. At first it didn't bother me because he's now a Christian, he's been forgiven, and he chose to marry me. However, I still feel inadequate and inferior to these other women. I'm afraid he may compare me to them—even if he doesn't mean to. How can I not allow this to affect our sex life?

Our society tells us that being sexually experienced will enhance marriage. Your question highlights one of the reasons why that notion isn't true. Nevertheless, there you are, haunted by the ghosts of your mate's former sexual partners. So let's turn on some lights and try to dispel the goblins.

Here are some things to consider:

You have no way of controlling your mate's thought life. You've said your husband has changed as a Christian. We assume

also that he's tried to reassure you about his former girlfriends. What may enter his mind from time to time is something that only he can control—with God's help.

Both of you must erase tapes. All of life's experiences become encoded into our memory and may be triggered into consciousness. We can choose to replay the old tapes or let them go. It's just as important for you to erase your tapes about your husband's former girlfriends as it is for him to erase those memories. When images of those women, whether real or imagined, slip into your thinking, toss them out. Only you can control your doubts and fears.

You're not competing with the past. You're the only wife your husband has. There's no reason for you to feel inferior or inadequate to any of his former girlfriends. You and your husband should get on with enjoying the sexual intimacy that's uniquely and exclusively yours.

Q & A

How Can I Forgive Myself?

When I was single, I had sex with a number of people. Now I'm a

Christian, and I want to give myself wholly to my wife. I'm tormented by knowing that I've already given myself away to others. What can I do?

The most remarkable thing about Christianity is the potential for redeeming what has been lost. God's redemption extends even to our sexuality—a perfect gift that frequently gets tarnished by our humanity. Here are some ways to appropriate the process of God's healing:

Seek and accept God's forgiveness. God created us with strong sexual desires, and he knows how easy it is for us to fall into sin. Still, sin brings consequences. The saddest cost of promiscuity is the devaluation of sexual intimacy. It's true that you've lost the innocence and mystery of sexual union with only one partner. However, the sin has been dealt with. The formula for healing is the same as for all other sin: confess, repent, ask God's forgiveness, and receive his grace. God does the rest, even to the point of cleansing your guilt.

Forgive yourself. When something reminds you of past sexual sin, remind yourself that your sin has been forgiven and forgotten.

Then think about the most delicious, ecstatic sexual experience you have had with your wife, and celebrate the healing God has given you.

Ask your wife to forgive you. She may already know about your promiscuity, but perhaps you have never seen it as a sin committed against her. If she doesn't know about the promiscuity, we advise you to carefully consider the impact of a confession. If you decide to talk about prior involvements, don't name your partners or give details. A simple confession of having been sexually active, then asking for forgiveness is sufficient. When those three areas of guilt and remorse are bathed in forgiveness, there is no reason why you can't celebrate the pleasurable mystery of sexual union in marriage.

Q & A

WHAT ABOUT OTHER SOUL TIES?

As a teenager, I once heard a Christian speaker warn against the dangers of premarital sex. He said intercourse creates a "soul tie" between two people. My husband and I have been married for eighteen months, and our sex life is OK. But I worry about the soul tie he created with his college girlfriend. He says his repentance removes that, but it's hard for me to believe he feels no connection with her. Why can't I stop thinking about this?

Louis: Premarital sex has many effects on individuals, but the depth of impact and strength of the experience over time varies considerably. The variables include: the intensity of the relationship, the length of the involvement, the morals of the individuals, the guilt or remorse experienced, what intervened in the romance, and the way the relationship ended. The idea of a soul tie would not apply in every relationship.

More important is the true soul tie that you and your husband have created. That will be strengthened by your accepting his word, dismissing your doubts, and deepen-

ing the trust you feel for him. Ask God to help you take your doubts captive and to focus on the oneness he's created for your marriage.

Melissa: Many couples who come to us for counseling had premarital sex, either with each other or with another partner. The primary result is usually lack of trust. One or the other spouse brings up the issue, especially during arguments.

Even if the past behavior was painful, it's foolish to allow that pain to carry over into your marriage. Getting past that pain into forgiveness is a choice well worth making—and it is a choice.

You don't like the feelings that go with your lack of trust. Your husband (or wife) doesn't like your accusations. Your solution seems simple: Forget the past and move toward oneness and a great marriage.

3

FIRST ENCOUNTER:
Expectations and Preparations

We're convinced after counseling more than a thousand couples that waiting for sex till marriage is the least complicated route to sexual initiation. The notion that having sex early, often, and with many partners offers important experience has often resulted in disappointment, disease, and disaster. That doesn't have to be a part of one's sexual history.

If you lost your virginity before marriage, do some damage control now and redefine your boundaries. If you were sexually promiscuous prior to marriage, you have already discovered how each experience with a new partner becomes less meaningful. Don't rob yourself of deep sexual intimacy.

If you are a virgin, congratulations. You have the opportunity to celebrate the richness of a committed monogamous relationship.

YOUR ATTITUDES ABOUT SEX

Your attitudes about sex began when you were an infant. You got signals with every diaper change as you were uncovered, wiped, dried, and wrapped. You felt a warm touch and heard happy sounds, or you felt rejection as someone groaned in disapproval.

Never mind that you didn't understand the words. You were already recording the impression that sexuality was either a delight or something disgusting. Such messages played back as you discovered the feelings you could generate as a toddler by touching your genital area. Even though touching your genitals as a three-year-old was as inevitable as learning to undress and run around naked, the feedback may have been shame.

Your earliest exposure to sexual stimulation with another person also affected you. Many five- and six-year-olds compare anatomy while playing house or doctor. Some more adventurous and observant children may even attempt the motions of intercourse. While such experiments are quite common with preschoolers and rarely leave emotional scars, sexual activity with adolescents or adults is very destructive. The effect of such abuse permanently links fear or shame with sex.

During adolescence, you may have experimented with masturbation. You also may have attempted to prove sexual prowess by heavy petting or premarital intercourse. Formal teaching about sexuality at home or in the classroom blended with locker-room talk or sleepover tales to set cultural norms for you.

Some teaching encourages sexuality; some does not. Many Christians were raised with such strong taboos about their sexuality that they concluded sex was sin. A friend of ours said she was so strongly urged to remain a virgin that she had to struggle for years to let herself be sexually playful with her husband.

MYTHS ABOUT SEX

People have all kinds of misconceptions about sex, many of which can be harmful to a couple about to be wed:

You'll know what to do by instinct. Our instincts about sex are self-focused urges to mate. Without

---

Talk about It

Take a stroll into your earliest impressions of sexuality. When did each of you first become aware of sex? When your body began changing in adolescence, were you comfortable with the changes, or did they make you feel uneasy? What helped you accept or reject the sexual part of you? In what way does your attitude toward sexuality affect lovemaking with each other?

mature efforts to change that into mutually satisfying lovemaking, instincts may fail miserably. There can be a lot of fumbling and groping, especially in newlyweds, which does little to foster intimacy. In a way, becoming effective lovers is like learning to waltz. Lovemaking takes some good instruction and lots of practice.

If you love each other, sex will automatically be great. Love isn't enough. What's also necessary is proper timing, good arousal, gentleness, honesty, relational closeness, a safe setting, elimination of fears, and physical relaxation. There's nothing automatic about those.

You don't have to be married to enjoy sex to the fullest. The key word here is *fullest.* One can certainly have an intense orgasm outside of wedlock, but something deeper happens in marital sex. Relational intimacy, mutual pleasuring, and the security of commitment moves sex beyond a physiological reflex to spiritual oneness.

Sex will be the best thing you've ever experienced. The first time you have sex may be a big disappointment. Orgasm is great, but many experiences in marriage rival

or surpass that. Just to suggest a few: the birth of a child, being reunited after an absence, seeing a child succeed at a task, surviving a tragic event together, having a deeply spiritual experience, or welcoming a grandchild. Sex gets better as each partner is more vulnerable, trusting, and appreciative of each other.

The more you know about sex, the more you'll want it. How much you want sex has more to do with the depth of love in your relationship than your knowledge of sex. When you have both an understanding of sex and a commitment to your spouse, desire will grow.

The more partners you have, the better you'll get at making love. You could also get more turned off. Having more partners can reduce the wonder of sex to a trivial physical act that's not much different from masturbation, except for the dangers and self-loathing involved.

It's best to find out if you're sexually compatible before committing to marriage. Just about any male and female can copulate. Real sexual compatibility is a response to a deepening relationship, not the prelude to it. Indeed, statistics show that couples who cohabit before marriage are more likely to divorce.

Five Reasons to Wait Until You're Married

To establish trust. Finding out that your spouse has had other sexual partners before you plants seeds of doubt and mistrust. (You may wonder, *If she was promiscuous as a teen, why would she be faithful now?*) Knowing that you've both waited makes sex a gift to each other. It allows you to learn lovemaking techniques together.

To build confidence. When marital conflicts arise, which they invariably do, a wife or husband might remember the former lovers of a spouse and feel inadequate. The erosion of self-confidence leads to feelings of sexual inadequacy. (*I wonder if I'm as good as the others?* you may ask yourself.) A couple isn't burdened with this problem if husband and wife have saved themselves for each other.

To stay grounded in reality. Sexual intimacy is energized by fantasy and lively expectations. When physical reality fails to live up to those dreams, disappointment can tap into idealized memories of a previous romance. For example, I floated home without touching the ground after my first kiss. If that ecstasy had been with some girl other than Melissa, I might still be fantasizing about being with that girl, especially when things aren't going smoothly with Melissa and me.

"I haven't gotten to that part yet!"

To stay loyal. The same can be said about surrendering your virginity. Through the rough spots of marriage, the memory of some other exciting sexual partner who first claimed your body could easily breed disappointment with your spouse and inspire longing for another partner.

To encourage intimacy. Marriage is a private bonding of two people. When that relationship is secure, being vulnerable with each other is easy. Only after we felt confident in each other did Melissa and I feel free to express our desires without fear. We still don't agree on all the nuances of sexual pleasures, but we're no longer afraid to discuss preferences with each other.

What Most Honeymooners Really Experience

We've come to think most honeymoons are anything but sweet. The bride is worn out and fearful of having sexual intercourse. The groom is so eager to consummate he can hardly wait.

The first night, both nervously undress and begin to discover each other. They soon realize how little they know about sexuality. She is frightened by his genitalia and large erect penis. He worries that he might not find her vaginal opening. They manage to have intercourse, but she hurts and he ejaculates prematurely.

That's one scenario. Another is that the bride and groom decide to unwind from the busyness and excitement of the wedding by toasting each other with champagne. Unfortunately, the old bubbly makes them a bit sleepy. It also dulls their sexual sensitivity. Both fall asleep before consummating the marriage.

What couples expect on a honeymoon are thrills, romance, and nonstop sex. The reality is far different. Here's what many—if not most—couples feel during the honeymoon:

Disappointment. The couple is having too much sex—or not enough.

Fear. Bride and groom are stymied by fear of intercourse, fear of failure, fear of pregnancy.

Regret. After all the excitement of the wedding, both bride and groom realize that marriage—and putting up with this person in every part of their life—is for real, not just some romantic fantasy.

Homesickness. The bride or groom has an overwhelming longing to bail out and go back to a place where things are familiar and comforting.

Discomfort. Bride or groom are disconcerted by unfamiliar surroundings, noise, bugs, car trouble, upset stomachs, headaches, interruptions, and fatigue.

HONEYMOON PLANNER

We'd like to suggest a more glorious honeymoon experience—more like the one you've fantasized about since adolescence. We envision a relaxed, fun wedding with no intertribal warfare, a reception glowing with the support and affection of friends and family, warm farewells, and a stress-free getaway. Next we'd see a smooth trip to a private spot that you've both always wanted to visit, where you'll enjoy days and nights of leisurely romance with no intrusions.

A honeymoon like that won't happen by accident. It takes serious planning. In preparing for the honeymoon, mark these on your to-do list:

Plan your first hours together. Now, be honest. You may be so impossibly in love that you'll say, "Whatever you want, dearest honey-bun." But doing that may set you up for a major fight, especially when your honey-bun fails to anticipate your secret desires and to magically fulfill your wildest dreams. Do not rely on guessing games. Talk honestly about what you'd like.

Decide where you'd like to go. A fishing or hunting trip to a mosquito-infested swamp may sound exciting to a guy, but most women wouldn't plan that kind of venue for a honeymoon. Likewise, most guys wouldn't be thrilled with days of shopping and nights at the ballet.

Where you go doesn't have to be exotic, but do consider the possibilities. The Internet offers countless options. However, website photos can be deceiving. If at all possible, check out the facilities in person. Evaluate what amenities and activities are available. Find out what restaurants are nearby.

A bride and groom may not like doing the same things. One may prefer not to go on a cruise because of potential seasickness. The other may not like the limited activities at a resort. Determining what you each want offers you the opportunity to learn the art of compromise. Make lists of places and activities that both of you like, then highlight the important ones.

By the time you make a choice, you should both be comfortable with it and looking forward to it. Even if your dream trip has to be delayed till later on, that's OK; it will give you something to look forward to. We spent our honeymoon at a relative's beach house and took our dream trip to San Francisco about eighteen months later. Both experiences were great.

Decide what you will do. Wedding events can be brutal. The more elaborate the wedding, the higher the stress. Considering all that frenzy, it's no wonder that many newlyweds are exhausted on the honeymoon. It's very important to plan rest for the first few days. That precaution may not be so crucial if you have a simple family wedding. Whichever you choose, plan your honeymoon accordingly. A quiet morning wedding offers the rest of the day for an unrushed journey into paradise.

Prepare yourselves sexually. Don't just assume that you and your mate will be fine "doing what comes naturally." You'll be much better off talking to and asking for some advice on sex from a wise person or couple prior to the honeymoon. However, choose your mentors wisely. Some doctors, counselors, and pastors will walk you through premarital counseling without ever dealing with sex. They may ask if you have any

"We've been so in touch with each other on our honeymoon . . . our married life will be like that always, won't it Jack . . . Jack?"

questions about it, probably hoping you don't. Even if you did, you might be too embarrassed to ask.

If you can't find the right person to counsel you on sex, at least get a good book and read it together. Learn about your bodies and how everything works. Whatever physical contact you and your partner are having should be teaching you something about how your body and your partner's body are responding to touch.

Deal with issues. If you haven't already, discuss such issues as frequency of intercourse, desire for children, contraceptive choices, sexual techniques, fears, and fantasies. If you've had sexual experiences that have affected your perceptions, get those into the open. (See "What to Say about the Past," 39–41.)

Find each other's language of love. If she responds to romantic words, write her a love poem. If he is longing for physical affection, give him some loving! If gifts express love, find something that he or she really wants. If acts of service are perceived as love, fill your honeymoon with acts of kindness. Bring him breakfast in bed, fetch the contraceptives, help him

---

Why Make the First Time Special?

⌒

- ❧ The first experience can affect your view of sex for the rest of your life.
- ❧ The first time can be embarrassing, messy, awkward, and uncomfortable.
- ❧ The first encounter makes you totally vulnerable.
- ❧ The first encounter shows you what you don't know.
- ❧ The first encounter may rouse deeply rooted fears.
- ❧ The first encounter takes planning and sensitivity to be pleasurable.
- ❧ Done right, the first encounter is something to treasure and build on.

disrobe for bed, turn off the bedside lamp. Be a thoughtful lover.

Be creative. Your honeymoon doesn't have to be disappointing. Make it the world's finest love feast. It will become a story of love to share for many years to come.

THE PREMARITAL PHYSICAL: WHAT THE GROOM CAN EXPECT

It's not customary for the groom to have a premarital exam, but it's not a bad idea, especially since many men go through adolescence and early adulthood without a checkup. We recently had a client whose doctor discovered a testicular tumor during the premarital exam. It saved the groom's life.

A premarital physical for the groom includes:

- A general exam of the entire body, including height, weight, blood pressure, heart rate, and urine.
- A check of the condition of eyes, ears, nose, skin, and the inside of the mouth.
- An exam of lymph nodes that might be swollen in the neck, armpits, and groin.
- Listening for abnormal sounds in the heart, lungs, and abdomen.
- Feeling the abdomen for abnormalities, especially in the spleen, liver, and kidneys.
- Examination of the penis and testicles for lumps, swelling, disease, sores, warts.

Talk about It

Take some time, preferably prior to the honeymoon, to discuss your thoughts and fears and expectations about sex. A premarital exam can be the impetus for getting you started. You can begin by talking about what the doctor said about your physical condition, then go on to other things, such as what scares you about sex, what you expect of each other in lovemaking, and what you should do about birth control.

❧ A rectal exam of the prostate. (See "Prostate Checkup," 78.)

❧ Blood tests for general counts, such as white cells, red cells, and hemoglobin; sexually transmitted diseases (if you've been sexually active before marriage); and HIV.

❧ A discussion of questions you might have about sex, including birth-control issues. The more open you are, the more a doctor can help.

THE PREMARITAL PHYSICAL: WHAT THE BRIDE CAN EXPECT

The first gynecological exam of her body can be frightening if the bride doesn't know what's involved. The premarital physical includes:

❧ Routine examination of the entire body, including height, weight, blood pressure, heart rate, and urine.

❧ A check of the condition of eyes, ears, nose, skin, and the inside of the mouth.

❧ An exam of lymph nodes that might be swollen in the neck, armpits, and groin.

❧ Listening for abnormal sounds in the heart, lungs, and abdomen.

❧ Feeling the abdomen for abnormalities, especially in the spleen, liver, and kidneys.

❧ Blood tests for general health as well as HIV and other sexually transmitted diseases.

❧ Examination of the breasts plus instruction on self-examination and mammograms.

❧ Examination of the vagina and cervix (may include a Pap test, in which cells from the cervix are examined under a microscope for abnormalities). The doctor uses a speculum to spread the walls of the vagina to examine the cervix and vaginal sheath.

❧ Examination of the uterus and ovaries. The doctor checks the uterus, Fallopian tubes, and ovaries by placing one hand on the abdomen and one or two fingers of the other hand in the vagina or rectum. The internal structures can be examined between the two hands to check for any abnormalities. This can cause some discomfort, but it's minimal.

∞ Discussion about intercourse. The doctor may advise a bride to begin to stretch the vaginal entrance with a series of dilators or with an increasing number of fingers to prevent pain on penetration during intercourse. If necessary, a too-tight hymen can be surgically incised.

∞ A discussion about birth control methods. (See 90–96 for a discussion of birth control.)

GETTING NAKED TOGETHER: HOW WILL IT GO?

On the wedding night, even couples who indulged in a great deal of premarital petting may grasp at fig leaves. A bride, particularly, may be reluctant to undress in front of her groom. Or she may enjoy the fun of titillating him in a seductive negligee. Indeed, his discovering the delights of her body that are veiled in lace is part of the fabulous dance of sex.

OK, maybe it doesn't always work out that way. Maybe the bride hides out in the bathroom or stays under the bedcovers. Maybe the groom loses control and ejaculates prematurely when he first sees his bride naked. After all, that first exposure to your mate's naked body is a singular moment during which many concerns creep out of the hidden corners of our minds, such as:

∞ Will he like the way I look? I'm hardly a Hollywood actress.

∞ What if I can't make love well?

∞ Can I bring her to orgasm? I hear that's really important for a woman.

∞ Will my childhood sexual trauma make me unresponsive? I've never told anyone about the abuse.

∞ I really should have lost another ten pounds. What if she finds me repulsive?

∞ What if he thinks my breasts are too small?

∞ What if she thinks my penis is too small?

Don't be surprised if questions like these pop into your mind—they do for most anyone who bares all for the first time for a spouse. What's crucial is that the two of you respect each other's feelings and attitudes about undressing. When you do, you can begin to marvel at the mystery of your uniqueness and celebrate being together, naked and unashamed.

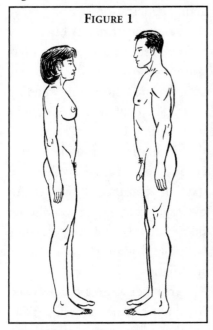

Figure 1

Two Essentials for Intercourse

The ultimate goal, of course, is for the man to insert his erect penis into the woman's vagina. For this to work well, you'll need:

Adequate lubrication. Preferably this will be supplied by natural fluids from the labia, vagina, and penis. Over-the-counter lubricants such as KY Jelly are also useful. There are a variety of these lubricants on the market, but beware—some may weaken the latex of condoms. You can also use saliva as a lubricant.

Whatever you do, don't try penetration without lubrication. It will irritate a man's penis and cause bleeding in a woman or a reflexive painful spasm of the vaginal walls called vaginismus. (See "Vaginismus," 160.)

Something to clean up. You will need something to deal with the ejaculate. If you're using condoms, there should be no mess

---

What to Expect the First Time

- ✂ Anxiety
- ✂ Awkwardness
- ✂ Arousal
- ✂ Ecstasy
- ✂ Pain
- ✂ Discomfort
- ✂ Disappointment
- ✂ Sadness
- ✂ Elation
- ✂ Any or all of these

until the condom is removed. If you're not using condoms, some sticky seminal fluid (about a teaspoonful) will be spilled. If the wetness doesn't bother you, you can simply cuddle, go to sleep, and let things dry. Your body and the sheets will come clean in the wash.

If you find the ejaculate and lubricants unpleasant, provide something to clean them up with. Some couples lay a towel on the bed to absorb the fluids. Others may use tissues or washcloths. Some people like to get up right after intercourse and shower.

ADVICE FOR THE FIRST TIME

Don't expect too much. Treat your first time as a time of discovery. Prior to this, you may have experienced orgasmic release through masturbation or foreplay. Even without clitoral or penile stimulation, sexual arousal through kissing or caressing can be intense enough to produce orgasm.

A woman may not experience orgasm the first time she has intercourse. By contrast, a man, who takes less time than a woman to move from foreplay to orgasm, generally has little prob-

lem with ejaculation. His problem may be ejaculation before actual penetration.

Take your time. A bride may be too distracted to enjoy intercourse, at least initially. She may be exhausted from the wedding week. She may be nervous about intercourse. That can cause tension in her pelvic muscles, tightening her vaginal walls and making entrance difficult. An overeager groom only complicates matters by failing to take time with foreplay, arousal, and clitoral stimulation.

Treat sex as an art. Lovemaking doesn't come naturally. It's an art that takes time and practice. Adequate caressing and tender, passionate foreplay lubricates the labia and vagina and prepares the way for successful penetration. Gentle manual stimulation of the clitoris leads a woman to orgasm. The angle of penetration in pelvic thrusting is important for maximal clitoral stimulation.

It takes time for a couple to learn what works best for them in various positions, timing of foreplay, and use of lubricants.

Work with your differences. You and your mate will differ in what you view as erotic—count on it! You'll also differ in how long it takes you to progress from arousal to orgasm. The intensity of your climaxes will vary each time you make love. Don't expect to have simultaneous, explosive orgasms every time you make love. "Rarely" is more like it.

What you can expect with each satisfying sexual experience is to feel more loved and united in body, soul, and spirit. That's what the Bible means by saying that in sexual intercourse a man and woman "become one flesh."

Q & A

WHY AM I SO SCARED?

My fiancé and I were both taught that sex outside of marriage was wrong, so we've saved ourselves for each other. The problem is, I'm really terrified about having sex. I'm worried about getting naked too. And I'm really scared about going away with my fiancé for a whole week. What should I do?

Congratulations on saving yourselves for marriage. What a special gift you can give each other! Be assured that your anxiety is quite normal. It's good you're

expressing those fears. Now share those concerns with your fiancé. He probably has some of the same worries. Talk about these issues and lay some ground rules for your honeymoon. We suggest:

No rushing. If you don't achieve penetration the first time, back off. Explore other forms of sexual stimulation until you feel comfortable with each other. Then try again.

Be honest about your feelings. Don't pretend you feel passion if you don't. Don't pretend you're elated if you're not. If you're hurting, say so. If you're thrilled, say that too.

Don't keep score. You are both rookies, so don't try to judge each other's responses. Lovemaking is not a performance.

Enjoy each other's bodies. Learn the pleasure of getting naked with each other.

Q & A

WHY WON'T HE TALK ABOUT THE HONEYMOON?

I've been so busy planning our wedding that I've hardly had a chance to think about the honeymoon. I've tried to talk with my fiancé about where we're going and what we'll be doing, but he tells me it's a surprise. Is it wrong for me to want to know more?

There's nothing wrong with your wanting to know more about your honeymoon. It would be nice to know what kind of climate to prepare for. Kayaking in Glacier Bay requires a different wardrobe from cruising in the Caribbean or seeing Broadway shows in New York City.

Ask what kind of clothes to pack. Then look forward to the surprise. It sounds like you're about to have a great adventure.

Q & A

WHO WILL TALK TO US ABOUT SEX?

My girlfriend and I are getting married. Our church offers premarital counseling, but we've heard that the sessions never address questions about sex. Our married friends aren't much help either—they just joke about sex. What are some ways we can prepare ourselves for a good sexual relationship? Who should we talk to?

You're very wise to ask such questions now. Seeking help prior to the honeymoon is so much better than bumbling your way through problems. We recommend that you and your fiancé read and discuss together some good Christian books on sex (start with this one!). Then find a therapist or doctor to talk with about any questions you have.

Don't try to wing it. Your entire sexual relationship in marriage may be affected by what happens on your honeymoon. Dealing with issues now can clear the way for a lifetime of lovemaking.

4

AFTER THE HONEYMOON:

Facing Reality

When we think of a honeymoon, we think of a sweet-sounding escape that will get marriage off and sailing. However, the reality can vary considerably—from an extended trip abroad or a getaway in Hawaii to a one-night stay in a nearby motel or a bed at Mom and Dad's (with them just down the hall).

The sexual experience also varies. Ideally a bride and groom come together in passionate, painless pleasure the first night of their marriage. They make love over and over again, delighting in their discoveries of each other. More often than not, however, postnuptial fatigue, anxiety about sex, "honeymoon cystitis" (a urinary tract infection resulting from frequent sex)—even sunburn—dim the celebration.

The honeymoon also ends quickly. Newlyweds come home to a new apartment or house with their pictures, souvenirs, and memories. They both rush off to work. She writes thank-you notes for wedding gifts. He unpacks boxes. In all the busyness, they probably don't take time to talk about how the honeymoon went for them sexually. Yet, years later in counseling for some relational crisis, a husband or wife may blurt out, "I knew already on our honeymoon that this would never work. You practically raped me!"

"I was tender and sore. But you insisted on sex three times a day!"

"You refused to have sex for the first four days!"

"When we were dating, you were eager and passionate, but ever since the wedding you've been uninterested. What happened?"

FIRST-TIME PROBLEMS

Your first sexual experience may be glorious—or not. You'd be surprised how many couples find that long-awaited experience disrupted by unexplained barriers. Other couples begin marriage with ecstatic sexual experiences, only to drift gradually into unfulfilling mechanics or, worse, avoidance of sex altogether. Whatever problems you have, you must deal with them. Denial and avoidance will only make things get worse. So don't be afraid to talk to each other about your difficulties and, if necessary, with a professional who can help you both work through them.

The reasons for sexual barriers can be as different as we are as people. But generally, sexually frustrated couples can trace their problems to one of these causes:

Pain. The usual causes for pain in a woman during intercourse are an intact thick hymen, lack of adequate lubrication, and aggressive pelvic thrusting. These each have simple solutions, although they may require an exam by a gynecologist. The problem is that once a pain response develops, the reflexive tightening of the vagina and pelvic muscles aggravates the pain.

Called "vaginismus," the spasms intensify the discomfort and reinforce avoidance.

If intercourse is painful for the bride, genital union should be put on hold until solutions can be found to prevent vaginismus. The couple can continue to have enjoyable sexual stimulation manually or orally until the pain problem is resolved. (See "Sensate Focusing," 161.) Then genital union may resume.

Premature ejaculation. Some guys can't sustain an erection long enough to satisfy their wives. Quick ejaculation may be a genetically determined response allowing for quick impregnation. It also might be a learned response to masturbation, in which the combination of risk taking and sexual arousal prompts a hurried response. The epinephrine associated with risk taking and the endorphins released at orgasm become a reinforcing chemical charge. The result is addictive rapid discharge. The anxiety of a wedding and excitement of the honeymoon may also cause premature ejaculation.

Recognizing these dynamics and taking a more relaxed approach to lovemaking may be sufficient to ease the problem. However, if it persists, the couple could try the Squeeze Technique (see page 158).

Fear of sex. This may be based on actual experience or reports from others. Sometimes fear of sex is caused by completely unconscious factors that are mystifying to the person who has it. Such avoidance should be explored with a knowledgeable counselor.

Other fears may inhibit desire for intercourse. These include fear of inadequacy, fear of sexually transmitted disease, fear of pregnancy, or fear of religious condemnation by parents or religious leaders who emphasize the dangers of sexual sin and believe intercourse is only for procreation. In many cases the possibility of such a negative reaction can be discovered and dealt with through honest discussion prior to marriage.

One source of fear is the anticipation of pain, either physical or emotional. That is particularly true if there has been a history of sexual abuse. Old images may threaten to emerge, creating intense anxiety. Old coping devices such as physically hiding or becoming emotionally absent may also come into play.

For example, on her honeymoon, Kristin leaped from the bed, crying, "Get away from me!" Her new husband, Paul, found himself listening to Kristin's sobbing from behind a locked bathroom door. When the couple told me about this, I immediately asked whether there had been an earlier traumatic sexual experience. The boundaries of courtship had protected Kristin's old scar, but the prospect of intercourse exposed the wound.

Erectile dysfunction. Failure to have or sustain an erection is not usually a honeymoon phenomenon. More commonly men in their forties to seventies experience erectile dysfunction because of fatigue, stress, medication side effects, alcohol or drug abuse, guilt over past sexual behavior, or medical problems such as diabetes. If the problem happens early in a marriage, relational issues should be considered. Treatment of these underlying causes should precede taking a supposed wonder drug such as Viagra, Cialis, or Caverject.

Anger. Hear me out, guys. Imagine you and your wife have a disagreement. You quickly forget the argument, particularly as your testosterone level increases toward bedtime. But your wife still feels hurt. Is it realistic to assume she's going to invite you into her body? No way. She's still thinking rationally, since testosterone isn't clogging up her central nervous system. To her, you're the cause of recent pain, not an irresistible hunk.

Unresolved anger is one of the most common blocks to sexual freedom. Having sex dissolves a man's anger while it relieves his sexual tension. Yet while he's mellowing out in the afterglow of orgasm, his wife's sense of violation has intensified. The old saying "Kiss and make up" doesn't work. Couples need to make up before they make love.

Shame. Shame is good when it means accepting the reality of right and wrong. But things run amuck when a person feels shame about behaviors or desires that are not sinful. Unfortunately, this frequently occurs in the area of sex. Shame causes intense anxiety, which often is expressed in extreme modesty, resistance to sexual playfulness, or guilt over sensual pleasure.

The best antidote to unjustified shame is the Bible's teaching on sex. God's Word clearly affirms the physical body and celebrates the joys of sexual pleasure. Jesus' comments about celibacy and marriage (Matthew 19:3–12; Mark 10:2–12) endorse sexual oneness in marriage. Paul strongly reinforces the same view in his epistles (1 Corinthians 7; Ephesians 5). God created us as sexual beings and saw that it was "very good."

Ignorance. Many adults have gaps in their knowledge of sex, particularly of the differences between men and women in sexual interest and response patterns. Ignorance is largely due to a lack of teaching about physiological variables and the distortions perpetuated by our culture.

Couples usually develop a mutually satisfying sex life when they have the information they need. We're hopeful that this book provides what men and women need to explore and enjoy their sexuality, making the most of their differences. That was God's design in creating us male and female.

Fear of failure. The prospect of performing at the level portrayed on television or in movies is enough to scare anyone's pants on. When sexual intimacy is equated with bedroom Olympics,

4 ⌐ AFTER THE HONEYMOON

the possibilities for failure are frightening. This anxiety inhibits sexual freedom and function.

Past sexual experience. If a husband or wife has had previous sexual experience, comparisons are difficult for the spouse to avoid. He or she asks, "Am I as good as he was? Does he find me as exciting as she was?" Questions like these should be dealt with immediately.

Loss of control. Let's admit it: The intense feelings that come with erotic stimulation erode one's sense of control. One woman I know had never experienced orgasm because she feared what might happen if she lost control. Giving yourself to your spouse makes you extremely vulnerable. Any power struggle in a marriage can make sexual vulnerability risky. Resolving power issues between you and your spouse is critical.

None of these barriers to sexual joy is so complicated that it can't be overcome. It's worth the effort. The sexual part of your love story that develops over the years will reflect your personal efforts to deal with problems and move beyond them to passion that only sweetens with age. However, the first step to dealing with your problems is to acknowledge them.

Q & A

WHY CAN'T I ENJOY SEX?

My husband and I were both virgins when we married. I was told sex for the first time would be painful. It was—and still is. My gynecologist suggested going slower and trying a lubricant. We did, and the pain lessened. But I still experience no pleasure. Can you help us?

It's sad that you were taught sex would be painful. However, whatever discomfort you felt the first time can easily be overcome. Proper lubrication and a slow, relaxed time of foreplay can usually lead to a pleasurable experience. However, experiencing pain in any activity, including sexual intercourse, can create anxiety about having pain again. That fear then becomes a barrier to arousal. Here are steps to overcome that:

Discuss the problem. What were your expectations and early experiences with sex? What physical stimuli have been pleasurable? Are there specific situations that trigger a shutdown? What situations are most romantic to you as a couple? These beliefs and desires form the foundation of sexual intimacy. So get to know each other. If you discover guilt or resentment about your lack of sexual intimacy, offer understanding and forgiveness to each other.

Relax. Reprogram your behavioral responses. Learn to pleasure each other. For now, forget about having intercourse and focus on having fun. Take turns pleasuring your mate with physical touch. Begin with such things as back rubs, foot massage, and scalp or neck stimulation—anything your mate enjoys except genital touch.

Proceed with caution. When these actions become natural and positive, move toward erotic stimulation. Try kissing around the head and neck, then go south to breast stimulation, thighs, buttocks, and finally, genital massage. Allow these to develop gradually. Don't rush or force each other.

Enjoy each other. Don't worry about genital union until it's a natural and desired culmination of your play. Above all, realize that pain is not a natural part of sex. Sexual satisfaction is a reasonable expectation. Relax and enjoy it!

Q & A

WHY IS HE SO ROUGH?

I've been married eight years, and I dearly love my husband. But sometimes when we make love, it seems like he has no feelings for me. He is a little rough at times. Afterward, I can't help feeling I've been taken advantage of. I want to enjoy sex, but I feel degraded because of his approach. What can I do to resolve this problem?

Melissa: Do you feel like you've prepared a scrumptious feast of your husband's favorite foods, then found no plate set for you? Feeling left out of your own sexual relationship must be lonesome and frustrating. Not much can happen to change this until your husband listens to your feelings. Pray that he will begin to understand the problem.

Your letter doesn't indicate that you've talked to him about this. Don't expect your husband to read your mind or automatically know how to change. Be prepared to verbalize your needs, feelings, and desires.

Maybe your husband will catch on if you express your feelings a different way. It may help to use first-person statements or emotional word pictures. As you express your feelings, find out about your husband's feelings. Don't assume that he intends to be unfeeling or unkind. What comes across as sexual selfishness may be something else, such as fear or frustration.

In time, your husband may realize that unselfishness on his part will benefit both of you. Maybe he has even been wishing all along that you wouldn't hold back, not realizing that his own behavior was keeping you from doing that. He may actually welcome your suggestions.

THE STORY OF DOUG AND SUE

Doug and Sue are one couple who discovered honeymoons can have lasting consequences. They had been married for twenty-three years when Doug had a heart attack. He almost died. When he was still in intensive care, Sue found their marriage was in crisis—and had been since the honeymoon.

Sue told us, "Doug has always been the most kind, thoughtful guy you could imagine, but while he was in the intensive care unit, he became cold and distant. Before he was released from the hospital, he told me he had filed for divorce. I wondered if Doug had some brain damage."

Doug said, "Sue and I have been married a long time. We had a great time dating—she was one hot chick. On the first night of our honeymoon, though, I knew I had made a terrible mistake. Not only was she cold sexually, but she turned out to be a whiner and manipulator. She has controlled me every day of our marriage since.

"About a year ago I had a pretty serious heart attack. While I was lying in the ICU hooked up to all kinds of machines, I began to assess my life. My biggest regret was marrying Sue.

"When I realized I could die with all that bitterness and frustration, I decided I just couldn't do it anymore. I decided to leave her and start a life of my own."

Doug was asked if he had ever told Sue about his frustration with her. He confessed he never had the nerve.

A POST-HONEYMOON GIFT

Although the experience of Sue and Doug is extreme, we've

heard many similar stories. In all of them, the key dynamic was silence—the couple avoided discussing a problem that had started way back on their honeymoon.

So, before unpacking your wedding gifts, give each other the most precious gift of all: an honest discussion of your honeymoon experience. Before you do, though, realize there will be differences because two people rarely experience things the same way.

For example, the bride might recall the room in which the couple stayed. Maybe she remembers what he ordered on the first dinner out or how far they walked on a moonlit beach. The groom might focus on his new wife's body and the feeling of genital union. Her kisses were so passionate, his climax so intense, especially when they had sex first thing in the morning.

Or, each may have come away with serious disappointments about sex. An honest discussion about what worked and what didn't would help the couple make the necessary adjustments in future lovemaking.

Ground Rules for a Post-Honeymoon Talk

Keep it nonthreatening. Either person might bring up the desire for the discussion, saying, "Darling, I've had some concerns about the level of our intimacy. I've enjoyed having sex with you, but I think it could be better. I want to know if you're really satisfied. When can we talk?"

There should be no angry accusations, no blame, just an honest first-person expression of a desire to connect—relationally and sexually.

Accept your differences. You might say, "I realize that my experience on our honeymoon may be very different from yours, so I want to really hear and understand what you experienced. I also hope you'll hear and understand mine." Then truly listen to what the other person is saying without becoming threatened or defensive.

Work for understanding. It's crucial that you do not act like trial lawyers or judges to establish who's right or wrong. Acknowledge that each person's perception is truth to her or him. As you explore differences, try to identify behaviors that led to those interpretations.

Listen to each other. After affirming his love for his bride, the husband might admit that the sexual part of the honeymoon wasn't quite what he had expected. "I had this fantasy that you'd want sex as much as I did," he might say. "Then, on our wedding night, you were too tired to make love."

She might apologize, then explain, "I was frustrated by how uptight and controlling my mother was. I began to feel like it was her wedding, not mine. I just wanted to get the whole thing over with and find a place to hide. I knew it was unfair to you, but I wanted the first time we made love to be really special."

Plan on further discussion. He begins to sense her hurts; and she, his. Both view this talk as the first of many honest sessions that can clear the way for better sex. The sooner a couple deals with hurts, disappointments, and misunderstandings, the sooner they can discover the true keys to sexual intimacy.

Anticipate a gradual learning curve. Don't expect miraculous, wonderful sex each time you and your spouse have sex; rather, work toward growth. For many people, talking face-to-face about the specifics of sex is too intense or embarrassing. So consider reading a book on sex together. You might also try writing to each other. Use affirmation to stimulate closeness. Share with each other the intense "wow" sexual experiences of your past.

If your first time is less than what you hoped for, don't despair. Considering your high expectations for the long-awaited fulfillment of your dreams of erotic ecstasy, it would be remarkable for the event to live up to those expectations. First-time sex rarely measures up. Yet we can assure you that better lovemaking will come as you become more comfortable with your mate and more skillful at pleasuring each other.

Q & A

WE LOVED SEX BEFORE MARRIAGE; WHY NOT NOW?

I love my husband immensely, but our sex life is terrible! We have sex barely once a month. This surprises me, because we had intercourse before we were married, and I had no problem getting turned on then. I've been to a doctor, and there are no physical problems holding us back. We know that having sex outside of marriage was sinful. Did premarital sex ruin our married sex life?

Louis: What happens between the steamy days of courtship and the marriage bed is as unpredictable as winter snows in the Rockies. Things can turn frigid overnight. Some of the problems are complex and require professional help. Others are relatively simple and easily resolved. Here are some problems:

Guilt or anger. Whether you were carried away in passion or felt coerced, surrendering your virginity before marriage prompts regrets. This problem may require some counseling so you can come to mutual forgiveness and a sense of God's grace. It's also good to remember that your sexual passion didn't surprise God, and that he still redeems sinners.

Unromantic intimacy. It's pretty unromantic to crawl into bed with the same guy who smells up the bathroom. Likewise, seeing a woman without her makeup and in oversize flannel pajamas may be a real turnoff to a guy. Try loving each other as you really are, not as idealized fantasies.

Everyday chores. When we were courting, Melissa and I saw each other once every two or three weeks. We put enormous energy into creating a few hours of paradise—great dinners, romantic picnics, spiffy clothes, and bottled fragrances. Now we have bills and chores and responsibilities that we have to intentionally set aside to make way for whatever romance we can muster.

Arguments. Hurt or anger can cool off lovemaking. Some men go directly from a heated argument to a heated sexual encounter, but most women can't. Clearing out the backlog of negative emotions is crucial.

Expectations. The best sex happens when both partners contribute. Any man we counsel invariably says he wants a wife who makes him feel that she craves his body. When a woman initiates lovemaking, sex becomes more erotic for her and her man.

Q & A

HOW CAN HE PRAY BACK HIS LOST DESIRE?

On our honeymoon, my husband got a bad chest cold. Let's just say that the honeymoon wasn't what I had been waiting for all those years. Both my husband and I were virgins when we married, and I thought that our sex life would be exciting once he felt better.

Now, three months later, I am the one who makes the move to get intimate. Not having sex doesn't seem to bother my husband. He thinks that because he prayed all his life to keep sexual thoughts away, he's still in that mode. How do we get my husband's sex drive back?

You and your husband should openly and honestly explore your attitudes about sex, asking such questions as:

How did each of you learn about sex?

What were your earliest sexual experiences?

What were the constraints and teachings that helped you maintain your virginity?

Are there expectations about sexual performance that may have made you anxious about sex?

Understanding yourselves and each other may help you find a more agreeable level of interaction. In the meantime, I encourage you to be patient. If your husband has been praying for so many years to reduce his sexual thoughts, it may take some time for those inhibitions to diminish. Your patient acceptance of his sexuality can help him do that.

In addition, affirm and reward his signs of affection, and continue to gently invite him into sex whenever you want. You mentioned wanting him to have his sex drive "back," so I would expect his libido was once quite active. With patient wooing, I assure you, it will return.

Q & A

WILL WE EVER HAVE SEX AGAIN?

Since our honeymoon, our sex life has gone slowly down the drain. My wife doesn't even like to kiss me anymore. I find myself dreaming that I'm dating other women, then wake up to find I'm still in my disappointing marriage. I love my wife and I'm attracted to her, but I'm tired of feeling rejected. Is this what the next forty years are going to be like?

Louis: Early sexual adjustments are difficult. The popular culture's notion of dynamite sex on the honeymoon and ever after is explosive only in its inaccuracy. In the first place, you have to deal with vast gender differences. These range from a woman's typical view that sex expresses relationship while a man sees sex as physiological gratification. But men and women also view sex differently when it comes to turn-ons and turnoffs and in how long it takes to achieve orgasm.

Since sex is such a personal and often threatening subject, many couples retreat quickly when their love life is not working well. Not wanting to admit problems, they begin building up fearfulness and anger. Men are particularly defensive about sexual difficulties.

I encourage you and your wife to talk with a competent counselor at your earliest possible opportunity.

Melissa: If you and your wife think sex isn't what you thought it would be, you have lots of company. Great sex needs to be cultivated and nurtured. If we

knew that going into marriage, it might have cut down on some of the disappointment.

Every part of marriage requires adjusting to another person's wants and needs. Sex may be one of the toughest adjustments of a new marriage. So learn as much as you can about sexual approaches and techniques that would heighten your wife's interest and enhance her comfort level. It's a great investment of time and energy. Take it from us, forty years of great sex is worth it.

THE RIGHT SETUP FOR SEX

- ✤ Realize that sex begins with the brain. So learn all you can about making love.
- ✤ See having sex as a way of expressing love to your partner,

Talk about It

Take a few minutes to recall the first time you made love. What expectations did each of you have about that encounter— what did you think would happen? What in that lovemaking was better than you expected? What surprised you? How has your lovemaking improved since the first time?

not just the means of satisfying your own need.

- Be sensitive to your surroundings; avoid situations that inhibit or threaten sexual desire.
- Supply the sexual organs and the brain with the greatest possible number of positive sensations.
- Tell each other what makes sex good and what doesn't.
- Make adjustments and do some experimenting.
- Have fun learning!

PART THREE: SEX AND OUR BODIES

5

MADE FOR LOVE:

Our Amazing Bodies

⌒

The adaptability of a man's and a woman's sexual organs is simply amazing. I can't imagine how such organs could have evolved without a Creator God. If you look at a flaccid penis, you'd have difficulty envisioning that it was capable of increasing five times its size. Then explore the vagina as a gynecologist would with a speculum. The vagina feels snug as it envelops the penis, but it, too, is capable of expanding—enough to allow passage for a full-term baby.

Remarkable!

I encourage you to examine yourself and your spouse. This may be a strange thought to a woman who has never used a mirror to identify her own genitalia. Men are generally more narcissistic about their organs, which are easy to see without a mirror. Nonetheless, a couple could benefit from exploring each other so they can know which areas are sensitive to touch.

A LESSON IN MALE ANATOMY

A man doesn't need to hold a mirror to his bottom to examine his sex organs. A straight look in the mirror is enough. (See figure 2.)

HIS PENIS

If your penis has not been circumcised, retract your foreskin to look at the head of the penis (glans) and its coronal ridge. Those are the most sensitive parts of the penis.

The fascination with the penis is so strong that some cultures, such as ancient Egypt, had cults dedicated to it. Carvings on the structures at Karnak show men with large, erect penises, which were symbols of power.

For today's men, an erection represents masculinity and power. From the time of adolescence, a guy focuses much of his identity as a male and his sense of potency on this bit of flesh that dangles between his legs.

What exactly does the penis consist of and how does it work?

The penis is made up of three parts: the base, or root, which is attached to the abdominal wall; the shaft, which extends from the wall to the head; and the head, or glans. Each is made of spongelike tissue encased in a fibrous sheath. (See figure 2.) The glans is rich in sensory nerve fibers and is the most sensitive receptor of sexual stimulation. The glans is covered at birth with a loose fold of skin called the foreskin.

With sexual arousal, the arterial blood supply to the three parts of the penis dilate, the venous outflow contracts, and the three spongy vascular compartments become engorged with blood. The strong fibrous sheaths enclosing each shaft cause the shafts to become hard and stand out from the body. (See figure 3.) There is no bone in the penis, just firm fibrous tissue. When the penis is erect, the foreskin retracts as the penis enlarges, exposing the sensitive glans, which then plays an important role in stimulating orgasm.

The urethra runs through the center of the penis. Urine is expelled from the bladder through this tube and out of the opening in the glans. This tube also serves

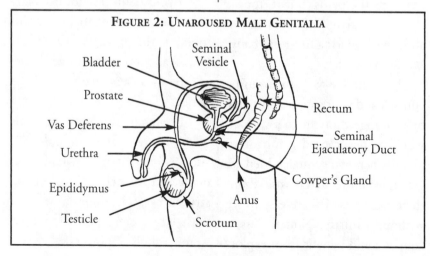

FIGURE 2: UNAROUSED MALE GENITALIA

Bladder
Prostate
Vas Deferens
Urethra
Epididymus
Testicle
Seminal Vesicle
Scrotum
Anus
Rectum
Seminal Ejaculatory Duct
Cowper's Gland

as a pathway for the ejaculate that is projected during orgasm.

HIS SCROTUM

The scrotum, which is a loose skin sack, has some important functions. Essentially, it is a temperature-control device. It is insulated with several layers of fascia and muscle and keeps the testicles warm to allow sperm production. The ideal temperature for producing sperm is slightly lower than body temperature, which is why, during embryonic development, the testicles descend from the abdominal cavity into the scrotum.

If a man gets into a cold shower, the small muscle fibers surrounding the spermatic cord and testes will contract, bringing the testicles closer to the body to keep them warm. Stroke the skin of the scrotum and watch it pull up the testicles. Of course, if a wife does that to her husband, she must be prepared for the arousal and erection that may occur.

HIS TESTICLES

Gently feel each testicle within the scrotal sack. There should be two. On each, you will feel a ridge along one side, the epididymus. This is where thousands of tiny tubules from the testicles join to form the vas deferens. The vas carries sperm into the ejaculatory duct, where they mix with secretions from your prostate gland and seminal vesicles. The seminal vesicles, vas deferens, and prostate

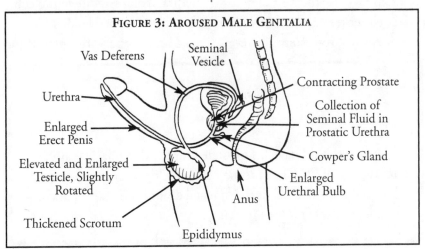

FIGURE 3: AROUSED MALE GENITALIA

Vas Deferens

Seminal Vesicle

Contracting Prostate

Urethra

Collection of Seminal Fluid in Prostatic Urethra

Enlarged Erect Penis

Cowper's Gland

Elevated and Enlarged Testicle, Slightly Rotated

Enlarged Urethral Bulb

Anus

Thickened Scrotum

Epididymus

gland contract at orgasm, forcing seminal fluid out through the penis.

The testicles are essential for male development and reproduction. They manufacture the male hormone testosterone, which is secreted into the bloodstream to act throughout the body, and they produce sperm cells in the testes. The sperm is collected in a system of tiny tubules, which join into larger and larger ones, finally forming the single vas deferens. These muscular tubes rise from each testicle and go up into the abdomen. Testosterone also acts in the central nervous system, stimulating the parts of a man's brain responsible for regulating libido and arousal.

Damage to the testicles can affect either testosterone or sperm production. Testosterone levels may also be affected by liver disease, some drugs, and chromosomal abnormalities. Male reproduction has vascular, hormonal, neural, and perceptive components. Any physical or psychological factor that affects a single component of the system can result in sexual dysfunction.

THE PROSTATE

This organ, which produces 20 to 30 percent of the volume of seminal fluid, is the shape and size of a walnut. The prostate surrounds the urethra as it exits from the bladder.

As a man ages, the prostate becomes enlarged. This is called benign *prostatic hypertrophy*. An enlarged prostate presses on the urethra, making it difficult to completely empty the bladder. Surgery may be necessary to enlarge the

Prostate Checkup

A man should have his prostate examined regularly, especially after the age of fifty. The prostate can develop a cancerous growth, which a doctor can feel during a rectal exam. The exam is uncomfortable, but it could be lifesaving.

passageway. If the enlargement is due to cancer, the prostate may have to be removed.

Another way to check the health of the prostate is through a blood test. The prostate-specific antigen (PSA) is produced by the prostate to help liquefy semen. A small amount of it circulates in the blood. If a higher than normal amount of PSA is detected, it could indicate cancer. A biopsy of the prostate is necessary to rule out or confirm cancer.

HOW IMPORTANT IS SIZE?

Penises come in various sizes, from about one inch to six inches long in the flaccid state to eight to twelve inches long during erection. Width may also vary, even between racial groups. The size of a penis does not affect the orgasmic reflex for a man. Neither does it affect enjoyment for his wife, since most sexual stimulation for a woman occurs at the clitoris outside the vagina and in the outer third of the vagina, often called the "G-spot" (see page 85). The shortest penis is adequate to bring pleasure to a woman.

Some women enjoy the feel of deep thrusting, which is enhanced by a longer penis, but many also find that uncomfortable. They may prefer shallow stimulation near the vaginal opening rather than deep thrusts.

We say all of this to make the point that a large penis may mean a lot to a guy's ego, but it doesn't matter anywhere else. We realize we may not convince any male that the size of his penis isn't important, but it isn't.

CAN A PENIS BREAK?

Penises are sturdy. Even with forceful thrusting in intercourse or vigorous stroking in masturbation, a penis will not break. However, lubrication is important for sexual activity. It is thus important for a man and woman to have adequate foreplay to provide good vaginal lubrication—or to use a lubricant, such as KY Jelly or saliva—for masturbation or intercourse.

CIRCUMCISION: WHY DO IT?

Circumcision, meaning "cutting around," is a surgical procedure in which the foreskin of the penis is excised so that the glans is always exposed.

Circumcision has been a religious rite for many people since the beginning of civilization. Today circumcision is done for health reasons. In an uncircumcised male, non-semen secretions can accumulate under the foreskin. This smegma can be a breeding area for germs if it is not frequently washed away. To clean this area, the foreskin must be pulled back from the glans so the area under it can be thoroughly washed. These secretions are produced by the foreskin; therefore, removing the foreskin reduces the risk of bacterial infection.

EJACULATE

Ejaculate is a whitish, sticky fluid primarily produced by the seminal vesicles and the prostate. The prostate is at the base of the urethra, just in front of the bladder. The seminal vesicles are attached to the prostate gland. They combine with the ductus deferens, which transports sperm from the testes to the urethra.

When ejaculation occurs, two to five milliliters of seminal fluid with a small volume of secretions (sperm) from the testicles containing twenty to one hundred million sperm cells shoot out of the urethra in rhythmic spurts. There are about four of these spurts per second for ten to twelve seconds. The force of the ejaculation decreases with age, as do the number of functional sperm produced, the volume of seminal fluid, and the number of rhythmic spurts. The power behind the ejaculation comes from the muscular structure of the vas deferens (the main duct through which the semen is carried from the epididymis to the ejaculatory duct) and muscle fibers around the seminal vesicles and prostate gland.

A LESSON IN FEMALE ANATOMY

After God created Adam, God said, "It's not good for man to be alone." So he reviewed all the living creatures he had made to see if he could find a match for Adam. None fit the bill—not even a good hunting dog. So God reached for a rib and fashioned the crowning achievement of creation: a woman.

Adam took one look and flipped. That's been happening ever since. From the start, visual impact hooked old Adam. Let's take a peek at what he saw.

HER BREASTS

We assume that one of the first things that caught Adam's eye was Eve's breasts. Psychoanalysts have tried to link man's attraction to breasts with nourishment in infancy. That wasn't true for Adam, and it may not be for modern man. There may just be something mystical about those two rounded structures with dark tips. Like mountains, they invite exploration and conquest. They certainly bring delight to both a man and a woman. Tender fondling, caressing, kissing, and suckling rouse the nipples and stimulate sexual excitement.

We've sometimes wondered why women have two breasts. One would have been adequate for feeding offspring, although two are more comfortable for a nursing mom. Perhaps a man needs two to keep both of his hands busy when he's amorous.

HER REPRODUCTIVE ORGANS

Before giving your husband lessons on your anatomy, take some time to examine your sexual equipment and how it works. Here's a step-by-step process:

Survey the area. Get into a relaxed, comfortable place with a hand mirror. Since some of your genitalia are hidden, you may have never seen them. So hold the mirror so you can see your bottom. (See figure 4.)

You'll see your entire perineum from pubis to anus. This is the floor

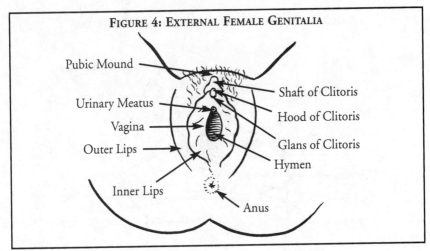

FIGURE 4: EXTERNAL FEMALE GENITALIA

Pubic Mound

Urinary Meatus

Vagina

Outer Lips

Inner Lips

Shaft of Clitoris

Hood of Clitoris

Glans of Clitoris

Hymen

Anus

of your pelvis. It is supported by a muscular sling, the pubococcygeal muscle—the muscle that's strengthened in Kegel exercises, which help with bladder control.

Put your hand over the whole area while tensing the muscles you use to stop urination. Do you feel your bottom lift? That muscle action is part of what happens in intercourse and orgasm.

Find your mons pubis. That's the rounded area just over your pubic bone. The old Latin anatomists called this the mons veneris, or mountain of Venus, who was the goddess of love.

Below this is your vulva, the collective term for all your external reproductive structures. The lateral, or outside, parts are called the labia majora, or major lips. These lips are quite prominent in little girls but flatten out later on. As that happens, the labia minora, or lesser lips, which are the inner folds, become more visible. These folds of tissue just inside the labia majora form a hood over the clitoris in the front and join toward your anus in the rear. (See figure 5.)

The clitoris is about the size and shape of the end of your pinkie. The clitoris has a shaft and a rounded end, the glans. The labia and clitoris are erectile tissue that swells with sexual arousal. Stimulation of the clitoris is primarily responsible for orgasm. Therefore it is very important for you to know where it is and what sort of stimulation feels best to you. Direct caressing of the glans is

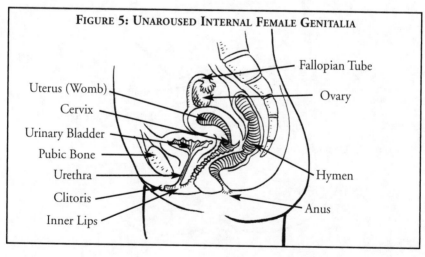

FIGURE 5: UNAROUSED INTERNAL FEMALE GENITALIA

Fallopian Tube

Ovary

Uterus (Womb)

Cervix

Urinary Bladder

Pubic Bone

Urethra

Clitoris

Inner Lips

Hymen

Anus

uncomfortable for most women, particularly early in foreplay, because it has so many sensory nerve endings. A gradual approach is best.

Find the entrance to your urethra and your vagina. Just below the clitoris is the urethral meatus, the end of the urethra, through which urine travels from the bladder. Because of the location of the opening, you can understand why women sometimes get bladder infections after extended sexual activity. These infections are sometimes referred to as "honeymoon cystitis." They can be prevented by urinating immediately after sexual activity to flush bacteria from the urethra. Consider applying a water-based lubricant to the vaginal area to ease penetration. If you do have problems, such as pain while urinating, drink plenty of water (eight glasses a day is recommended), drink cranberry juice, avoid coffee, and see a doctor.

Behind the urethral opening is the vagina. You'll see a somewhat irregular entry with the hymen or fragments of the hymen. What you won't see is the heralded G-spot. This supposedly is an area in the anterior wall of the vagina that has a dense network of sensory fibers which, when stimulated, creates intense pleasure. (See "The G-Spot," 85.)

The vagina expands during sexual arousal, accompanied by lubricating moisture from the mucous glands. During orgasm, the outer third of the vagina has rhythmic contractions. These embrace the penis and can be augmented by voluntary contractions of the pubococcygeal muscle (the pelvic muscle that holds back urine). The inner part of the vagina expands at orgasm to create a receptacle for the man's semen.

Examine the anus. This is the opening to your rectum and intestinal tract. The orifice is sensitive. Some men find that inserting a finger or erect penis into the anus is sexually exciting. We do not advise anal sex because of the risk of infections and damage to the lining of the anal orifice and rectum.

Get a physical. You can't see your internal structures—the vagina, cervix, uterus, Fallopian tubes, and ovaries. However, it's important that you know where they are and what they do. Have an annual physical exam to make sure everything is healthy and in good working order.

THE CLITORIS

During sexual arousal, the clitoris and labia minora of a woman become engorged with blood. These structures have erectile tissue much like that in the male penis and glans. They are extremely well supplied with sensory nerve endings. When sufficiently stimulated, the clitoris provides the buildup to orgasm. In fact the clitoris is the only structure in the body whose only function is to provide pleasure.

It is critically important for a man to adequately stimulate the clitoris during sexual foreplay and intercourse. For most wives, this means gentle caressing initially around the sides of the clitoris and then across the body of the clitoris. This stroking can be done with a man's penis, hands, lips, tongue, or other part of his body.

The key is providing the kind of pressure and rhythm that is pleasurable to the woman. She is the only one who can determine that, so it's important for her to communicate her preferences. She may also be the one to show her husband where her clitoris is. Once a husband finds it, he can be more skilled at providing the right touch.

We should mention that clitoral stimulation isn't absolutely necessary. Some wives experience orgasm from kissing and breast caresses alone.

HER RESPONSE

As a woman sexually awakens to touching of her breasts or clitoris, she experiences changes in her genitalia. The labia and clitoris swell. The cervical and labial or vestibular glands secrete lubricating fluids to ease the passage of a man's penis into her vagina. (See figure 6.)

After a man enters a woman, clitoral stimulation should continue. This can be done with manual caresses or with the thrusting of the penis—if the man is positioned to allow the shaft of the penis to rub across the clitoris or labia. If this isn't happening, the penis can be withdrawn and direct clitoral caressing resumed, which will carry the wife through the plateau phase to orgasm.

During orgasm, the walls of the vagina and uterus rhythmically contract. Tension that has built throughout the body lets go. A woman can be taken back to the intense plateau phase, then built again to further orgasmic responses. That kind of multiorgasmic response is usually only a fantasy for men.

Some people ask, "Is it better for a woman to reach vaginal or clitoral orgasm?" The question of vaginal versus clitoral orgasm seems academic to us. If a man's penis penetrates a woman's vagina at the right angle, rhythmic thrusts stimulate the walls of the vagina, which are sensitive and responsive. The thrusting also stimulates the labia, the perineum, and the clitoris. Clitoral stimulation, however, provides the most intense response.

THE G-SPOT

A concentration of nerve endings in the anterior vaginal wall has been the topic of much discussion. In the 1940s, a German gynecologist named Ernst Grafenberg announced that he had discovered a spot on the wall of the vagina that could produce a powerful orgasm when correctly stimulated. This area became known as the Grafenberg Spot, or G-spot. There is anatomic evidence of a G-spot; however, it's more of an area than a spot. This area, located in the anterior, or front, wall of the vagina, has a richer network of sensory nerve endings than the rest of the vagina. (See figure 7.)

HER HYMEN

In some cultures, it is very important that a bride has an intact hymen, or maidenhead, on her wedding night, to prove her virginity.

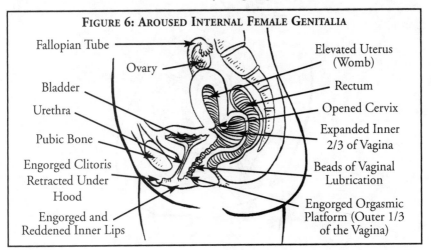

FIGURE 6: AROUSED INTERNAL FEMALE GENITALIA

Fallopian Tube

Ovary

Bladder

Urethra

Pubic Bone

Engorged Clitoris
Retracted Under
Hood

Engorged and
Reddened Inner Lips

Elevated Uterus
(Womb)

Rectum

Opened Cervix

Expanded Inner
2/3 of Vagina

Beads of Vaginal
Lubrication

Engorged Orgasmic
Platform (Outer 1/3
of the Vagina)

The hymen is the thin skin, or membrane, that partly or completely covers the external vaginal opening. The morning after a marriage is consummated, some cultures require bloody evidence that this hymen has been broken.

Actually the hymen may be torn in physical activity or in other ways prior to intercourse. Furthermore, hymens are of variable thickness and size. Some girls are born without them, while others have hymens that completely cover the vaginal opening. If a young girl has no opening to allow menstrual flow, this should be surgically corrected. Some young women have openings so small that a doctor may recommend that prior to marriage the hymen be gently stretched to allow penetration with minimal discomfort.

HER MENSTRUAL CYCLE

A prominent part of a woman's sexuality is her hormonal cycle. Her sexual organs are designed for reproduction. The primary effect of monthly hormonal stimulation is to bring an egg to maturity, to release it for fertilization by a man's sperm, and to welcome it as an embryo into the uterus where it will be nurtured until it is large enough to be born. If fertilization and implantation of the embryo into the uterine wall doesn't occur, the uterine cells are shed in the menstrual flow.

A woman's hormones affect other areas of the body too. Her

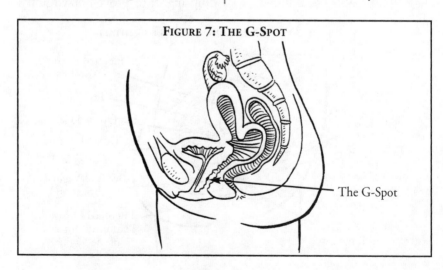

FIGURE 7: THE G-SPOT

The G-Spot

breasts swell and become tender prior to the onset of her menstrual period. She retains fluid, even in her brain; gains weight; and is tired, depressed, and moody. She may suffer headaches, dizziness, fainting, easy bruising, and heart palpitations. Premenstrual syndrome (PMS) is a physiological phenomenon, not an imaginary ailment, and is treated with hormones, diuretics, and diet changes.

Do a woman's hormonal changes affect sex? Some women don't seem to be affected; there's little difference in their sexual interest and response when they're premenstrual, menstrual, or weeks away from their period. Others note considerable variations during the cycle. They say sexual desire peaks around ovulation and drops prior to menstruation. It picks up again during menstruation, when fertilization is most unlikely.

WHAT ABOUT SEX DURING MENSTRUATION?

Realizing they're infertile during menstruation makes some women more responsive to sex. However, there are at least a couple of reasons for abstaining during this time:

Religious belief. Old Testament law said a man should not have relations with a woman while she was having her menstrual period, though we don't exactly know why. There doesn't seem to be any increased susceptibility to infection or damage during this time.

Inconvenience. The messiness of menstruation may be distasteful to either husband or wife. It's

---

Talk about It

⌒

Have either of you heard about the G-spot? What have you heard? As a woman, have you experienced intense pleasure in this area of the vagina? What led up to that? How can the G-spot be stimulated to enhance lovemaking with your husband?

untrue that the menstrual blood will harm a man.

HIS AND HER HORMONES

Hormones are critical in sexual function. For men, the process is fairly simple. They have a fairly consistent level of testosterone, which affects their sex drive, or libido, as well as their sperm production, hair growth, muscle mass, and aggressiveness.

A woman's hormones are more complicated. Her monthly cycle begins with a hormone manufactured in the hypothalamus, at the base of the brain. This acts on the pituitary gland, attached to the base of the brain. After a woman's menstrual period, the hypothalamus stimulates the pituitary to produce a follicle-stimulating hor-

mone, which prompts the ovaries to mature an egg. The maturing follicle secretes estrogen, which encourages growth of the uterine lining in case conception occurs. After the egg is released, the follicle corpus luteum produces progesterone, which stimulates the uterus to develop support for an implanted embryo, or fertilized egg. If pregnancy does not occur, the hormonal levels drop. The lining of the uterus is sloughed off in the menstrual flow. Then the whole cycle starts again.

The ebb and flow of hormones affect a woman's moods, vascular system, breasts, bone health, skin, hair, vaginal mucosa—and sexual receptivity. No wonder women are so fascinating—and so difficult to predict. We men could all benefit

Helen tries out her new "Not-Tonight" nightgown.

from the kind of early-warning alert system that Melissa uses. It's a T-shirt that says, "Beware! I'm out of estrogen and I have a gun."

When the T-shirt is on, sex probably isn't.

Q & A

WHAT SHOULD WE EXPECT FROM SEX?

My husband and I have been married seven months. We were both virgins when we married, so we really didn't know what to expect. Sometimes sex is really good, and sometimes it's not. Should sex always end in orgasm? Should we be climaxing at the same time?

Louis: Spending your first months becoming familiar with your sexual arousal patterns and preferences for pleasurable touch is important. For Melissa and me, being able to talk about our sexual interaction was crucial. We both had impressions and expectations about sex that just weren't true for our sexual relationship. For example, I thought that deep pelvic thrusting would bring Melissa to orgasm. It didn't because the angle of penetration was not promoting clitoral stimulation. We were able to dispel the myths by reading books on sexuality and by talking to a doctor.

Though our naïveté was embarrassing at the time, we're now happy we had the great experience of learning together. One thing we've learned is that, though simultaneous orgasm for both partners is an event to celebrate, it's also extremely difficult to achieve. Try not to let sexual play become a performance that holds you hostage. If only one—or neither of you—achieves orgasm, that's OK, as long as you're enjoying each other.

Talk about It

After reading this chapter, what have you each learned about your own anatomy? Your spouse's? Any surprises? How does understanding each other's anatomy help you in lovemaking?

BIRTH CONTROL:

Making the Right Choice

Let's face it: Pregnancy is one of the results of sexual intimacy. Yet some couples, even though they've never gone so far in love-making as vaginal penetration or ejaculation, have found themselves with an unplanned pregnancy. Sperm often leak out of the penis before ejaculation occurs. These sperm are aggressive little things that are viable for forty-eight hours. With more than twenty million of these guys in every ejaculation, odds are that *if* there is an egg anywhere in the neighborhood, it will be found and fertilized.

There are many ways to keep this from happening. Some contraceptives inhibit ovulation. Some block sperm production. Some prevent the sperm's passage to the urethra. Some prevent sperm from reaching an egg. Some prevent a fertilized egg from nesting in the uterus. All of these methods of birth control have some problems technically, physiologically, or theologically. We'll present a list and discussion of each with objections or cautions for consideration. We strongly advise you to discuss these options with a doctor and each other to decide what's best for you.

Be aware that some people believe sex is only for procreation; therefore, contraception of any kind is wrong. We do not hold this viewpoint, since the Bible celebrates the pleasure of sex as well as its procreation value. For some couples, parenting seems unwise altogether, and for most couples, pregnancy is better when planned.

PHYSICAL BARRIERS TO CONCEPTION

Theoretically the following methods of birth control should

be totally effective. They're not. Keep this in mind when considering each as an option for preventing pregnancy.

The diaphragm. This round rubber device fits over a woman's cervix to prevent sperm from entering the uterus and traveling up a Fallopian tube to connect with a waiting egg. It is essential to use a spermicidal jelly inside the cup-shaped diaphragm to ensure success. After applying the jelly, the diaphragm is folded, then carefully inserted into the vagina so that it seals off the entrance to the uterus. (See figure 8.) A doctor can help you work with the diaphragm.

The diaphragm fails when it is torn, is inserted incorrectly, or is a bad fit. The diaphragm can be inserted up to six hours before sex. After six hours, more spermicidal jelly must be added. The diaphragm should be kept in place for at least eight hours after intercourse.

Condoms. These latex sheaths, which fit over the erect penis to catch the ejaculate and prevent sperm from being deposited in the vagina, are probably the most advertised and overrated devices for birth control. A friend of mine who is an obstetrician says couples who depend on condoms for birth control keep him in the business of delivering babies.

A condom will not prevent pregnancy if it has tiny holes or tears. But most often, a condom fails because it's not properly put on or taken off. A condom should

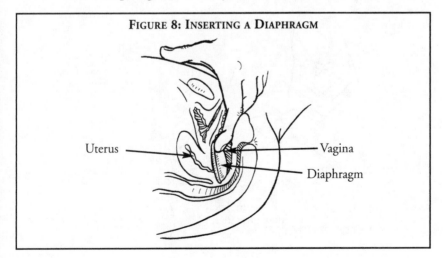

FIGURE 8: INSERTING A DIAPHRAGM

Uterus

Vagina

Diaphragm

be placed on the erect penis and rolled down the shaft, leaving a small pocket at the top to collect the semen. (See figure 9.) All condoms should be used with spermicidal foam that's deposited in the vagina before intercourse.

Proper removal of the condom is also important. To minimize any leakage of sperm, the condom should be held in place while the man pulls his penis out of the vagina. This should be done before he completely loses his erection.

Note: Condoms, or rubbers, do not completely prevent sexually transmitted disease (STD). They reduce the risk for HIV, syphilis, gonorrhea, and some other STDs, but they're totally ineffective for human papillomavirus, which causes cervical cancer. Your premarital exam should include screening for STDs.

CONTRACEPTION FAILURE RATES AND COSTS

According to the U.S. Food and Drug Administration, here are some figures for contraception failure rates and costs:

- Diaphragms with spermicides: 20 percent failure, cost of doctor visit ($25 to $50) and fitting ($35 to $150)
- Condoms: 14 percent failure, 50 cents apiece
- Coitus interruptus (withdrawal): 19 percent failure, no cost
- The pill: 5 percent failure, $360 per year

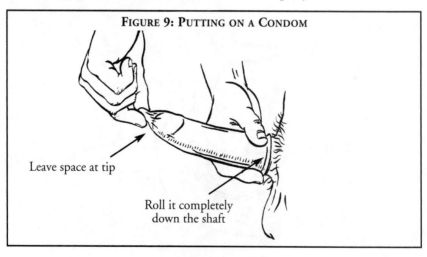

FIGURE 9: PUTTING ON A CONDOM

Leave space at tip

Roll it completely down the shaft

∝ Norplant: less than 1 percent failure, $450

∝ Depo-Provera: less than 1 percent failure, $180 per injection

∝ Tubal ligation: less than 1 percent failure, $1,000 to $2,500

∝ Rhythm method: 25 percent failure, no cost

∝ Spermicides (jellies, foams, creams): 26 percent failure, 25 cents per application

∝ Vasectomy: less than 1 percent failure, $500 to $1,000

∝ IUD: 1 to 2 percent failure, $240

INTERRUPTING THE REPRODUCTIVE PROCESS

Each ovary in an adolescent woman contains 200,000 primordial follicles, or potential eggs.

Once a month, usually ten to fifteen days after the onset of a woman's menstrual flow, an egg matures and is released (ovulation) into a woman's pelvis. The egg is swept up by a Fallopian tube and moves toward the uterus.

If sperm enter the cervix through intercourse and swim through the uterus into a Fallopian tube, one may penetrate the egg and fertilize it. (See figure 10.) The embryo that results travels down the tube into the uterus, where it plants itself and continues to develop. (See figure 11.)

There are several ways to prevent pregnancy by interrupting this reproductive process.

Coitus interruptus. This is an attempt to prevent sperm from

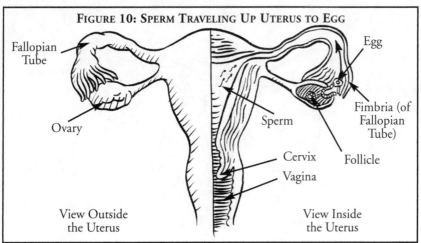

FIGURE 10: SPERM TRAVELING UP UTERUS TO EGG

Fallopian Tube

Ovary

View Outside the Uterus

Egg

Fimbria (of Fallopian Tube)

Sperm

Follicle

Cervix

Vagina

View Inside the Uterus

being deposited in the vagina. A man inserts his penis into his wife's vagina during intercourse, but he withdraws it prior to ejaculation.

This type of birth control often fails because sperm can escape from the penis prior to ejaculation. It is also ineffective because of pilot error; in the passion of the moment, a guy may find it too difficult to interrupt such intense pleasure and fail to withdraw his penis in time. Either way, the sperm is well on its way to an egg, which is waiting to be fertilized.

The pill. Ovulation is halted by altering a woman's normal hormonal cycle. The pill prevents the release of the follicle-stimulating hormone (FSH) from the pituitary gland. Consequently no egg matures or is released for fertilization.

The pill is a reliable contraceptive as long as it is taken faithfully. If a woman misses a pill, however, ovulation can occur. Each day a pill is skipped, the risk increases. If two pills are missed, some other birth control device should be used for that cycle.

Implants. Two hormonal preparations can be implanted or injected into a woman to prevent ovulation. Norplant contains synthetic progesterone in small plastic capsules that are inserted under the skin. It lasts five years. The effects of Norplant are reversible, so when a woman wants to stop the drug, she asks her doctor to remove the device. The most

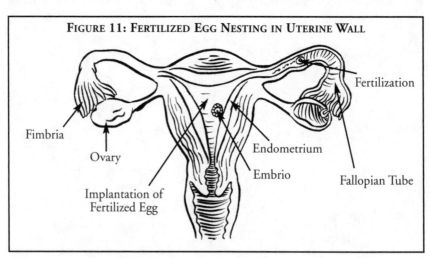

FIGURE 11: FERTILIZED EGG NESTING IN UTERINE WALL

Fimbria

Ovary

Implantation of Fertilized Egg

Endometrium

Embrio

Fertilization

Fallopian Tube

common side effect of Norplant is irregular bleeding. The device is costly to insert and remove (about $500 to $750 to implant and up to $200 to remove).

Depo-Provera is similar to Norplant, but it is given as an injection every twelve weeks. It blocks ovulation for three months. Those effects cannot be reversed; the drug continues working for three months.

Surgical intervention. Tubal ligation, or cutting and tying (or cauterizing) a woman's Fallopian tubes, keeps the egg and sperm from meeting. (See figure 12.) If the two Fallopian tubes are cut and tied, the eggs and sperm cannot come together. In rare cases, the tubes grow back.

Tubal ligation is a surgical procedure that can be done on an outpatient basis, under local anesthesia, either in a clinic or hospital. Complications include bleeding, infection, or reaction to the anesthetic, but these are rare.

Other surgical procedures. A hysterectomy, or surgical removal of a woman's uterus, prevents pregnancy. So does an ovarectomy, or removal of a woman's ovaries. However, neither of these procedures are ordinarily used for contraception.

The rhythm method. Ovulation normally occurs about halfway through a woman's cycle, or about ten to fifteen days after the onset of the menstrual flow. The egg can be fertilized for roughly twenty-four hours after it is released from the

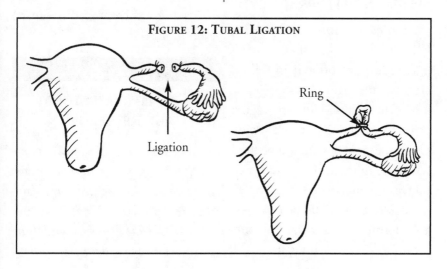

FIGURE 12: TUBAL LIGATION

Ligation

Ring

ovary. So fertilization is possible from days ten through eighteen of a woman's monthly cycle.

That sounds pretty predictable. But it isn't because the rhythm method depends on the regularity of a woman's menstrual cycle, and many women's cycles are not 100 percent reliable. Predicting ovulation becomes difficult, and the chances of pregnancy increase.

Ovulation is more accurately identified by a woman's body temperature. When a woman ovulates, her temperature rises slightly. To prevent pregnancy, sexual relations should cease the day before ovulation, during ovulation, and twenty-four hours after, because sperm remain viable for forty-eight hours.

SPERM INHIBITORS

Jellies, creams, and foams. Chemicals that kill sperm (spermatocides) are offered in jellies, creams, and foam. These spermatocides are injected into the vagina prior to intercourse to eliminate viable sperm. They should be used with a diaphragm or condom to increase their effectiveness. Spermatocides are not 100 percent reliable. Remember, it takes only one sperm to penetrate an egg.

Vasectomy. The most reliable way to avoid pregnancy is by surgically blocking the pathways for sperm and eggs to meet. A vasectomy, which closes the route for sperm to leave the testicles, is an effective method of birth control. (See figure 13.) However, even surgical intervention can fail if a man's vas deferens, which carries sperm from the epididymis to the ejaculatory duct, manages to reconnect. Reconnecting is rare. One caution: some sperm remain in a man's system after the operation, so another form of contraception should be used for at least twenty to thirty ejaculations following a vasectomy.

A vasectomy, which costs up to $500, is less costly than tubal ligation, which costs up to $2,500. Reversing either procedure costs even more.

Q & A

CAN HIS VASECTOMY BE REVERSED?

My husband was previously married. He had four children by his first wife and had a vasectomy before she died of cancer. Now that we're married, I'd like to have a child. Is it possible for my husband's operation to be reversed? Could he still father a child?

Louis: Yes, your husband's vasectomy can be reversed. The surgery should be done by an experienced microsurgeon using specialized instruments. One type of reversal stitches the cut ends of the vas deferens together. If there's too much scarring and sperm is blocked from getting to the vas deferens, the vas deferens can be directly connected to the epididymis. The cost of the surgery ranges from $5,000 to $15,000.

Recent studies indicate that sperm appears in the semen in approximately 85 to 97 percent of men who have vasectomy reversal surgery. Approximately 50 percent of couples subsequently achieve a

pregnancy. Consult a urologist to explore this option.

Q & A

WHAT IF SHE FORGETS TO TAKE THE PILL?

My wife and I decided to use the pill for birth control. The problem is that she sometimes forgets to take it. So we're now in the midst of the second pregnancy in three years of marriage. Obviously this kind of birth control isn't working. What do we do now?

Louis: You and your wife should share with each other your feelings about having children. Your wife may just be forgetful about taking a daily pill, but she may also "forget" to take it because she really wants to get pregnant. If

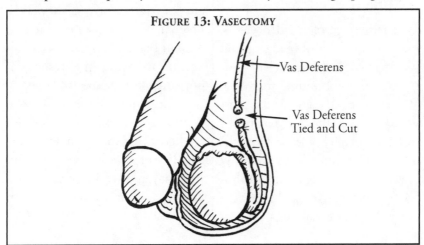

FIGURE 13: VASECTOMY

Vas Deferens

Vas Deferens Tied and Cut

you both agree on contraception, at least for a while, we encourage you to consider other alternatives, such as a diaphragm, Depo-Provera injections, Norplant, or condoms. Remember, none of these are 100 percent effective in preventing pregnancy. If you're ready to discontinue having children altogether, consider tubal ligation or vasectomy.

Use the months you have left in this current pregnancy as a decision-making period. Explore options with your obstetrician. Talk to trusted friends or a pastor. Pray for guidance from God in making this important decision about birth control. Most important, make sure you are both comfortable with whatever you decide.

THE BOTTOM LINE ON BIRTH CONTROL

In this age of rapid development in the fields of medicine and pharmacology, the science of contraception is continuing to evolve. We've addressed some of the most widely used methods of birth control, but not all. Some newer methods include Lunelle, a monthly injection of hormones; the Ortho-Evra contraceptive patch; and the Nuva Ring, a vaginal ring with hormones. Before choosing your own method, we recommend you discuss new developments with your doctor, and that you supplement this discussion with your own research on the medical and ethical implications of each option. We suggest you look at *The Contraception Guidebook: Options, Risks, and Answers for Christian Couples* by William Cutrer, M.D., and Sandra Glahn, Th.M. It's a great guide for exploring options.

All methods of contraception can fail but one: abstinence. Understandably, very few couples choose abstinence as a method of birth control. Even the apostle Paul and Jesus indicate that abstinence requires a special calling (1 Corinthians 7:1–7; Matthew 19:10–13).

Abortion and abortion drugs are not contraceptives. They end a pregnancy. They take the life of a human being. Abortion is not an option to avoid the results of unplanned or irresponsible sex.

The emotional and physical complications following abortion are becoming increasingly apparent. If you have had an abortion, you may receive forgiveness and healing for the wounds abortion has caused.

PART FOUR:
MAKING MARITAL
ADJUSTMENTS

7

IT TAKES TWO:

Loving through Differences

As a male, I have a broader range of sexual curiosity than my wife. That's because men generally like more variety. I've needed to exercise restraint in my adventurous spirit while using gentle persuasion to woo Melissa out of her comfort zone.

Still, I've never been as wild as one guy I talked to who had this fantasy of making love in a canoe on a lake in the moonlight. He and his wife pulled it off—capsizing only once. He noted it to be a very satisfying, once-in-a-lifetime experience.

Our riskiest lovemaking happened during blanket parties in a remote mountain meadow. Sex was exciting and not too threatening until a helicopter came over the ridge one day. That was the end of that!

You and your spouse each have definite ways you expect love to be expressed. Chances are that is the same way you choose to show love. Couples who take time to discover each other's love language are more likely to connect sexually. That's a no-brainer, really. When two individuals make frequent deposits into each other's emotional bank accounts, they create a solid base for expressing themselves sexually.

Still, we've known hundreds of couples who miss each other's signals. One expresses love verbally, the other with physical affection. One offers love through acts of service, while the other looks for material gifts. One hugs and touches, while the other is busy buying nice things. With such different languages, expectations, and preferences, both feel neglected because each is not getting what each wants.

To find understanding—and good sex—in the midst of such diversity, look at your basic differences. Communicate your sexual desires and preferences about what brings you fulfillment. And give each other the grace to explore the delights of your sexuality without shame.

THE CRUCIBLE OF LOVE

Men and women aren't alike. Like the old nursery rhyme says, one gender is snips and snails while the other is sugar and spice. How then can men and women reconcile their differences?

To blend such disparate elements, we might put everything into some sort of crucible, force them together with heat, stir them around, then watch for fusion to occur. That's a pretty good description of sexual intercourse. In the heat and friction and intense pleasure of lovemaking, the differences between male and female begin to dissolve. Two people begin to bond together. In the words of Scripture, "The two become one flesh."

The breakdown of defensive boundaries allows a relationship to grow. As two people learn to honor, love, and trust each other, they also become better equipped to handle stress in other parts of life.

Q & A

HOW CAN HE KNOW WHAT I WANT?

My husband is really gentle and loving, but he also thinks he understands exactly what I want in lovemaking. It's like he doesn't believe me when I say something else would feel better or arouse me more. What do you recommend?

Melissa: You have taken a great first step in communicating your sexual likes and dislikes to your husband. But you may need to try new ways of communicating. There's the old two-by-four approach, but I can't really recommend clubbing him over the head.

Perhaps you could come up with a good example that would get his attention. You know your husband better than anyone, so listen to the way he talks, and try to use illustrations or ideas that he's most familiar with. Keeping the discussion light, you might try a direct challenge: "If I told you what turns me on, how would you use that information?"

You say your husband is loving and gentle. It tells me that he wants to please you and will eventually listen if you can get on the same wavelength.

Four Ways to Bridge Differences

Men and women have different approaches, expectations, and hormonal drives for sex. Here are some necessary ingredients to help them overcome those differences and click for a lifetime:

Long-term commitment. A couple in a long-term, committed relationship build a more secure and trusting territory with each sexual encounter. In that context, intercourse becomes making love rather than just having sex.

Mutual submission. Men usually want more frequent sex and greater variety in sexual play. Women usually want more emotional connection through conversation and tender touch. They also prefer more consistent lovemaking techniques. These differences can lead to tension over positions for intercourse, frequency of sex, and experimentation with different sources of stimulation.

But differences can also provide a great opportunity to develop mutual submissiveness as each partner looks for ways to show love to the other. For example, to please her husband, a wife may engage in sex more frequently or try techniques that go beyond her comfort zone. A husband may relinquish a sexual fantasy or adjust his demands for more frequent intercourse so he can please his wife. These exercises in personal restraint are not easy, but they can help build the oneness of intimacy.

Mutual pleasure. If a sexual activity doesn't bring both of you enjoyment, repeating it eventually causes resentment. Self-focused sex often involves power or control. Sex becomes an invasive, dominating behavior that violates the personal dignity of another person.

God wants us to enjoy the passion and pleasure of lovemaking. Some definite boundaries were established to protect and enhance the maximum enjoyment of the gift. One is that both of you agree on what you do to find enjoyment and pleasure in lovemaking.

Honest talk. Melissa and I are lousy mind readers. When we assume we know what the other is thinking, feeling, or wanting, we're often wrong, even after forty years of marriage. We do much better when we talk—actually saying words that reveal ourselves.

The old way of hinting and guessing and assuming produces lots of frustration. Yes, of course we can sense each other's moods through nonverbal cues, but being able to talk about our feelings, desires, and spiritual concerns is essential to the kind of bonding that leads to super sex.

CAL AND CINDY: MISSING EACH OTHER'S SIGNALS

Cal's parents and siblings were fantastic servers. Family members each knew they were loved because other people in the family sensed their needs. Someone was always there to take you where you needed to go or to keep your clothes clean or to serve you your favorite food. Everyone helped each other.

Cindy's family showed love through physical affection. Someone was always ready to hug you or pat you on the back when you needed affirmation.

What to Expect in Lovemaking

- ✑ Expect that you and your mate will differ in what you each experience as erotic.
- ✑ Expect each of your timing from arousal to orgasm to be different.
- ✑ Expect the intensity of your climaxes to vary each time you make love.
- ✑ Expect to not have simultaneous, explosive orgasms every time you make love.
- ✑ Expect to feel more loved and united in body, soul, and spirit as you increasingly bond together. That's what the Bible means by saying a couple becomes one flesh.

You can imagine what happened when Cindy failed to offer Cal acts of service or when Cal was short on kisses and hugs for Cindy. Each tried to connect with the other, but without knowing each other's love language, their efforts were meaningless. Cindy didn't care that Cal washed the dishes—she just wanted a hug. Cal got tired of Cindy's clinginess when he couldn't find a clean shirt.

Sex became a minefield of disappointments. The difficulties eased after the couple learned to understand each other's languages of love and to court each other accordingly.

FULL DISCLOSURE NEEDED

For a healthy sex life, spouses should tell each other what they like and don't like in sex. They should ask questions about things they don't understand. Sure, talking about sex is uncomfortable at first. Melissa and I have found that reading a book about sexuality together can provide a good starting point.

Whatever you do, don't assume anything. It's surprising how much misinformation is accepted as truth. You may be missing out on a lot of sexual pleasure by not talking to your mate about sex. Some examples:

- Edgar thought women didn't enjoy sex so he never bothered to learn what Mabel wanted. During therapy, he was pleasantly surprised to find out that she enjoyed orgasm. He also learned that she had occasionally masturbated because she thought he couldn't bring her to orgasm. Both were like honeymooners after they made those discoveries and learned better lovemaking skills.

- Sylvia gave birth to her fourth child before she and her husband realized that douching after intercourse was not an effective contraceptive.

- Norman assumed his wife wouldn't want oral sex. Judy had been curious about trying it for some time but had never said so. After therapy they began some fun experiments.

- Tim and Theresa thought the missionary position was the only Christian way to have intercourse. They later discovered that Theresa had more effective stimulation when she was astride Tim.

Q & A

WHY DOES SHE WANT SEX ONLY ON SUNDAY?

My wife and I have fallen into a pattern of having sex once a week—always on Sunday night. This suits her fine; she's a schedule-oriented person. But I don't feel that she really wants to have sex; she's just checking off another item on her weekly to-do list. I try to understand that this is just who she is, but I'm starting to resent her.

Louis: Try writing a letter to your wife, expressing your love and desire to be a thoughtful husband. Point out the things you appreciate about her. Then let her know about your hurt and frustration—even how awkward you feel about telling her that.

Then talk. Discuss male sexuality in general, then mention how you feel about being controlled in your sexual interaction. Indicate your longing to discover a more spontaneous solution for achieving oneness with her.

Open, vulnerable, straight talk about your feelings and desires is the only way to avoid sounding critical or delivering ultimatums or being forced to beg.

Melissa: While you resent this path toward sexual intimacy, your wife may be unhappy about other issues, such as emotional intimacy. Sex for sex's sake is not very appealing to a woman. But sex as the natural outcome of relational intimacy is very appealing.

You may be surprised to discover that neither of you is very happy with the status quo. As the two of you talk openly, you may discover a better way toward mutual satisfaction.

FREQUENCY OF SEX: WHY IT'S SUCH AN ISSUE

Of all the areas of tension in marital sexuality, frequency of sex is the most troublesome. Here are some reasons for that:

It's a two-person decision. Usually men have a higher libido (because of the colossal impact of testosterone), but not always. Whichever spouse has the higher desire for sex feels the most frustration. This difference is not something that could be anticipated from your dating days. In the excitement and romance of courtship, both partners showed an intense need for physical affection and for expressing their love sexually.

It's connected with performance. When a wife turns down a husband, for whatever reason, the husband tends to interpret her refusal as a rejection of his manhood. When a woman pushes for more frequent sex, she might wonder what's wrong with her femininity if he doesn't want intercourse.

The frequency question is not just a matter of negotiating a satisfactory compromise, because each partner's self-acceptance hangs in the balance.

It's loaded with other issues. How often to have sex can be strewn with emotional baggage, such as anger, guilt, fear, jealousy, and shame. Emotions such as anger, guilt, and shame affect a woman's sexual response more than they do a man's, perhaps because in intercourse a woman opens herself to being penetrated. Becoming vulnerable is hard to do when a woman is in emotional turmoil.

Since marriage begins with a vow of exclusivity, it's crucial for spouses to feel 100 percent loyal to each other. If a partner struggles with jealousy, he or she must express that to the spouse, who may be oblivious to actions or attitudes that feed into such jealousy. In con-fessing feelings of jealousy, the spouse must take care not to blame the other partner. Statements such as "You're giving her too much attention" or "Stop it or else!" do not ease the way for change.

How Much Sex Is Enough?

We've heard from couples who were satisfied with sex once a month. Others weren't happy unless they had it three times a day. So how often should you have sex? You decide. There is no outside standard.

If you're struggling with differences in your sex drives, keep working toward sexual oneness. Discuss your individual barriers to desire to make sure these issues aren't skewing your experience of mutual enjoyment. Sexual oneness is a process—but it's worth working for because it can bring satisfaction into every level of your marriage.

When She Won't Initiate

Some factors that contribute to a woman's hesitation to initiate lovemaking:

She doesn't have testosterone. The hormone testosterone

stimulates sexual drive and circulates at far higher levels in the bloodstream of men than in women. The result is that men think about sex more often than women.

She's been told not to. Girls traditionally are taught to be sexually reserved. This modesty about sexual exposure and aggressiveness often extends into the marriage relationship. We often counsel women who avoid initiating sexual play and are also reluctant to let their husbands see them naked. That is unfortunate, since men respond primarily to visual stimulation.

She'd rather have relationship. I've rarely talked to a guy who didn't fantasize that women had an irresistible drive for sex with him. By contrast, a woman is more satisfied by relational intimacy. Sensing that men only want her sexually makes a woman feel like a sex object.

LESSONS IN SEDUCING HIM

A woman may not be innately wired to seduce a man. However, on occasion, it can be fun to vamp your spouse. Here's a step-by-step way to overcome inhibitions and get you and your mate going in the bedroom:

1. Make a list of all aspects of sexual play you can imagine (in private, of course).

2. Rank them according to the degree of difficulty each represents for you.

3. Beginning with the easiest activity for you to do, gradually move down the list, mastering each level in turn. Your first exercise might be to signal to your spouse that you're available. The next might be to show up in a sexy nightie or to lower the lights. The next could be to reach over and caress him in a stimulating area of his anatomy, and so on.

4. Allow each new, more assertive behavior to become comfortable before moving on and letting your husband know you are purposefully (even if timidly) working on that aspect of your sexuality.

Q & A

WHY MUST I BEG HIM TO LOVE ME?

My husband and I are intimate, on average, every month-and-a-half.

I've reached the point where I can no longer talk to him about this because I feel like I'm begging to be made love to. I love my husband, but I am afraid that if this continues, one morning I am going to wake up and have absolutely no feelings for him. Can our marriage last with this type of problem?

Love can outlast sexual frequency issues. It can also grow to richer levels of intimacy. Focusing on other ways to express your love besides sex is crucial. As you develop these ways, you may adjust better sexually. Having said this, we realize it's hard to live with frustration. Working together toward a better sexual rhythm is essential.

In our culture, a man usually has a higher drive for sex than a woman. That makes your situation especially painful. It probably doesn't help for your friends to say, "I wish that were my problem." You may even question your own attractiveness as a sexual partner.

Understanding your husband and accepting his individuality is an important first step. He may be struggling with his self-image. Or there may be other issues. Talking about them in an open, nonblaming way is essential.

WHEN HE WON'T INITIATE

Here are some things a couple can do when the husband isn't interested in sex:

Get some counseling. You might assume that a husband with libido problems would resist talking through the problem with a professional counselor, but sometimes a husband is surprisingly ready for that step.

Try a little seduction. A husband might fear the risk of initiating sex. A wife could minimize this by asking for some loving. Expressing her need in a straightforward way isn't begging. It's clear communication.

Focus on other things. Think about his nonsexual needs. Discover his language of love and sublimate your sexual needs till he's more ready for sex.

Have a physical. Realize there is a huge range in sexual drive in males. Libido is affected by physical factors such as testosterone, thyroid function, diabetes, vascular and neurological systems, drug and alcohol use, side effects of medication, and fatigue. A thorough physical evaluation would be helpful. (See "Why His Equipment Fails," 173–74.)

Q & A

Why Doesn't He Want Sex?

I am coming to you desperate for answers. My husband never wants sex. He doesn't understand the importance of this intimacy to me or how it affects every other aspect of our marriage. I am miserable and frustrated. I feel completely unattractive, despite his constantly letting me know that it's not me and that he is very attracted to me. His actions certainly show differently. Please help me.

Louis: Yours is an unusual but not unheard-of situation. We occasionally counsel couples whose pattern is like yours. There are some men who have lower libido, and a once-a-month pattern for intercourse seems to satisfy their needs. There are two factors to consider.

The first factor is your feelings. Your sexual desire and the frustration you're experiencing are important. It is healthy for you to have the release of an orgasm and to enjoy a sense of intimacy. Your husband should be providing that for you. You've tried to communicate your feelings, but you might also explore how your husband feels about your frustration. Often a man feels threatened by any suggestion that his wife is dissatisfied with him.

The second factor is your husband's libido. There are many possible reasons for your husband's lower sex drive. For most males these reasons are scary to look at. Denial is usually the first line of defense. A man doesn't want to admit that he may not be able to meet his wife's sexual needs. We all like to think of ourselves as studs (whatever that means).

Get your husband to talk openly with you about the issue. Start by talking about your sexual histories, asking questions like:

- What did your family think about sex? What were their attitudes about it?
- Were you ever sexually abused? By whom? How was it handled? Did you get therapy for it?
- What were your experiences with masturbation? How did your family react to this activity? How do you feel about doing that?

⮸ What experiences have you had with pornography? How has that affected you?

⮸ What premarital experiences with sex did you have?

If your husband is unwilling to discuss these issues with you, perhaps he would talk to a trusted male friend. Ultimately it would be helpful for you to go together to a competent counselor. One way or the other, do something to move the situation forward. The status quo is creating too much tension for you.

Melissa: I am wondering if you need to take a good look at yourself. Ask a woman friend if there are things about you that might be a turnoff to your husband. He says he is still attracted to you, but to say otherwise would be risky for any man. Check out such things as cleanliness, odors, weight, the way you dress, your playfulness, attitudes, or anything you and your friend can think of that might be objectionable to him.

Choose this friend carefully. She should be someone who can be trusted to keep this matter confidential.

Ask the Lord to let you know what the problem is. His plan for you and your husband is oneness. You can count on him to help you achieve that.

Q & A

WHY IS SEX SUCH A LOW PRIORITY FOR HER?

I love my wife dearly, but I'm frustrated by our sex life. Sex is good, once we get going, but I always have to initiate it. Even then, I get rejected a lot because my wife has so many excuses—she needs ten hours of sleep, she wants to watch the soap operas she recorded earlier, she needs to finish the ironing. I can't figure out why lovemaking is such a low priority for her.

Louis: Your wife—and mine—are quite normal. In the thousand-plus couples Melissa and I have counseled, we can recall less than twenty in which the wife had a greater sexual appetite than her husband. So I've tried to accept that reality in my wife and adjust to it.

Part of the adjustment was understanding that my wife's disinterest was not an indictment of my sexual prowess. Early in our marriage I assumed, like most guys, that if I was an adequate lover, Melissa would be more interested. I imagined she would want my body so much that she'd seduce me every chance she could.

Eventually I realized that her lack of interest was primarily biological. That took us both off the hook—me from doubting my desirability, and Melissa from feeling frustrated by my demands.

Now we try to minimize the frustrations caused by our differences in several ways:

⊱ I accept my God-given sex drive as a sensible reason for me to take the initiative in lovemaking (even if it's all the time).

⊱ I look for creative ways to awaken my beloved's passion.

⊱ We agree that sex is beneficial to our marriage, so we try to maximize our relationship outside the bedroom. That increases the chance that sex will follow.

Melissa: I used to think Louis had a one-track mind. Now I know he does! But I've also learned that he is normal. Another thing I've noticed is that Louis's work, moods, attitudes, and behavior in general seem to improve when he is sexually satisfied. I like enhanc-ing his effectiveness in these areas, so I've tried to take more initiative in sex. This hasn't been difficult—it doesn't take much to seduce Louis!

A DIFFERENCE IN NEEDS

Over the years, Melissa and I have learned a few things about gender needs that could help you:

Men usually have stronger sexual needs. If women had our testosterone levels, they'd be a lot more interested in sex. Of course they'd also have beards and hair on their chests. They might also have liver damage—so don't slip testosterone into your wife's coffee.

You might suggest she do some reading on male sexuality. Helping her understand normal male sexuality will take you further than accusing her of frigidity.

Women usually have stronger emotional needs. The most effective way to enhance a woman's sexual responsiveness is to get close to her emotionally before reaching out for her physically. For a woman, sexual intimacy blossoms out of a sense of relational intimacy, spiritual bonding, and emotional safety. Without these as a foundation, sexual vulnerability is too frightening.

We've often heard a wife say that getting a glimpse into her husband's soul—his needs, fears, hurts, and dreams—makes her want to get physically closer to him. His emotional openness allows her to become more sexually vulnerable.

Q & A

WHY DOES HE SWEAR DURING SEX?

My husband sometimes uses coarse language when we're making love. At times I'm glad there's some passion and earthiness between us. But other times I feel that swearing cheapens our experience. I'm embarrassed to bring it up, but I'd like to confront this problem. What do you suggest?

Louis: In Colossians 3:8, Paul tells us not to let filthy language come out of our mouths. Certain forms of earthy language that are intended to be playful and erotic might be acceptable, but words that demean either one of you are out-of-bounds.

Since you feel uncomfortable with coarse language, you should talk about that with your husband. Pick a good time, then say, "There's something I'd like to ask you; is this a good time?" Then, in a nonaccusing way, express your curiosity about the language your husband uses during sex.

Ask him what the words he uses during sex mean to him. His response may be related to how sex was first explained to him. Most guys first heard about sex from their grade-school buddies. As they got older, they began to associate sex with what was dirty or hidden or wrong. Some men still have trouble breaking the habit of thinking about sex as forbidden.

It's also crucial for you to explore your response to earthy expressions. Are you offended by such talk because of the words or the way they're delivered? Talk to your husband about your reaction. Then decide how you want to deal with this problem. Like all communication, this exchange should invite honest response and comfortable agreement about what's enjoyable and what's offensive.

Q & A

HOW CAN I MAKE LOVE WHEN SHE MAKES ME FEEL BAD?

At times my wife says or does things to me that she knows will upset me.

Or she'll embarrass me in front of others. Five minutes later, she's all sweet and lovable and wants to be intimate. I feel cheap and used. She never says she's sorry. How can I enjoy sex with my wife after verbal abuse?

Louis: A couple's sexual relationship is often a barometer of their overall relationship. Usually, as a husband and wife develop basic attitudes and skills for relating with each other, their sex life improves. So, take a look at the foundational principles of marriage, begin to apply them, and see how they affect your sexual relationship:

Principle One: View marriage as a lifelong process. Marital experts and professors Les and Leslie Parrott discovered while giving a basic relational skills course that the majority of their students didn't have a clue about relating to a marriage partner. Concepts like courtesy, mutual respect, apologizing, accepting differences, and resolving conflict were foreign to them. Yet marital intimacy depends on those skills every day. If you and your partner lack such skills, ask for help early in your marriage rather than waiting until

resentments are layered like coats of paint on a thrift-shop chair. You can then begin to peel away the hurts and get down to the valuable mahogany.

Principle Two: Discover what's important to you. It's important for you and your spouse to identify your differences in emotional sensitivity, expectations, sexual preferences, and styles of dealing with conflict. One way to do that is to each write a history of your relationship. Describe events that seem important to you, how those events affected you emotionally, and what you concluded about each other afterward. For instance, you might describe a time when your wife embarrassed you in front of others, how you felt when that happened (ashamed? angry? discounted?), and what conclusion you came to ("I can't trust her," "I'm overly sensitive to criticism," or "She enjoys putting me down").

Principle Three: Share your thoughts. The primary goal of any relationship is to understand the other person's point of view—not to prove who's right or wrong. So work toward understanding, not blame, and forgive each other for hurts you may have caused. You'll probably find that each of you has blind spots in your relationship. For example, you are painfully aware of your wife's insensitivity toward your feelings. Insensitivity is her blind spot. Your blind spot may be doing things that fuel her hostility and make her lash out at you. As each of you listens to the other, the need to justify behavior should diminish.

Principle Four: Realize that change begins with you. As much as you'd like to change your spouse, that is futile. With better insight into yourself, you can begin to focus on how you can be a better mate. Changes in yourself plus better communication between you and your wife offer the real promise of change. A visit with a marriage counselor can speed up the work you are doing.

WAYS TO SATISFY BOTH MALE AND FEMALE DRIVES

Women tend to want touch and affection that doesn't lead to intercourse while men typically push for the sexual release of orgasm. Short of emasculation or deprivation, how can you satisfy both of these drives?

When people with contrasting perceptions are polarized by dif-ferences, they become enemies. Rather than being considerate of each other, they dig into defensive postures or make aggressive demands. This can certainly happen in marriage over the issue of how affection is given. A better way is for spouses to become allies in a quest for mutual satisfaction.

For example, let's say Sally wants to have some cuddling from Bill without it leading to intercourse. If they approach each other on principle ("A good husband cuddles when asked" or "A good wife wants to satisfy her husband's sexual needs"), both will feel shorted. Sally will become resentful because Bill won't hold her, and Bill won't hold Sally because she won't have sex.

A better way is for the couple to negotiate from interests, or what they each want in their marriage. Their lists would probably include words like *intimacy, trust, caring, closeness, affection, respect, consideration, selflessness,* and possibly *sexual pleasure.* Chances are that in reviewing each other's lists, Bill and Sally will find they have many of the same desires. Realizing that they both want some of the same things can help them shift from being adversaries to working together as allies.

They might discover that Bill likes loving touch (back rubs, gentle fingers through his hair, cuddling on the couch) and that, when the time is right for her, Sally enjoys the exciting release of orgasm. Defining the parameters of touching no longer is a win-lose proposition.

WORKING THROUGH DIFFERENCES

So here you have it: the husband with surging hormones, fragile self-confidence, and emotional protectiveness; and the wife who desires relational intimacy, is sexually reserved, and resists being reduced to a sex object. No wonder becoming one flesh is a challenge! To work through this:

- ∞ Understand that these differences are natural and give each other some space.
- ∞ Commit to change. In any marriage there are countless opportunities to show love. View changes in initiating lovemaking as a gradual process.
- ∞ If you can't initiate lovemaking, explore the origins of your shyness.
- ∞ Discard the negative beliefs that inhibit you.
- ∞ Celebrate your sexuality. Men and women are remarkable creatures capable of intensely pleasurable sexual experiences. Find ways to accept and celebrate the wonders of your body. When you do, it will be easier for you to give yourself without inhibitions.

Talk about It

Begin by each making a list of three ways you differ on your approach to sex. Then discuss those differences. Talk about ways you might each adapt to each difference so that it does not divide you. Then talk about ways that those differences might actually enhance your sexual relationship.

8

GETTING IN THE MOOD:

Touch Points to Love

Humans need more than food, water, oxygen, and physical shelter. About fifty years ago, psychiatrist John Bowlby discovered that as infants we could receive all of those things and yet waste away if we lacked one other essential element: touch. Babies who were not cuddled sank into depression, quit eating, and died.

We never grow out of the need for physical contact. Of course, there are cultural and family differences about how to show touch and affection, but the basic need persists.

Even men brought up as nontouchers are driven by the need for touching in sex. We might sanctify the need for sex by calling it a drive for procreation, but let's face it, sex usually has little to do with reproducing ourselves.

That's where conflict arises. We need touch and cuddling long beyond childhood, but that need gets complicated by testosterone. One touch inevitably leads to more intense touch, which ultimately results in sex. Women often complain about that. Each will say, "I'd like my husband to just hold me, but it won't stop there. Once he starts touching, it's going to end up in the bedroom."

Both men and women have a healthy need for touch. While women want more of the kind of touch that does not lead to sex, men want the kind that does. So what are some ways to satisfy both of these needs without depriving either? Read on.

PREAMBLE BEFORE YOU TOUCH

We do much better at connecting with each other when we talk—actually saying words that reveal ourselves. One form of communication is what we call "preambles." That's giving the other person a signal that you've got something important to say. You may even indicate what kind of response you would like to have. For example, if I'm feeling the need for nonsexual touch, I might have this kind of conversation with Louis:

Melissa: Louis, I have some feelings I need to express. Is this a good time to talk?

Louis: Sure, what's on your mind?

Melissa: We've been so busy lately. I'd love it if you'd just hold me for a while.

Given our history, Louis might want to clarify things at this point. Here's what he'd probably ask.

Louis: Ah, just wondering: is this a seduction?

Melissa: No, just a request for some cuddling.

On the other hand, the preamble might go something like this:

Louis: Sweetheart, I'd like to talk about something that's bothering me. It's nothing you have to respond to—just something I want you to know.

Melissa: Can we talk after dinner? I'm pretty busy right now—and I know you don't want your food burned.

Louis: Sure, how about if I help you with the dishes later? Then maybe we can talk.

Later, while washing dishes, the preamble continues:

"Helloooo, honey, your Love Machine is home for yooooooou!"

Melissa: OK, now what did you want to tell me?

Louis: Well, I realized I've been kind of crabby. I think it's because I feel unloved. It's been several days since we made love. I'd like to make a date with you. When are you available?

Melissa: I was wondering if something was wrong, but I didn't realize you felt unloved. I can be available in five minutes, but don't expect too much. I'm really tired. If we wait till tomorrow morning, though, I'd have more energy. Which would you prefer?

Louis: Both!

Q & A

WHY WON'T HE KISS ME FIRST?

When my husband and I have sex, he won't caress or kiss me. He just wants intercourse. When I ask for some affection, my husband gets angry and says I shouldn't tell him what to do. I've tried to let this go, but I really crave his touch! Why is it so difficult for him to be affectionate during sex?

Louis: We men have a lot riding on our ability to make a conquest, and that drive is fueled by testosterone. Therein lies the problem; once we're aroused by testosterone, our brain changes its focus, and we don't think right. Most of us also seem to have a hard time realizing that by investing in foreplay and showing affection to our wives, we will reap huge dividends not only sexually but also relationally.

We recommend that you have a serious discussion with your husband to help him understand your needs in lovemaking. Find a good time and place so that your husband will be especially receptive. Then let him know in a non-threatening way that you're struggling with something and need his help.

Explain your frustration in terms of your feelings, not his behavior. Resist the temptation to accuse him of anything; that will only shut him down and close him off to what you want to say. Stick to talking about your desire for sexual fulfillment and what will make you responsive to him. Assure him that he's the man you want.

SEX TRIGGERS

The things that sexually excite us are as unique as our personalities.

Candy and flowers, sweet nothings whispered in moonlight, soft music and candlelight, tight sweaters and bikinis work for most. But seeing a girl in hose without shoes wildly excited one of my college buddies. Go figure!

What's important about triggers is to share them with your spouse. Melissa and I frequently see people who know what their personal triggers are but refuse to share them with their spouses, saying, "If my spouse really loved me, he/she would know what I like without me having to say it." That cockamamy notion assumes mind-reading abilities beyond most human capacities. It is much more effective—and loving—to tell each other what arouses you, then to accept those confidences as a genuine gift of love.

WHAT GETS US IN THE MOOD?

Louis: Bing Crosby used to croon: "I'm in the mood for love simply because you're near me. Funny, but when you're near me, I'm in the mood for love."

As an old romantic, I really identify with that mushy male stuff. Still, I've rarely met a woman who gets in the mood just by being near a guy. She's a lot more complicated.

Melissa: I wouldn't say we're complicated, just mysterious. Think about the sexual response curve in a woman. My arousal curve is a gentle slope, like a woman's breast. Feeding into that curve are attitudes, expectations, my love language, your approach, my sugar level, my selfishness, my feelings about my body,

---

Talk about It

To discover your mate's sexual triggers, you can guess what they are. Or you can simply talk about those sexual triggers, eliminating the need to guess. Ask each other: What two or three things could I do to warm you up to lovemaking? What might I eliminate that might cool off your passion?

and my level of fatigue. Just to name a few.

Louis: Well, that sounds too complicated for my simple brain. Would you be willing to sort through some of that to help me know when you're in the mood for love?

Melissa: I don't mind at all, but remember, I may leave something out so I can remain mysterious. Let's sort through these one by one.

THINGS THAT AFFECT THE MOOD

Melissa: Here are several things that affect my mood:

My attitudes toward sex. Those started in my childhood. My family was very modest and raised me to have firm boundaries about boys. Mom probably never used the word *sex*. I knew what she wasn't talking about, though, and knew that I should bring my virginity into marriage. The message was clear: Good girls don't do sex.

The problem was, this message never got updated. No one ever told me sex would be OK after marriage or that it could actually be fun. I sensed that, but

on a deeper level I was afraid to let myself go.

Lots of messages from childhood get stuck in our minds. We counseled a woman recently who'd been sexually abused and thought the only value she had was as a sex object. She had a hard time saying no to her husband. Another woman learned from her mother that sex was dirty and painful but a duty she had to endure in marriage. Sure enough, the daughter saw sex as a painful, dirty duty.

By contrast, girls who learn from parents that sex is a natural part of a loving marriage look forward to sex as a healthy, enriching experience.

My expectations for marriage. One thing I expected in marriage was that the man of the house should be able to handle anything that came along. I saw my daddy that way. "Red" Morris was the strong, silent type who had everything under control. Naturally I expected my husband to be the same way. What follows is that when I feel secure because everything is under control, I'm more likely to be in the mood for love. Conversely, the more anxious

I feel, the less able I am to respond positively.

The way love is expressed. Louis's language of love has always been physical affection, while mine has been acts of service. Many couples have difficulty understanding such differences. But when your mate doesn't understand the way you show love, it's hard to get into the mood.

It used to be awkward for me to touch and caress Louis the way he wanted. It's not so difficult anymore, especially when he is speaking my language. When he is doing thoughtful things for me during the day, I'm much more likely to want to make love with him at night.

We once heard about a young man who married a girl from a hostile tribe. Anytime the newlyweds were having conflict, someone said, "You know, he married outside the tribe."

I think we all marry outside the tribe. What's more, the love language of one family may be very different from the love language of the other. For example, when we first married, Louis expected me to do things the "McBurney way," which to him was the right and only way. That approach turned me off sexually.

Something else that put me off was his assuming that I'd be turned on by all the things he liked. Frontal nudity and ear nibbles did nothing for me. That was hard for him to believe, but he finally got it. At least he never tried the Neanderthal approach of forcing me to do what he wanted. Some husbands we've counseled still act like junior high bullies and expect their wife to be turned on.

My level of anger. If I'm feeling angry about something, it's hard for me to emotionally shift gears and try to make love. Of course, it's worse if I'm angry with Louis. That's why I try to keep short accounts. It's much better to express anger and not let it simmer inside so lovemaking isn't put on hold.

My level of selfishness. Sometimes I don't want sex because other things are more important to me. If that level of selfishness gets too strong, I can ignore all the signals Louis may send about lovemaking. I don't like to be selfish, and I certainly can't defend it, but confession is supposed to be good for the soul. That's not to say I'll never be selfish again, but at least Louis knows I feel guilty about it.

How I feel about my body. I saw an ad the other day about getting a makeover. What came to my mind was, "Sure, I'll have one. Make me tall and thin." (I am short and plump.)

Almost every American woman has some flaw that she sees when she looks in the mirror. I wasted years hiding myself from my husband. He is an honest man, and he is easy to read. When he tries to keep something from me, I know. So I believe him when he says that he loves the way I look. Yet I have hung on to my perception of myself as short and plump. Such lack of self-acceptance can easily feed into reluctance to make love.

Q & A

WHY IS SHE
LIFELESS IN BED?

My wife is the sweetest person in the world. She's really easygoing and never gets angry with me no matter what I do. The problem is that she's also lifeless in bed. She never says no to sex, but I can tell she doesn't really like it—she just tolerates it. What gives?

Since anger is a normal human emotion, we wonder what your wife is doing with hers. Unless you're a saint, I doubt that she has no reasons for irritation or frustration from time to time.

You said, "She never gets angry with me no matter what I do." That makes us suspicious that she's stuffing her anger instead of dealing with issues. Stuffing can keep one's surface smooth, but suppressed anger will come out somewhere. Some people who suppress their anger get headaches or stomach ulcers—even heart disease or cancer. Some get paranoid. Others build emotional barriers.

The problem is that when negative feelings are buried, positive feelings get pushed under as well. That may be happening with your sweet wife. She's keeping such a tight lid on anger and other emotions that there's not much energy or passion available for sex.

It's also quite possible that your wife doesn't want to get close to someone who irritates her from time to time. Yet she won't do what's necessary to express her anger at you because it violates inner controls.

Your wife needs counseling to help explore what she was taught about anger by her family or church. Chances are, there was a strong prohibition on expressing anger. She may have heard, "If you can't say something nice, don't say anything at all." This assumes that talking about negative feelings such as hurt, anger, irritation, frustration, loneliness, or abandonment is bad.

Negative feelings can be expressed without attacking another person. Scripture says we should deal with anger in a straightforward, prompt manner (Proverbs 13:3; Ephesians 4:25–27). One way to do that is to use first-person language in sharing feelings and reactions rather than making second-person accusations about another person's behavior. For example, a person might say, "I've been really frustrated lately. I love being with you and having quality time together, but that hasn't been happening. I feel lonely and abandoned. Can we work on this situation?"

We suggest that you and your wife discuss how you each feel about expressing anger, how you might express it in an appropriate way, and how you might deal with issues in constructive ways. When your wife is able to clear out her backlog of anger and hurt, her energy will be freed up for loving. Some of our most passionate moments have come after we cleared the air of conflict.

WHAT IF I'M NOT IN THE MOOD?

"Is it OK if I'm available but not involved?" Melissa asks me sometimes. Although that kind of sex isn't my preference, it is an acceptable alternative from time to time. I have to stop thinking of myself as a superlover to enjoy it. But Melissa has finally convinced me that she finds satisfaction in giving me pleasure. And because we have other times of mutual intensity, we can enjoy these occasional times when one—rather than both—finds sexual satisfaction.

Q & A

WHY AM I NEVER IN THE MOOD?

My husband tells me he often thinks about sex during the day, but I never do. I don't think I'm a very sensual person. I like being close to my husband, and I almost never turn him down when he initiates sex. But truthfully, I'm never in the mood. Should I just accept the way I am, or is there something I can do to become sexier?

Louis: Enjoying sexual feelings in response to a spouse's advances is a wonderful thing. So is participating in sexual play in the context of trust and safety. That's what God intended for us when he created Adam and Eve, naked and unashamed and willing to share their bodies with each other. However, if you don't enjoy sex or do not have orgasms, you may need some helps to move you toward a better experience:

Think more about sex during the day. Focus on the most romantic, most sexually fulfilling encounters you've had with your husband. Do that before he comes home. It might increase your level of response when he initiates sex.

Show him that you want him. Most men yearn to be wanted sexually. Although you may never need your husband sexually as much as he needs you, you might occasionally initiate sex. Do it as an act of the will, motivated by your desire to give love.

Melissa: You may have some ideas about sex that are blocking your enjoyment of sex. Now is the time to alter these ideas. Perhaps you can get a trusted friend or counselor to help you with the process. Above all, be assertive and positive in your approach to this problem. Don't back off. Let your husband know you care. Keep on making yourself as attractive as possible. If your sexual disinterest continues, see a marriage counselor together.

John and Amy: Finding Each Other's Triggers

We recently worked with a couple who'd been at a stalemate for years. Each was sure the other was refusing to do what was romantic out of spite.

John wanted Amy to signal sexual readiness by wearing a seductive teddy to bed. She had no idea that's what he wanted, so night after night she'd put on a pair of old, comfortable pajamas. Amy really loved the notes or poems that John would write expressing how much he cared for her. Yet he thought those notes were meaningless to her because three years ago she had failed to react to one.

It wasn't hard to persuade this couple to share those secrets. The night they did, an erotic note and some seductive nakedness triggered a gratifying response.

EXPRESS YOUR NEEDS

Let's face it. It's hard for a man to cuddle without being sexually aroused and wanting to continue to orgasm. That's the reason most women want to maintain a safe distance.

To overcome such barriers, we must get better at expressing our needs—not just sexual needs and desires but wants and preferences in general. The almost universal assumption is that if a mate really loves you, he or she will know your needs and preferences. Most of us don't operate that way. If we did, we'd be more thoughtful, kind, and considerate. The truth is, we're not very good at sensing what our mate wants. It seems better, then, to just tell each other what we need.

For instance, telling your wife that you love it when she initiates sex and that you're feeling particularly needy right now would be better than seething about her sex put-offs. Of course that works both ways. She should let you know she'd love to seduce you if you'd first vacuum the living room and get the kids to bed. The important thing is to tell each other plainly what you need, and not expect the other person to read your mind.

Q & A

WHY DOESN'T HE LIKE KISSING?

My husband doesn't enjoy kissing. When I kiss him, he pulls away quickly. I love kissing and miss it. He just seems to think it's icky. This is a first marriage for me, but a second marriage for my husband. Is there anything we can do?

Louis: Don't be offended by this question, but have you checked your breath lately? Seriously. One reason some people don't like to kiss is that their spouse has chronic bad breath. If you pass the breath test, ask your husband what it is about kissing that he finds icky.

Melissa: If he doesn't like kissing, what does he like? Focus on those things. That will say to him, "You are important to me, and I want to please you." You will then have a happier man (and it's a lot more fun living with a happy man). Maybe someday your husband will change his mind about kissing, or he'll kiss you as a gift to you. In the meantime, provide what pleases him most.

Marriage is like a laboratory in which we're becoming more Christlike by becoming more selfless. When you're serving, caring, being considerate, and giving up your wants, you're putting faith into practice. You do this in many aspects of your relationship, not just sexually. Happiness is an excellent by-product of your giving behaviors. So is better sex.

Lovemaking: Plan It Like a Symphony

Microwave cooking, email, instant oatmeal, and cell phones are great; so is an occasional "quickie." But some things, such as sex, should be savored and prolonged. Sex is lots more enjoyable when it can be slowly orchestrated—each movement arranged with passion and finesse.

An erotic symphony requires careful planning. Here are some suggestions:

Find the right venue. The bedroom is often filled with reminders of other demands—telephone calls to make, computer email to check, laundry to be put away. That isn't conducive to sex. Finding a different locale for lovemaking can break the power of old habits and leave you free to improvise. As long as you can be reasonably assured of privacy, why not try the woods, the beach, or a comfortable spot in front of the fireplace? We'll admit it: we've even enjoyed an "auto-erotic" experience. Just don't try it while driving.

Vary the time of day. Most couples have a set time for lovemaking: late night after the lights go out. Varying that can be a real boost to sexual enjoyment. Take off a half day from work and spend it in bed with your sweetie. Or wake up early and reach for each other.

Set the atmosphere. Soft music, candlelight, aromatic fragrances, and no television blaring away in the other room creates a relaxed setting. Along with these special effects, begin with some easy conversation about your favorite things and how much you care about each other. All those elements set the tone for slowing things down.

Melissa and I have found that the more familiar we are with each other's "melodies and harmonics," the better we can orchestrate more exciting lovemaking. Building crescendos and soft interludes create an experience that demands an encore. Lovemaking like this takes time and planning, but it's worth it.

It always amazes me how many busy people in all walks of life find time for adulterous relationships. Why not use that creativity to have a torrid affair with your spouse? The rewards are so great you'll want to get together again and again.

Q & A

HOW CAN I WARM THINGS UP?

My wife doesn't want or need sex as often as I do—I understand that this is typical. But if my need seems great and she's not in the mood, is it OK for me to try to warm things up? I'm wondering if there's any way I can be considerate and self-sacrificing, yet get enough sex, too?

Melissa: The way to approach sex with a woman is through rela-

tionship. To warm things up for lovemaking, try doing the things your wife says she needs. Listen to her talk—even to what you might consider irrelevant topics. Share your feelings—even when they seem trivial to you. Give her lots of attention and plenty of eye contact. Do not pressure her for sex. Rather, offer her lots of nonsexual touching and attention.

When you're sharing your feelings, you can make clear to your wife what you have in mind. Make sure you stress that you want that time to be pleasurable for her. It might be a good idea to try this approach when you are not feeling desperate for sex.

I find there are times when I'm not really in the mood for sex, but I'm still willing to be available to Louis. It's helpful if he understands this and is able to lower his expectations for how much pizzazz I can offer. You might discuss that possibility with your wife.

Above all, strive for openness and honesty with each other. Talking is a wonderful way to connect emotionally before you try to connect sexually.

Louis: Understanding female sexuality can be a real challenge, but it's essential if you want to connect with your wife. You might also try focusing on giving rather than getting. True relationship is built on reciprocal giving to meet each other's needs. It's also based on the spiritual principle of reaping what you sow, and it works in marriage as well as in other relationships. Because of our desire to meet each other's needs, I fill Melissa's emotional bank account through nonsexual touch, and she responds with red-hot lovin'. Works well for us. Try it!

SIX WARM-UPS FOR SEX

Rather than progressing directly to sex, we suggest some pleasant ways to lead up to intercourse more gradually.

1. Take a shower. A nice warm shower together gets things warmed up and your body fresh and clean for pleasure.
2. Make a date. Melissa and I plan time for sex when our schedules are too packed for spontaneity.
3. Say what you want. Differentiate between an invitation for intercourse or just wanting a hug. That's better than guessing wrong.
4. Shed some clothes. Dressing down is a signal that your interest is up. There are other signals evident in what you are—or are not—wearing.
5. Get moving. Physiological arousal signs such as flushing, sweating, breathing hard, groaning, erection, and lubrication are obvious.
6. Relax and enjoy. Don't become a spectator who makes judgments on performance.

Q & A

MUST I STRIP FOR HIM?

My husband asks me repeatedly to strip for him. I understand men are visual creatures, and that by my doing this he'd have a pleasing experience. While I'd love to do this for him, I feel self-conscious. I'm not the thinnest woman. How do I get over this negative self-image so I can please my husband? And anyway, is stripping even a healthy sexual suggestion?

Stripping is a healthy sexual suggestion. And believe us when we tell you your weight doesn't matter. Love is blind and lust quite myopic. It's wonderful that your husband has a touch of both.

If you're really self-conscious about your weight, ask your doctor if you should lose a few pounds. But if this is more than just a weight issue, we encourage you to work at removing your fear of sensuality. God gave you the right equipment to be a Song of Songs woman. That Bible book teaches that a lover is a delight to the eyes of her beloved. He is eager to feast on her loveliness.

Ask God to help you relax your inhibitions with your husband. Learn to undress one bit of clothing at a time with some stimulating music in the background. Practice alone until you're less self-conscious. Then turn down the lights, light some candles, and surprise his socks off.

Q & A

WHY DOES SHE LOSE INTEREST?

Sometimes my wife seems to be really turned on, but then, just when things are going great, she gets distracted by a noise, a book on the dresser, the dinner dishes that haven't been washed—anything! Believe me, once my engine is running, nothing would distract me. How can I hold her attention?

Louis: Compared to men, women have a lot more associative pathways in the brain. That allows them to process many stimuli at once. Men have a simpler construction. That explains why when a man's testosterone level is high and sex is on his mind, nothing will distract him, short of a four-alarm fire. (See figure 14.)

Melissa takes a long time to get unhooked from the rest of life and warmed up to sex. I sometimes forget that and think she's ready when she's not. I've learned to give Melissa plenty of time to shift her focus. She may need to talk about her day, do the dishes, and call her mom before she's connected with my agenda.

Melissa: Women are wired this way for good reason. Motherhood requires that we be able to do several things at once. So your wife's distraction is neither deliberate nor a reflection on your skill in lovemaking. Louis doesn't make me feel guilty when I get distracted. That helps, because trying not to be distracted is like being told, "Don't think about green monsters." Of course you start thinking about green monsters.

It's still frustrating to Louis when I interrupt the process with an unrelated question or piece of information. So I try to pick up on the subtle signs that sex is on the evening's schedule and prepare myself by eliminating potential distractions ahead of time.

Talk to your wife about your frustrations. Find out how you can help her prepare for times of intimacy. She may find that concentration is a worthy goal because sex is important to you. Philippians 4:8 says that controlling our thoughts is possible. Don't expect miracles, but do expect improvement.

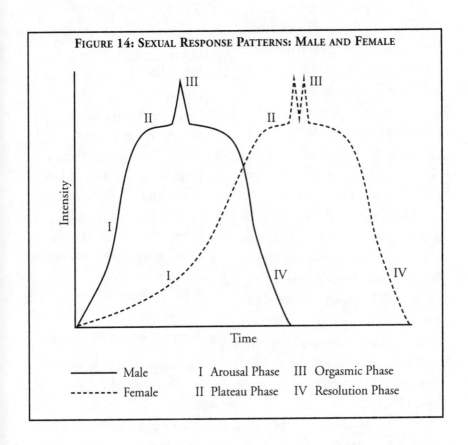

FIGURE 14: SEXUAL RESPONSE PATTERNS: MALE AND FEMALE

——— Male   I Arousal Phase   III Orgasmic Phase
------- Female   II Plateau Phase   IV Resolution Phase

9

MAKING LOVE:
Pleasure Zones and Positions

Did you know that lovemaking begins in your head?

That's right. The brain is the largest, most powerful part of the sexual system. It is where your sexual identify is formed, your sexual development is organized, your sexual fantasies are stored, your methods of approach are conceived. It orchestrates your excitement and registers pleasure.

The cortex of the brain stores memories and regulates motor behavior. The limbic system is the center for reflex behavior and pleasure. The hypothalamus regulates the pituitary gland, which controls your hormonal output. And we can't overlook the sensory systems that connect you with your spouse.

You've probably never thought of your brain as sexy. Well, it is. To get your brain involved in creating a great sex life, ask yourself:

- What builds up his and my interest in sex?
- Who should initiate lovemaking and how?
- What kind of stimulation gets her and me going?
- What do we each prefer as preliminaries to lovemaking?
- What kind of foreplay works best for her and for me?
- How much time should we each expect to spend in foreplay?
- What positions for intercourse will we choose?
- Who will decide the positions?

The answers to these questions can be discovered through experimentation and clear communication. Just don't assume your mate perceives things as you do. It can lead to all kinds of problems in lovemaking.

PLEASURE ZONES

Sit down together and examine figure 15. Think about your best lovemaking experiences. Then take a red ink pen and mark on the figure the areas of your body that like to be touched in foreplay. If you're a woman, you will realize that your pleasure zone moves during lovemaking. As your level of arousal increases, pleasure shifts from your face, neck, and lips to your breasts. Then it moves to your abdomen, thighs, and ultimately your clitoris and vagina.

Guys—just color the penis red. Seriously, guys may find that their erogenous zone also moves during foreplay. Most men enjoy kissing, particularly French kissing. Men also like caresses of the

---

Faulty Assumptions in Lovemaking

- I'm turned on visually, so I'm thinking that if I parade out of the bathroom in my birthday suit, she'll go crazy with passion.
- I like lots of conversation, then some cuddling before any heavy petting. So I'll arrange things so that he and I can just sit and talk awhile.
- I can hardly wait for her to touch my penis, so I'll begin to massage her clitoris right away.
- I know the husband is supposed to initiate sex, so I'll wait for him to make the first move.
- I've seen lots of movies where the babe wants the guy to tear her clothes off. Then she goes after his.
- Sometimes my breasts and nipples feel tender, so I'm sure he'll be very gentle with them.
- We've both saved ourselves for this moment. I bet she's as eager to have me inside her as I am to be there.

head, neck, and chest, and being invited to enjoy a woman's breasts. Men tend to focus on their penis as a pleasure zone and sometimes want to rush toward pleasing that area. Slowing down is not easy, but it will lead to more satisfying sex for both partners.

Now that you've got some better understanding of your individual preferences for erotic touch, talk to each other about the areas you colored. Be honest. Of course you won't know all the answers when you first marry or even through the years as you change

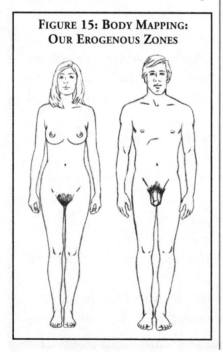

FIGURE 15: BODY MAPPING: OUR EROGENOUS ZONES

and grow. You'll just have to keep experimenting with sex, learning as you go. What a price to pay!

Q & A

HOW CAN I STAY FOCUSED DURING FOREPLAY?

For years my wife has told me that conversation is an important part of foreplay for her. I try to stay focused during the chatty time, but I soon get sleepy and lose interest. The result? My wife gets the conversation she needs, and we don't have intercourse. I'd feel selfish if I didn't provide the kind of foreplay she needs, but how can I stay awake long enough to close the deal?

Louis: Conversation is an important part of foreplay for most women. So the most obvious solution to your dilemma is to find a better time of day to enjoy unhurried conversation, foreplay, and intercourse. You might make love earlier in the evening or before work in the morning. If you live close to the office, you could even schedule a midday rendezvous.

Tell your wife about your frustration and ask for her help. You may find other creative solutions. Sometimes it's hard for men to share such thoughts. But your wife is probably thankful for your concern about her needs and will welcome the opportunity to reciprocate.

Another solution is to be satisfied by an occasional quickie sex without lengthy preliminaries. We've found that kind of sex can be mutually enjoyable. Melissa receives the gratification of bringing me pleasure, and I accept her gift without feeling guilty or selfish. Abbreviated lovemaking is not our first choice, but it's better than ongoing frustration.

Turning Each Other On

Relax first. For most erotic stimulation, relaxation and comfort is essential. Try holding hands, massaging feet, rubbing the back, or playfully tousling the hair to ease the way for more intense genital touching.

Turn him on. Men are more genitally focused, so they find gentle caressing of the penis very stimulating. The scrotum, where it attaches to the underside of the shaft of the penis, and the coronal ridge around the head of the penis are particularly sensitive. Men are also aroused by stroking or kissing their ears, lips, and nipples. The thighs, knees, buttocks, and toes are also erogenous zones.

Turn her on. For a woman, relational and emotional closeness are necessary preludes for sex. Once that's assured, pleasure begins at the head and moves downward. Early foreplay starts with hand-holding, gentle kissing, and nuzzling the hair and neck. It progresses to more passionate kissing of the lips and neck. Then it moves south to the breasts in gentle caresses, kissing, or sucking and to the small of the back, buttocks, inner thighs, and lower

Talk about It

Review the body map of your erogenous zones. How does understanding your own and each other's anatomy help you in lovemaking?

abdomen. Finally—and preferably with the woman's guidance—caressing moves to the mons pubis, the labia, the clitoris, and vagina.

Warning: A man who progresses too fast might hear: "Wait a little." It's a signal to slow down and enjoy each step of the process.

WHAT POSITIONS ARE OK?

We say that any way a wife and husband can fit together for pleasure is OK. If it feels good, do it—but only if both of you like it.

A man tends to be more creative about positions and is willing to try almost anything. A woman tends to be less adventurous and prefers a more predictable approach. The key to finding alternative positions is good communication. If something doesn't feel good, say so. Don't be coerced into doing it. The problem with ongoing experimentation is that one spouse may not like doing something but is afraid to say so. Here are some guidelines:

1. Both husband and wife should agree to what is chosen and not feel coerced into doing something sexual against their will.
2. The act should not cause pain or humiliation for either husband or wife.

3. The act should not regularly take the place of genital union unless that's physically impossible.

Be creative. Any way a husband can insert his penis into his wife's vagina can be fun. Sitting, standing, facing each other, upside down—try it all. Just be sure your body can cope with the position without injury. Spare yourself the embarrassment of having to tell a doctor how you managed to break or sprain something in the bedroom.

FIVE POSITIONS: YOUR CHOICE

There are some fairly tried-and-true positions for intercourse that comfortably accomplish the basic goal. Whichever one you choose—or any other you might think up—keep in mind that both partners must assent to it. It's also a good idea for the wife to guide her husband's penis into her vagina when she's ready and at an angle comfortable for her.

Man on woman. This position is commonly referred to as "the missionary position," though we have no idea how it got the name. With this position, the woman is on her back and the husband on his side during fore-play. They can kiss and caress each other freely in that position. He also has easy access to her breasts and clitoris in this position.

When the woman is aroused and lubricated, the man lifts him-self above her, supporting his weight with his arms. If he intends to use a condom, one should be put on before he gets in this posi-tion. At this point, the woman may take her husband's erect penis in her hand and rub it across her clitoris to move her toward orgasm. When she's ready, she may guide the penis into her vagina. Both the man and woman may engage in pelvic thrusting at this point to intensify the movement toward orgasm.

The couple may remain con-nected after orgasm. If the man is using a condom, he should with-draw his penis from the woman before the penis becomes flaccid and some of the ejaculate escapes around the base of the condom.

Woman on man. Foreplay can begin in any configuration, but as arousal rises, the wife straddles her husband, guiding his penis into her. As they move together, she has more control of the rhythm of their movements, the angle of his penis, and the depth of penetra-tion. She can also reach around to fondle his scrotum and testicles.

The husband's advantage in this position is seeing his wife's naked breasts and being able to stroke or kiss them. A pillow under his shoulders makes this more pos-sible. He also has the erotic experi-ence of feeling his wife move her pelvis in and out on his erection. Some women prefer to have chest-to-chest contact in this position, but others like to lean back for more intense clitoral stimulation. Leaning back changes the angle of the man's penis and puts more pressure on the woman's clitoris.

Side by side. In this position, the man and woman lay on their sides, facing each other. The woman raises her leg to allow pen-etration. Both partners are free for maximal pelvic movement in this position. No one gets squashed or smothered, and neither is worn out by holding body weight off the other. A couple can stay in this embrace for the rest of the night if they want.

Sitting or standing face-to-face. In this position, the wife sits astride her husband on his lap. She may be on her knees or have her feet on the floor atop some pillows. That can be good for viewing and caressing each other. However, it's hard for the man to do much pelvic thrusting in this position.

Standing face-to-face also works well; however, if the wife is much shorter than the husband, she may have to stand on something to be the right height for penetration. Or her husband can raise her up and she can wrap her legs around him. This position isn't recommended for a couple who aren't in excellent physical condition.

Rear entry. The man penetrates the woman's vagina from behind her. For this approach, both can be lying on their sides. Or, the woman can be lying facedown with her hips elevated on a pillow. Or the couple can be standing with her bent over. Or the woman can be seated astride the man.

The angle of penetration may be uncomfortable for the woman in this position, so care should be taken not to create pain during penetration. Also, there is no clitoral stimulation by the penis in this position. The man should be able to provide this with his hands. The man can also caress the woman's breasts and nuzzle her neck.

IS ORAL SEX OK?

Oral sex isn't for everyone. Certainly, one partner should not demand it if the other is unwilling or refuses.

In one version of oral sex, also called fellatio (from Latin "to suck"), the wife stimulates her husband's penis with her lips or tongue. She may take his penis in her mouth and suck it or move it in and out to simulate the moves of intercourse. The penis should be washed thoroughly before oral sex. Some women enjoy this kind of foreplay all the way to orgasm. They do not mind the somewhat salty taste of the ejaculate. Others prefer to withdraw before that happens, catching the semen in a tissue or hand.

The other variety, called cunnilingus (from Latin for "vulva" and "to lick"), is when the husband stimulates his wife's genital area with his lips and tongue. He may use his tongue or lips to stimulate the labia minora or clitoris.

He may also insert his tongue into the vagina. The wife may want to hold her husband's head in her hands to pull him tighter or push him away for lighter or firmer pressure on her clitoris. The woman's genital area should be thoroughly washed before this type of oral sex.

In our counseling experience, we find about as many couples who say they practice oral sex as those who don't. That said, here are some considerations:

∞ Generally the problem is not so much with cunnilingus (the husband stimulating his wife with genital kisses) but with fellatio (the wife stimulating her husband's penis by mouth). He wants her to do it; she doesn't.

∞ A wife's resistance may be due to a variety of causes. Rarely is it related to childhood sexual abuse in which she was forced into fellatio. Sometimes she resists because of the insistent demands by her husband. Sometimes she resists because she thinks oral sex is unclean. Sometimes she resists strong genital odors.

∞ Medically, oral sex is safe unless there are infectious genital lesions (e.g., herpes, condyloma, chancres, etc.). The anal area is not sterile and should be avoided in sexual play.

∞ The Bible offers no clear directive on oral sex.

∞ Sexual intimacy is best when it's mutually satisfying. If oral sex causes dissension, then it's destructive—especially if a husband and wife don't talk openly about the disagreement. Trying to understand each other's perspective helps.

Q & A

IS IT RIGHT FOR HIM TO DEMAND ORAL SEX?

Lately my husband has asked me to perform oral sex on him even if we don't have full-blown sexual intercourse. He says that if I love him, I'll do this to please him. I'm not opposed to oral sex, but I feel cheap when he demands it. Am I silly to feel this way?

Mutuality is an important component of sexual intimacy. It applies not only to forms of stimulation but also to frequency, initiation, preference of location, and right of refusal. That seems to be the dilemma here.

It sounds like you see your husband's desire for oral stimulation as a self-centered demand for service. It's important to identify whether that is a distortion of reality on your part or a behavior disorder on his.

At times, a wife's perception of such a request may be related to what she was taught as a child. A controlling parent may have sensitized a wife to any message that sounds like an order. That would explain why the wife negatively reacts to a husband's "demand" for oral sex. If the wife's perception is not distorted, here are some approaches she can take:

Understand the male psyche. Men are bombarded with sexual images that they may build fantasies around. Because of this, your husband may think you're just waiting for the opportunity to gratify your desire to "have him" orally. Check it out with him. Maybe he'll share his sexual fantasy. Imagine his surprise, then, to find out that oral sex is the last thing you'd dream of doing.

Reconsider your attitude about his self-centeredness. We can respond to the desires of each other by seeing the other person's desires as problems that he or she should deal with. Or we can view those desires as opportunities for us to show love.

Talk to each other. Just as you can benefit from understanding your husband's sexuality, he can benefit from understanding yours. Avoid talking about his behavior with blaming "you statements." For instance, rather than saying, "You are selfish in demanding this kind of sex from me when it's just for your pleasure," try, "I want us to be closer sexually, and that works better for me when lovemaking focuses on both of our needs. Can we work on that?"

Such straight talk can include an expression of love that responds to his desires. Imagine your husband's surprise if you said, "I want you to know how completely I love you, and how excited I am that I can show it in such a private way. I hope this is a delight for you!"

Q & A

Should I Submit to Anal Sex?

I enjoy lovemaking very much; however, my husband tells me he wants anal sex to keep things interesting. The idea of this is completely disgusting to me. I cannot understand why he would want to do something that would be painful to me when there are other ways to spice things up. He says he would do anything for me, and I should do the same even if it is just for him. Is this an area in which I should submit?

Louis: The condemnation of homosexual practices in Sodom gave us the word *sodomy* to describe anal intercourse. Paul's comments about "unnatural" sex in Romans 1 may also apply.

Medically, anal sex is problematic. The rectum contains potentially harmful bacteria and viruses. If a couple chooses to practice anal penetration, the husband should use a condom. He should not alternate penetration of the rectum and vagina. Another consideration: the rectum is not designed for this kind of treatment. Serious medical problems, such as tearing of the rectal mucosa, may result from anal intercourse.

Now let's consider your feelings about having anal sex. Any sexual practice that is forced on someone violates that person's sense of safety and mutuality, both of which are required for marital intimacy. Sex is intended for mutual pleasure. It requires giving by both husband and wife.

If my desire for a certain sexual activity becomes more important than protecting and honoring Melissa, then I have stepped over the line. It wouldn't matter how convincing my arguments were; I would have damaged her.

THE GLORIOUS AFTERGLOW: DON'T SHORT IT

Afterglow—the time after orgasm and sexual union when both partners feel warm and relaxed and oh-so-close—lasts from ten to fifteen minutes. Of course, it can be the time you both roll over and zonk out. But we don't recommend this. Use this time to affirm each other's stupendous lovemaking or to describe how much you love each other.

Melissa and I often take this time to say, "Let's do that again sometime." Then we kiss each other and fall asleep in each other's arms.

Q & A

WHY IS SHE SO SCARED?

My wife and I have been married three months, and she hasn't yet had an orgasm. She has certain fears of sex and a lot of inhibitions. There are distinct boundaries that never get crossed: she won't try any position other than the missionary position, she won't touch my penis, and she won't get naked outside of bed. I don't blame her, but she faults herself for being so inhibited. What can we do to help things get better?

Louis: Since sexual development is such a private experience, there can be many reasons for your wife's difficulty. It might be helpful for her to see a qualified counselor to help her work through feelings that block her orgasmic response.

Some of your wife's inhibitions may be related to early teaching that sex is dirty. Many women were never given the message that marital sex is a God-given gift meant for our pleasure.

Another common cause for such feelings is a woman's need for emotional control and her related feelings of anxiety as erotic stimulation increases. The intensity of preorgasmic excitation is threatening for a woman who has learned to stay on guard.

Your wife could also be feeling guilt about sexual fantasies or pre-marital experiences. Both of those can create barriers to full sexual enjoyment.

Early sexual abuse can stimulate fearful associations. But don't let an overzealous counselor convince your wife that her problems with sex mean that she was abused as a child. Such ideas may be planted by a well-intentioned therapist but often have no basis in reality.

Melissa: Sometimes worrying too much about having an orgasm can inhibit a woman's response. If your wife is too preoccupied with orgasm, she may become a spectator more than a participant. An orgasm usually comes more easily when a woman stops striving for one.

Your wife may be suffering from false guilt. The Bible has clear instructions about how to deal with real guilt: Repent and accept God's forgiveness. But false guilt is based on notions that are not true yet seem so real that our hearts worry over them. Once your wife has dealt with real guilt, she can trust God to free her from listening to the lies (see 1 John 3:18–20). Treat your wife tenderly and accept her totally—inhibitions and all.

Louis and Melissa: Examine your sensitivity as a sexual partner. How willing are you to do what it takes to bring your wife to orgasm? Do you know what relaxes her? What type of touch gives her pleasure? What areas of her body respond and in what order? Most important, have you talked to her about this?

Q & A

WHO'S RESPONSIBLE FOR SEXUAL SATISFACTION?

My wife blames me when she isn't fully satisfied during sex, but isn't this a two-way street? How can I make her realize that sexual satisfaction is partly her own responsibility?

Louis: I don't like to hear blame applied to something as joyful and playful as sex. Pointing the finger shifts sexual intimacy into a performance with orgasmic intensity or frequency as the ultimate goal. Both partners need to encourage and help each other rather than cast blame.

Don't get me wrong. I like a good orgasm as much as the next guy, and I want Melissa to experience total satisfaction with every encounter. But our attitudes toward sex make a big difference. When we approach sexual interaction with a desire to bring each other mutual pleasure, we both take responsibility for what happens.

Taking responsibility involves three steps:

1. Be aware of each other's sexuality. What gives you pleasure? What is erotic for your wife? When are you or your wife ready for the next level of stimulation?

2. Allow space for each other to be less involved. There are times when your levels of interest and drive are markedly different. The times when you're less interested are good times to offer your mate sexual satisfaction. In turn, your mate should not insist on full sexual satisfaction for you.

3. Keep your sex life interesting. Avoid drifting into a stupefying pattern of sameness. Try different positions. Take turns pleasuring each other in new ways. Surprise your spouse with a weekend getaway so you can make love in an exciting new venue.

Melissa: Consider whether some other area of your marriage is causing this problem. Perhaps your wife has unresolved anger in another area besides sex. Stuffing her anger or frustration can cause an accumulation of negative feelings that affect the entire relationship.

If your wife is angry, it will be almost impossible for her to let herself be sexually vulnerable. It's natural, then, for her to feel that her inability to enjoy sex is your fault. To address this effectively, encourage her to get her feelings out in the open and deal with them.

UNSELFISHNESS IN SEX

When Melissa and I attend weddings, I listen to the vows each couple makes. They promise to love, honor, support, and forsake all others. I then wonder, *Does a promise to forsake all others include forsaking myself, particularly sexually?*

That's a hard question to answer. Selfishness is a natural part of every one of us—just look at any two-year-old. It's scary to discover that same infantile selfishness reasserting itself in the marriage bed, where it has the power to be very destructive.

Ironically, I've learned it's in my own best interest to act unselfishly toward my wife. It's one of those paradoxical spiritual truths the Bible talks about. When I take an honest look at my own desires in marriage, what I want from Melissa is a pleasant companion and fantastic sex. That is to say, I want to be affirmed and praised and have someone support me in my goals. I also want to have my physical needs met.

In describing what she wants, Melissa would add words like *cherish, emotional security*, and *intimacy*, but her list of major wants and needs would be similar to mine.

The paradox is that the more I devote myself to meeting Melissa's needs, the more she becomes the kind of companion I desire. Conversely, the more self-seeking I am, the more resistant she is. Friendship is built on giving to meet the other person's needs. It's the spiritual principle of reaping what you sow—a principle that works in marriage too.

SEX, BUT:

Dealing with Put-Offs to Lovemaking

A couple can find lots of reasons to not have sex. Some reasons are pretty compelling. Some are convenient excuses. Some are playful. Others are substitutes for expressing more important issues in a relationship, such as anger or fear.

You may be thinking, "Well, I really am too tired by 10:00 p.m., when I've finally got the kids in bed, the laundry finished, and the kitchen cleaned up." We'd affirm that. There are days and seasons in a marriage that interrupt sexual intimacy. Recognizing those times and adapting is crucial. Otherwise the interruption can begin to feel like rejection and abandonment. That creates a dangerous vulnerability to extramarital relationships.

Q & A

IS SEX A USE-IT-OR-LOSE-IT PROPOSITION?

If we don't have frequent sex, will our sex drive be diminished? Also, is it true that sexual activity helps prevent prostate problems later in life?

Louis and Melissa: The drive for sex isn't easily daunted. After most short periods of abstinence, the sex drive increases and sexual release intensifies. If decreased frequency is rooted in relational problems, the drive for sex may also diminish. But that's not a matter of physiology. The causes of the slow-down must be dealt with; then nature can take its course.

Louis: Urological studies support the notion that regular ejaculation decreases the incidence of prostate disease. But don't let the medical concern become an excuse for coercive sex. Saying, "I've gotta have sex or I'll get cancer!" is out.

Melissa: I hope women don't dismiss this letter too lightly. Frequent sex is a gift of love from you to your husband—and, evidently, good preventive medicine as well!

JANE AND JIM: ONE EXCUSE TOO MANY

Jane was married to a success-driven guy. He worked twelve-hour

---

Excuses We've Heard (and Used)

- ✀ I have a headache.
- ✀ I'm too tired.
- ✀ It's too late.
- ✀ You haven't spoken to me in days.
- ✀ I don't want you to get pregnant.
- ✀ My mother is in the guest room.
- ✀ Your mother is in the guest room.
- ✀ I have to get up early.
- ✀ You haven't showerd.
- ✀ I need a bath.
- ✀ The kids are still awake.
- ✀ I forgot to take my pill.
- ✀ I ran out of Viagra.
- ✀ I have my period.

days and brought work home on weekends. Jane felt abandoned. She tried to find fulfillment raising their two boys. She kept busy, but looking after children didn't meet her need for adult companionship. She was also sexually frustrated. She enjoyed sex but could rarely entice Jim into bed. His usual excuse was that this next deal was crucial; as soon as he got the contract he would take time for her.

Jane eventually shut down toward Jim, but her sexual drive didn't lessen. She turned to romance novels and self-stimulation. When that got old, she found herself looking at other men. One looked back. Soon they were meeting for coffee. Later they became sexually involved.

That wasn't what Jane wanted. She confessed her infidelity to Jim. It got his attention. It took some hard work and marital counseling to rescue their marriage. Jim had to reorganize his priorities to include his wife and family.

Making marriage a priority has never been easy. We must be vigilant about not allowing other commitments and responsibilities to get top billing.

FRANK AND KAY: EMOTIONALLY DETACHED

Frank was a brilliant guy. Kay was attracted to his no-nonsense approach to life and his organizational skills. She determined to marry Frank.

At times during their courtship, Kay wondered if Frank had emotions. He seemed to live in a world of thoughts and ideas, but he often seemed distant and aloof. He was much like other members of his family, who were wealthy and highly educated but had trouble connecting with each other.

After their wedding—the social event of the year—Frank began working on a doctorate. The couple's sex life became one more item in his highly disciplined schedule. Frank and Kay had sex the same way at the same time every week. There was nothing playful or tender about it. Kay suspected that Frank was timing the event and measuring her response.

RELATIONAL TENSIONS THAT AFFECT SEX

Troublesome as they are, life-phase stuff such as pursuing a career, attending graduate school, having a child, or retirement aren't as destructive to marriage as underlying relational tensions. Relational issues tend to become fixed patterns that persist in spite of life circumstances. For example, Frank was emotionally detached. Beneath that aloofness, however, was a lonely, fearful boy. Fearing the risks of emotional involvement, he buried his feelings by taking control of his environment. He could experience sex only as a physiological phenomenon, not as a joyful bonding of souls.

For a successful marriage—and fulfilling love life—a couple must recognize and get help for dealing with these relational difficulties:

- Perfectionism
- Criticism
- Control
- Unrealistic expectations
- Fear of emotional intimacy
- Detachment
- Self-absorption
- Fear of growing up

Q & A

IS SHE HOLDING OUT FOR PERFECTION?

My wife wants sex only if our relationship is perfect. I know she needs romance and attention, but that's not enough. Any minor disagreement or stress becomes an excuse not to have sex. We end up having very little sex. Wouldn't being physically intimate improve our feelings of closeness?

Insisting on perfection as a prerequisite for anything practically guarantees that it won't occur. Does your wife have some underlying resistance to sexual closeness that isn't being addressed? Is she angry, hurt, fearful of losing control? Is she a perfectionist?

People who have impossible standards are insecure about their own worth. They can't relax unless everything is perfect. This tremendous pressure interferes with every aspect of life, including sex. Talk about this with your wife. See if you can discover factors other than your behavior that might be turning her off sexually.

You asked if physical intimacy would help you feel closer. Men tend to feel more open, relationally, to their wives after sex. But women need to feel emotionally close to their husbands prior to sex. Since men and women come at intimacy from different directions, take a look at how she sees the problem.

Ask your wife if she thinks you're trying to control her. She may be withholding sex because it's the only area of your relationship where she feels in charge. Check out her definition of minor disagreements or stress. You may have different ideas about those. The only way to find out is to ask.

MY PROBLEM WITH PERFECTIONISM

Louis: When we married, I often told Melissa how she could improve herself. I thought I was being a very loving husband by giving this advice to my bride.

Melissa: At first I tried to do things Louis's way, but before long I felt rejected. I couldn't please him no matter how hard I tried—even sexually. I had felt cherished and desired before we got married, but I no longer felt it. I didn't have much motivation to make myself available sexually because when I did, I just ended up feeling inadequate as a lover.

Louis: Thankfully, Melissa didn't shut down emotionally. She valued our relationship enough to confront me with her feelings. I

was devastated by what she said. I had no inkling that I'd been systematically diminishing my sweetheart. I deeply cherished Melissa and had worked seven years to win her heart. Hearing that she viewed my helpful advice as critical rejection was like a slap in the face.

After we talked, I began to catch myself each time I had one of those perfectionist perceptions. I'd remind myself of how precious Melissa was to me and bite my tongue.

Q & A

WHY DOES HE BARTER FOR SEX?

I love having sex with my husband. But lately I feel turned off because he seems to expect sex as a reward for everything. If my husband fixes my car, if he spends time listening to my problems, if he takes me out to dinner, he expects sex. Do I owe him that?

Louis: Married life works best when both partners focus on ways to meet each other's needs. However, few of us find this easy to do. Several marital habits get in the way of unselfish giving:

The tendency to keep score. Keeping a legalistic ledger on who does what in a marriage ("I did this, so he owes me that" or "He hurt my feelings, so I won't be overly concerned about his") replaces the healthy give-and-take of a loving relationship.

Expressing needs as demands. If your husband commands you to meet his needs, no wonder you resist. Of course, we hope your husband will start communicating his needs in a less demanding way, but you can still choose how you want to interpret those requests. Try to see his desire for frequent sex as an opportunity for you to show love.

Cluelessness. Your husband may be trying to win your heart by performing acts of kindness and service. He thinks sex is an appropriate response. Try to see his gifts as acts of love. And help him understand how you would prefer to be wooed into lovemaking.

Melissa: Try beating your husband at his own game. If you suspect he's being helpful because he wants a reward, you could try outgiving him. Obviously, sex shouldn't be viewed as "payment for services rendered." But if you want to think in terms of cash

flow, determine in your own mind that what he does for you is twice as "expensive" as what you do for him. So when he fixes your car, decide that he should receive sex at least twice—maybe three times—before you ask for another favor.

If nothing else, his reward system will be thrown off. Perhaps you'll even be able to examine the issue together. Since you say that you love having sex with him, this should be a fun experiment for both of you.

Q & A

WHY WON'T HE GO ALL THE WAY?

My husband and I have been married for more than two years and we've never had sex. We kiss and touch each other, but when things start progressing toward intercourse, he pushes me away. When I ask him why he won't have sex with me, he says he wants a wholesome relationship, and we'll have sex when he's ready to have a baby. He refuses to use condoms because he says they're ugly. How can I tell him we're missing out on one of the best gifts of marriage?

Your husband clearly told you he doesn't want to use you, and intercourse is only for procreation. That's an unusual position. There are other possibilities you should consider:

Compulsive cleanliness. Your husband's aversion to "ugly" condoms could reflect a phobia about dirt or germs. For perfectionists, genital sex is too messy.

Erectile dysfunction. If a guy has experienced difficulty in achieving or maintaining an erection, he becomes anxious about it. Attempting intercourse is threatening. You haven't mentioned anything about your husband's arousal. If he can get and sustain an erection, this is not the problem.

A bad experience. Your husband may have had a bad experience with sex, perhaps even sexual abuse. If this is so, your husband should see a counselor.

Worry about pregnancy. With so many contraceptives available today, this fear can be minimized. Your husband may be concerned about fatherhood—now that's scary. Being a dad is no easy job.

Sexual identity disorder. Your husband may be struggling with his sexual orientation. Ask him!

If one or more of these factors is evident, you should discuss them with a counselor. In the meantime, it's understandable that you feel as though you're missing out on a wonderful marital gift. Share your feelings with your husband. (See "Four Ways to Approach a Problem with Sex," 167.)

Q & A

WHY DOES HE INSIST WE GO ALL THE WAY?

My husband and I have been married three years. I used to have much desire for him, but now I have none. His attitude that sex equals love has turned me off. I feel that if I even kiss or hug him, he'll immediately want to go all the way. How can I get back the feelings I once had for my husband?

Louis and Melissa: Have you talked with him about this problem? When you talk about your feelings and come to understand his, you'll have a better chance of working through this. Be sure to settle this issue, even if it takes a counselor to help you do that.

Once you've responded to each other's feelings about sex, work on rekindling your love. Think about some of the exciting times of your early relationship. You're probably not as hormonally driven as you were back then, but there were other elements—special attention and acts of love—that you could re-create.

Now identify actions that may have eroded your feelings toward your husband. List some of the disappointments, unrealized expectations, hurtful words, selfishness, or feelings of abandonment. Perhaps you had unspoken expectations about marriage that your mate failed without knowing he was being tested.

Go out of your way to build up your husband. By focusing on good memories and your husband's good points, your love for him will increase. Don't wait for your husband to change. Increase your desire for him by remembering the passionate times you used to enjoy together.

WHAT MAKES PROBLEMS GROW?

A headache or fatigue excuse may be OK periodically. But a pattern of avoiding sex indicates deeper conflict between you and your spouse. In trying to resolve such conflict, it's tempting to take easy ways out:

We avoid the issue. We run from it, pout about it, and complain about it to others. Sometimes we pretend it's not really happening. All of this seems easier than actually facing what's behind our excuses for avoiding sex.

We intimidate. We threaten, cry, create power blocks, and quote Scripture, trying to get our mate to go our way.

We manipulate. We entice, offer bribes, or withhold something.

We deflect. Instead of focusing on the real issue, we bring up issues that are safer, more urgent, and more comfortable.

SEVEN STEPS TO RESOLUTION

Conflict resolution takes determination, hard work, and the following:

Finding a solid basis for solving this problem. Ask, "Is resolving this issue part of our Christian commitment?" You each vowed in marriage to love and be faithful to your spouse. That vow requires you to resolve any conflict that comes between you.

Identifying the real issue. Are unfulfilled expectations causing the conflict? Are you denying sexual intimacy because of who has the power or who's going to have the last word? Is it a problem of trust? Find out what's really the problem.

Sharing your feelings. If you're begging off sex, you might say, "You know, I've really felt neglected lately; that's why I haven't wanted to make love." Or, "I've been feeling angry—or lonely, or tense." Because it's difficult to share feelings, compare them to what you felt on other occasions: "I feel like I did on our vacation when you went out without telling me, and I got very upset. Then you wanted to make love."

Listening to each other. Usually we're so busy preparing our defense that we're not listening. If we don't listen, we don't want to resolve the conflict; we only want to prove we're right. We must listen in a nondefensive way.

Conceding. Even though you don't deliberately hurt your spouse by rejecting his attempts to make love, you should sense his pain. If you're really concerned, you'll be sorry that you hurt him. Whether the cause of the conflict is moral failure or simply insensitivity, be willing to face up to it and ask each other's forgiveness.

Forgiving. Often the reason we don't want to forgive is because we feel superior when we withhold forgiveness. This self-righteousness must give way to forgiveness.

Compromising. By the time you've gone through the preceding steps, you should be ready to negotiate the things that are really important to you and your spouse.

Talk about It

Review these seven steps and ask each other which ones have worked well. Which steps have been difficult? Name some reasons for the difficulty. Suggest some problems you can work through together, following these seven steps.

SEX CHALLENGES:

Premature Ejaculation, Failure to Reach Orgasm, and Other Concerns

The problem with sex is that nobody wants to admit there are problems with sex. There is a great gulf between the reality of a person's sexual experience and the facade that everything is ecstatic.

In reality, every couple has periods of difficulty in their sexual relationship. That should not come as a surprise. Consider for a moment how complex each person's reproductive system is, how distractions can interrupt the mood for lovemaking, how inconsiderate behavior can sabotage a romantic moment, and, well, you see what we mean.

Still, love is strong, and the good times we share bring us back to each other with hope and desire. What's more, most sexual problems can be overcome. So if

you've been afraid to admit you have some disappointments in sex, now is the time to admit that and work toward improvement.

In the rest of this chapter, we'll look at common sexual problems, starting with those experienced by both men and women, then looking at problems experienced by men, and finishing with problems experienced by women.

FEAR OF INTERCOURSE

We've mentioned fear of intercourse as a contributor to sexual dysfunction. Briefly, let's discuss some possible causes for this fear:

Sexual abuse. For several years, therapists assumed that any time a woman expressed fear about having sex, she probably had been sexually abused as a child. Families were torn apart by such assumptions. Even if a woman has suffered such abuse, the abuse must be carefully explored and verified before accusations are made. Then therapy can begin.

Pain during intercourse. No one wants to do something that hurts. If pain persists, the person who hurts should see a doctor.

Fear of pregnancy. This fear is a barrier to sex if a couple isn't practicing good birth control.

Fear of failing to perform. This fear is a problem if expectations are unrealistically high.

Fear of sexually transmitted disease. This fear is a concern if one partner has been unfaithful or had other sex partners prior to marriage.

Fear of being seen by others. This fear is not a concern for couples who have their own homes and are circumspect about where they have sex.

Each fear must be addressed separately to find healing. Often just discovering the source is all that's necessary, but that may take some work with a counselor. Remember: Fear is not of the Lord. Love is.

GENDER CONFUSION

Within marriage, gender confusion is quite unusual; however, when it does happen, it creates great difficulties for sexual intimacy. A physician's exam might be helpful in ruling out any physical problems, but that's not enough. Counseling is essential. (See "How Can I Live with His Attraction to Men?" 282–83.)

INCOMPATIBILITY

We've heard this expression many times, but we're still not sure what it means. If it refers to the size of a woman's vagina compared to the size of a man's penis, it's probably not legit. The vagina can stretch to allow the passage of a child. What's that compared to the size of a penis?

It is possible for a bride to have such a thick hymen that penetration is impossible. That condition can be easily remedied surgically. But it's no grounds for incompatibility.

Does incompatibility refer to the difficulty of matching two people of very different sizes? A large person with a tiny mate will necessitate some thoughtful adjustments in lovemaking positions.

LACK OF INTEREST

Don't assume this is a woman's problem. Some guys aren't turned on by sex. This problem can be related to a lack of testosterone, but it is much more likely due to emotional or relational issues. Indifference or hostility toward one's mate, fear of pregnancy, childhood abuse, or lack of self-confidence may turn one off to sexual intimacy.

LOW SEX DRIVE

One partner has a higher drive or need for sexual intimacy than the other. Or their timing isn't in sync. A wife yearns for romance, for example, and finds that her husband won't cooperate. He yearns for sexual release, and she rejects his overtures. The problem may be physiological, caused by stress, medication, fatigue, or illness, but the most usual issues are relational. They include:

Differences in showing love. If you find that you're both trying to express love to each other but are failing to connect, you may not understand each other's language of love. (See "Cal and Cindy: Missing Each Other's Signals," 104–5.) Work at identifying ways that you each use to show love, and learn to appreciate your differences.

Disappointment. Many couples describe their fantasies about sexual play and how real sex fails to live up to those. The wider the gap between a person's expectations and the reality of sex, the harder it becomes to look forward to sex.

Unresolved anger. We have worked with hundreds of couples who allowed anger to galvanize into bitterness. It effectively shut down their responsiveness to intimacy.

Relational issues are different from the occasional lack of desire that every couple experiences. All can become opportunities to give to each other by sacrificing personal grudges and offering sex as an act of love.

PROMISCUITY

Today, men and women are coming to marriage with a history of having had multiple sexual partners. This can contribute to marital sex problems in several ways:

- ✑ It establishes a pattern of behavior that is hard to break. The boundaries necessary for commitment have not been established, so commitment within marriage is difficult.

⊗ It sets up haunting comparisons with previous sexual partners. Those encounters are grossly unfair to a spouse. He or she can hardly compete with a relationship that was free from marital and family demands.

⊗ It creates an environment of mistrust that's hard to erase. This problem can be overcome, however. (See "Addicted to Adultery," 269.)

DISTRACTIBILITY

I have learned that it takes longer for Melissa than for me to unwind from the day's events. It is thus wise for us to wait awhile for sex so her thoughts can change direction. That's much better than starting to caress her, then hearing, "Oh, did I tell you? Mother called today."

To reduce distractions, try environmental controls: lock the doors, play soft music, unwind together, or get out of town together.

If distractions become disturbingly frequent, seek help. Distractibility could be related to attention deficit disorder, bipolar mood disorder, hyperthyroidism, or drug side effects.

DYSPAREUNIA

Dyspareunia refers to pain in intercourse. For men, the pain can be due to irritation of the penis, inflammation of the prostate, inflammation of the testicles, or angina pectoris (heart pain from the exertion of intercourse).

For women, pain during sex may be due to inflammation of the vagina or other pelvic organs. Less commonly, pain can be related to the position of a woman's uterus. At times, a woman will have a reflexive tightening of the vaginal walls in response to stress or fear of intercourse.

For either men or women, dyspareunia indicates the need for a medical evaluation.

PREMATURE EJACULATION

Young boys have great expectations about having intercourse. They use words for it I wouldn't repeat here, but the fantasy is the same: what it will feel like for a guy to finally push his eager penis into a woman's vagina. By the time the actual event happens, the guy probably has been masturbating to the fantasy for several years. He has learned how to climax so quickly that by the time he actually confronts his wife on the honeymoon, he can't sustain an erection long enough to enter his wife, much less bring her to climax. This hair-trigger response is frustrating to man and mate. Fortunately there's an effective treatment. The Squeeze Technique (see box below) helps a guy prolong an erection. It also encourages a sense of partnership between husband and wife to overcome a mutually disagreeable problem.

Q & A

WHY DO I COME TOO SOON?

During sex, my wife and I enjoy extended foreplay. She enjoys the time after penetration, too, and wants to prolong this time, but I can't wait any longer and often ejaculate before

---

The Squeeze Technique

The man and woman undress and get into bed. With the man lying on his back, the woman sits across his thighs facing him and begins to stimulate his penis. She continues to stroke him until he indicates that he is about to ejaculate. At that point the woman holds the penis in both hands and firmly squeezes below the head of the penis for four to five seconds. The man will experience an abrupt halt in ejaculatory urgency along with a slight loss of his erection.

After thirty seconds of rest, the woman repeats the process, stroking the man until he's ready to ejaculate, then squeezing till the urgency lessens. The process should be repeated two or three times. The couple then proceeds to intercourse, with the woman easing herself atop the man. Thrusting should be avoided until the man regains his erection. Ejaculation should be held off as long as possible.

The technique should be repeated for several months. It is not an instant fix, but it will work.

she comes to orgasm. I want to satisfy her without worrying that I won't be able to wait. Can you suggest a remedy?

There have been many approaches to the problem of premature ejaculation, some of which are effective and some not. Here are some:

Distract and delay. A guy delays ejaculation during sex by thinking about baseball or his work schedule—anything to divert his attention. I'm not sure this approach is physiologically effective, and I can guess it isn't much fun.

Focus on her. A man and woman avoid stimulating the man's penis while providing manual or oral massage of the woman's clitoris until she is close to orgasm. Then they have intercourse. Unfortunately that doesn't always work. Some guys have such a rapid response that little or no stimulation is needed for climax.

Squeeze play. The Squeeze Technique is most effective for men who ejaculate too soon. For a description of how this works, see the box on page 158.

Relax. Premature ejaculation is not a sign of sexual inadequacy. Thinking that only increases anxiety about sexual performance and hastens ejaculation. A calm, relaxed approach to the problem helps reconditioning.

ERECTILE DYSFUNCTION

From what I see in commercials for Viagra, I'd say that if a guy is affluent, athletic, and handsome, he has a higher-than-average risk for erectile dysfunction. Actually, as we guys age, it is very common for us to experience difficulties in achieving or sustaining an erection. Medications, fatigue, alcohol, stress, guilt, and relational tension can add to the breakdown of the genital neurovascular system.

Medications such as Viagra, Cialis, and Caverject can help with this problem, but they aren't 100 percent effective. (See "When the System Fails," 177.) By contrast, gradually accepting and adapting to your sexual changes, such as slower arousal and less intense ejaculation, can be satisfying. Taking longer can be fun.

A word to the wife: Your response and encouragement makes

a huge difference in how your husband adjusts to his changing performance.

PRIAPISM

Priapism is a persistent erection. Priapism can be due to disease (leukemia, sickle-cell anemia), but most often priapism is a side effect of taking certain drugs (cocaine, ecstasy, and drugs used to induce erections). Lest you think priapism is the fulfillment of fantasy, think again. The condition is painful and requires medical treatment for relief.

POSTCOITAL BLEEDING

Many women have spotting or bleeding the first time they have intercourse because of the tearing of the hymen. The bleeding should be minimal. If bleeding persists, the woman should see a doctor.

Other causes for bleeding after intercourse are a vaginal or cervical infection, a growth in the vagina, or abnormal uterine bleeding. A doctor should evaluate any abnormal bleeding in your body.

VAGINAL DRYNESS

Without adequate lubrication of the vagina, intercourse is irritating for both husband and wife. Dryness is due to inadequate foreplay or to insufficient estrogen in a woman's system. Lubricants or vaginal estrogen creams are helpful. Talk to a physician about treatment.

VAGINISMUS

These painful contractions of the vaginal muscles are generally due to irritation of the vagina or irritation of the psyche. Both of these conditions can be effectively treated. (See "Sensate Focusing," 161.)

FAKING ORGASM

Many women are not sufficiently aroused to reach orgasm. Some fake a climax to bring sexual play to a close. Husbands who rush through sexual foreplay toward ejaculation may not be able to recognize the charade.

One would think a woman would want to ask for the necessary stimulation to achieve the real thing. But some women would rather keep quiet than deal with the issue. That may be a reflection of a lack of openness in the marriage relationship. If a woman has tried to bring up the subject at one time and met only hostility or defensiveness in her husband, she may be reluctant to make another attempt. Or she doesn't bring up the subject because she has never experienced orgasm and doesn't know what she's missing.

If her reluctance is because she doesn't know how to talk to her husband about her inability to have an orgasm, we suggest she write a note to her husband, asking

---

Sensate Focusing

Sensate focusing is an exercise that helps eliminate a woman's pain in intercourse. It involves both the man and the woman. They take turns bringing each other physical pleasure—first through nonerotic stimulation, such as massage, then progress slowly over many weeks to erotic, sexual stimulation without penetration (gentle, well-lubricated vaginal massage with one finger, then with two, etc., halting at the first sign of pain). The woman directs the man in this process. The exercises should progress very slowly (over a period of months) to decondition the pain response. When the pain is gone, the couple proceeds to intercourse.

Sensate focusing can also help a couple learn (or relearn) how to give pleasure to each other.

Begin with nonsexual touch, where a husband and wife learn to enjoy touching each other without worrying about sexual performance. Then progress to more intimate touch. Over several sessions, allow more passionate kissing, breast stimulation, and some genital fondling. Each partner is the total focus of the pleasuring in a given session. One night it's the wife's turn to give pleasure; the next night, it's the husband's turn. Finally, when each partner is comfortable being the recipient of the lovemaking, help each other achieve orgasm. Throughout these exercises, intercourse is not allowed.

---

him to read a section on orgasm that she's marked in a book. They could then talk about her problem together and work toward resolution. If that fails, she could make an appointment with a counselor to help her talk to her husband.

Q & A

WHY ARE ORGASMS SO DIFFICULT FOR ME?

Sometimes I wonder if God created sex for men and not for women. I have to concentrate so hard and it takes so long for me to achieve orgasm that I often feel it's not worth the effort. Even though my husband is sensitive to my needs, nothing makes orgasm easier. It's not fair that God didn't make having an orgasm as easy for women as for men.

Melissa: You're right; it's not fair. But consider how wise it is. Just think how little would get done in this world if women were as obsessed with sex as men are. But that doesn't solve your problem, does it? Some suggestions:

Find the right position. A woman usually needs clitoral stimulation to achieve an orgasm, so finding a sexual position that enhances clitoral stimulation could make a big difference in how often and how easily you reach a climax. (See "Five Basic Positions," 136–38.)

Don't try so hard. Worrying about not having orgasms can turn you into an observer of your sex act rather than a participant. Since you mention how hard you concentrate on trying to achieve orgasm, you may have become an observer. Relax.

Take your time. Early in our marriage, it was hard for me to believe Louis didn't care how long it took me to come to a climax. He enjoyed every minute of foreplay and didn't feel any need to hurry. That helped me relax and enjoy the process.

Pray about it. Over years of spiritual growth, I've seen God respond to my requests for more pleasure in lovemaking. When I prayed for a higher libido and the ability to shut out thoughts that distracted me from lovemaking, God provided what I needed. It's not easy to trust God with this area of your life, but the results are amazing.

Don't give up. Intimacy—even without orgasm—is precious. But orgasm is a worthy goal.

Failure to Reach Orgasm

Eva and Frank had been married twenty-three years and had raised four children, but they were both frustrated in their sexual relationship. In all their years of lovemaking, Eva had never experienced an orgasm. Understandably, she had grown more and more resistant to having sex. When Frank insisted on making love, Eva would give in. But her heart and body weren't in it. She just didn't enjoy it.

Frank was totally unaware of Eva's passivity. He was increasingly frustrated at her unwillingness to initiate sex or act like she enjoyed it. He thought she was frigid. By the time the couple came in for counseling, they had reached an impasse.

We got Eva and Frank to talk about their problems. Once they realized what had been going on, they were dismayed about how they had been acting toward each other.

We suggested some exercises. (See "Sensate Focusing," 161.) Through these exercises, Frank helped Eva experience her first orgasm. Frank felt like a new man when he saw how much Eva enjoyed the experience. The couple fell in love all over again.

Failure to reach orgasm can be a big problem for a couple over time, particularly if they never talk about it. This problem is more common in females because of their complex sexual response system. Many variables affect a woman's arousal on the way to orgasm.

Some women are threatened by their own sexual response because it feels like they're losing control. In a sense, that's what orgasm is: losing control. It's giving way to the release of muscle tension and the consuming pleasure of an adrenaline and endorphin explosion. It's an escape into ecstasy.

So why would a woman fear such an experience? Here are some of the reasons we've heard:

- ⋙ Only a wicked woman would enjoy such sensuality.
- ⋙ I might not be able to maintain my standards of proper behavior.
- ⋙ My husband might get the idea that I'll be available anytime.
- ⋙ When I get really turned on, I have fantasies that scare me.

We encourage women to accept orgasm as a gift from God. Without such release, the natural congestion of blood in a woman's pelvic organs during foreplay can cause chronic discomfort. It's like preparing a fantastic gourmet dinner but never being able to eat it.

We also suggest that a woman experiment with self-stimulation or manual stimulation of the clitoris by her husband till she has an orgasm. That should be done in a safe, relaxed setting with soft music, massage oil, candles—whatever makes the woman feel special. The goal should be for her only to attain climax. Neither partner should expect to have intercourse.

During this time, the woman should tell her husband, either verbally or nonverbally, what feels good. For example, there are times when direct clitoral stimulation isn't comfortable. Each woman is the authority on what she wants and when. If it takes several sessions to bring her to orgasm, that's fine.

Wives who have experienced these times with their husbands have said it opened them up to a wonderful world of pleasure. They loved feeling fulfilled sexually and relished the time of bonding with their husbands.

Q & A

WHY DOESN'T HE EJACULATE?

My husband doesn't have a problem getting an erection, nor does he lack the desire to have sex, but he almost never ejaculates. Is it possible for a man to feel satisfied by intercourse even though he doesn't ejaculate? I know he used to ejaculate when he masturbated, but he can't now. Can you help me out here? I enjoy sex and want to make sure he does too.

Orgasm for a man is most obvious in ejaculation, the forceful emission of seminal fluid from the penis. But orgasm also includes contractions of the vas deferens, seminal vesicles, and prostate in rhythmic cycle; the intense muscular contraction of large muscle groups such as the buttocks, thighs, and abdomen; sweating; and the relaxation that follows.

A man may have a satisfying sexual experience without ejaculation. If other aspects of arousal and orgasm are present in your lovemaking, you probably have little cause for concern. Other possible reasons for his failure to ejaculate:

Retrograde ejaculations. The seminal fluid is directed up the urethra into the bladder rather than externally out of the penis. This is not a dangerous condition. It is very common after prostate surgery. A urologist may be necessary to evaluate this condition and prescribe drugs for treatment.

Psychological factors. Fear of pregnancy or guilt about one's sexuality in the past or present may inhibit sexual release.

Physical factors. Fatigue or alcohol can inhibit ejaculation. So can medications such as tranquilizers, blood pressure stabilizers, and antidepressants.

From your question, we assume you and your husband enjoy your sexual relationship. Since many women find the fluids of ejaculation a problem, you may have an unusual blessing to celebrate. If your husband is frustrated or disappointed by this condition, however, he should see a doctor. A urologist will reassure both of you if there is no physiological reason for alarm.

Q & A

WHY DOES HE WAIT TO EJACULATE?

My husband can't climax until after we have sex. I don't want to make the problem worse by complaining about it, but his failure to ejaculate inside me makes me feel unappealing. The doctors say the problem is psychological, but my husband resents the idea that he should see a therapist. Our marriage is great otherwise, but I'm frustrated about this. What should I do?

Louis: I assume your doctor has ruled out physical causes of delayed ejaculation, such as neurovascular disorders or drug side effects. I'm also assuming your husband has had this problem for a long time. You say your marriage is great otherwise, so I'm thinking, "If it ain't broke, don't fix it."

If your husband doesn't resist sex, is sensitive to your sexual needs, and can lovingly bring you to orgasm, I don't think the problem has anything to do with your attractiveness. Rather, the most common causes of this disorder are psychological and may include:

∞ A compulsive personality, marked by the need to control
∞ Anxieties about cleanliness
∞ Fear of getting someone pregnant
∞ A deep-seated ambivalence toward women

Intravaginal ejaculation is not necessarily evidence of commitment, attraction, passion, or love. Stimulation to climax can be mutually satisfying with a variety of techniques. If you find orgasm more intense and complete during penetration, then continue that. Follow it up by stimulating your husband to ejaculation.

FAILURE TO REACH VAGINAL ORGASM

We once received a letter from a woman who said her husband's first wife always had a vaginal orgasm during intercourse. "He says there must be something wrong with me because I've never had one," the woman wrote. "Am I doing something wrong? Can any woman have a vaginal orgasm?"

The human sexual response is personal. It's thus unfair to say that one person should have the same kind of experience as someone else. Furthermore, there is no specific way of making love that is superior or inferior for everyone.

What's more important than differentiating between a vaginal or clitoral orgasm is that a husband and wife become closer to each other and more loving in sex. Orgasm is the culmination of sex-ual arousal and occurs with erotic stimulation. Kissing, breast caressing, clitoral stimulation, and vaginal stroking all lead to orgasm. The more romantic the setting, intimate the relationship, and exciting the lovemaking, the more intense that orgasm becomes. One prominent aspect of a woman's orgasm is the rhythmic contraction of the vaginal wall. So in a sense, every orgasm is a vaginal orgasm, even when the primary stimulation is in another erogenous area. It's also possible for a woman to experience orgasm when the vagina is the primary stimulus. Because of its location just above the entrance to the vagina, the clitoris usually receives some of the effects of pelvic thrusting and penile penetration.

The thing to keep in mind is that when sex becomes a performance and a measure of sexual adequacy, intimacy decreases. Relax, put away the scorecards, and enjoy your love for each other!

Q & A

WHY DOESN'T SHE HAVE VAGINAL ORGASMS?

We've been married about eight months. Although my wife is willing to have sex as often as our schedules allow (usually two to four times a week), she doesn't seem to get much physical enjoyment from intercourse. She often achieves orgasm when I stimulate her clitoris, but she hasn't yet had vaginal orgasms.

We both think some of her problem may be due to her family's poor attitude about sex. I've suggested we talk to a Christian counselor, but she doesn't like the idea of discussing our sex life with someone else. Can you help?

We don't see your wife's failure to have a vaginal orgasm as a problem. Some researchers believe there is no such thing as a vaginal orgasm. Unless penetration is painful or repulsive to your wife, you should be able to enjoy each other without worrying about the quality of orgasm. You may not have simultaneous orgasms, but that isn't necessary for satisfaction. Few couples are able to have simultaneous orgasms on a regular basis.

You have only begun to discover the wonders of marital intimacy. As you continue to enjoy each other, you may find ways to overcome whatever blocks there may be to total pleasure. Exploring the attitudes you picked up from your families of origin with a ther-apist could provide new insights someday, but this should happen only when you're both comfortable with the idea. Meanwhile, relax. Enjoy each other.

FOUR WAYS TO APPROACH A PROBLEM WITH SEX

Realize everyone has problems with sex. One of the most healing aspects of our group counseling sessions is that couples discover that they're not the only ones who aren't perfect. So often we hear someone ask in amazement, "Do you feel that way? I thought we were the only ones!" Then there's a great sigh of relief.

Admit your problem. That can do a lot to break down walls of misunderstanding. One other common confession besides erectile dysfunction is a woman's never having had an orgasm. Talk about that usually begins with an honest question to a close friend: "I don't get it—what's so great about sex?" If you're wondering, you're probably missing out on the best part!

Explore your attitudes about sex. Begin with some private journaling about your unique sexual history. Share your history with your mate or a counselor. Then proceed toward finding solutions together as husband and wife.

Take corrective action. You do the same thing in other areas of your life. Why not with sex?

HOW TO CONFRONT A PROBLEM

Confronting a problem isn't fun. When the problem involves sex, the discussion is even more emotionally charged. Here are some communication tips that can help:

Reaffirm your love for each other. Commit to dealing with differences and disappointments.

Pick the time and place to talk. Maybe you need to go out and find a place where you can deal with this stuff without interruption.

Ease into the sore spot. Giving verbal warnings of what the agenda is helps ease the way into murky waters. State what each of you are looking for as a response. Finally, allow each other freedom to postpone the dialogue until a better time.

Use the right language. In expressing the problems you're having about sex, open with an affirmation of love and commitment, then talk about your own thoughts or wants or feelings rather than make blaming "you statements." Listen to the difference:

One way: He says, "You're never interested in sex! I work hard and don't run around on you, but you're always too tired to make love. I can't take much more of your indifference. What's your problem?"

A better way: He says, "Sweetheart, I love you and want our marriage to be great for both of us. But I've been feeling frustrated about

---

Talk about It

Talk about some of the problems each of you struggle with in your sexual relationship. Which of these can you work through as a couple? Which of these, if any, might benefit from outside help, such as counseling? Should you go to a counselor individually or as a couple?

how seldom we have sex. I try to be a thoughtful husband, but I'm stumped. I don't know what I can do to get you interested in making love. Can you help me out?"

In both scenes, the man says he's disappointed about infrequent sex. But the first way is heavy on blame, guilt, and defensiveness. The second way is a plea for understanding and compassion. In each case the response is likely to match the approach. For example, the response to the guilt trip might be, "So when's the last time you took me on a date or said a single kind word? If you'd pay some attention to me instead of watching the blasted TV, I might want to go to bed with you."

The response to the second approach might be: "I'd like to have a better sex life too. If we could have more romantic times together, I'd be more responsive. How about a date Friday night?"

Sex and Health:

When the Problem Is Physical

Failure to achieve and maintain sexual intimacy is often due to relational barriers. However, occasionally the problem is purely physical.

Well, maybe not. Hardly any sexual dysfunction is totally physical. Failure to function sexually prompts a strong emotional reaction that complicates the picture. However, it is important to recognize that many physical problems interfere with the desire or ability to engage in sex.

Do you feel romantic when you have the flu? When your

Physical Turnoffs to Sex

- ✵ Fatigue
- ✵ Too much alcohol
- ✵ Drug abuse
- ✵ Prescription-drug side effects
- ✵ Upper respiratory infection
- ✵ Vaginitis
- ✵ Arthritis
- ✵ A headache. Yes, really.
- ✵ Premenstrual tension
- ✵ Miscarriage
- ✵ Cancer
- ✵ Menopause
- ✵ Myalgia
- ✵ Heart disease
- ✵ Stomach or intestinal disorder

---

stomach is in knots over something that happened at work? What about a bad headache? The sexual side effects of these physical problems disappear after the cause is removed. After you have recovered from a cold or a broken leg, amorous notions return.

But some chronic illnesses have a profound effect on sexual function. Prolonged erectile dysfunction, orgasmic failure, or ejaculatory abnormalities should be medically evaluated. Conditions such as high blood pressure or diabetes should be brought under control. Specific treatment of these conditions is more important to your sex life than reaching for the latest erection-enhancing drug.

I can't list all the medical disorders that affect sexual function. That would take another book. However, we do want you to consider how you each respond to physical problems that can affect your sexual intimacy.

Q & A

IS HE TOO DISABLED TO MAKE LOVE?

My husband was in a bad accident, and now he's in constant pain. We haven't had sex in a long time. I love my husband and want to turn him on. I've exhausted every option trying to do that: sexy lingerie, taking a vacation, marriage counseling, sex toys. Nothing helps. I miss making love. Living without it is killing my self-esteem. Any ideas?

Have you and your husband pursued every way to get his pain under control? You might want to go to a pain management clinic for treatment.

In the meantime, the best way to deal with your need for physical affection is to tell your husband what you told us. You expressed love and concern for your husband, and you indicated your willingness to make things happen. You clearly stated your desire for his affection and explained what has happened to your self-esteem by not having sex. Your husband needs to hear those things.

If your husband hasn't read the letter you sent us, write those thoughts in a love note to him. Let him know he doesn't have to be a superlover to make you happy. Maybe you can remind him of the warmth you once shared. Then discuss some things you can both do to have a satisfying sexual relationship.

You may want to try marriage counseling again. This time, stick with it until you achieve more satisfying results.

Q & A

WHY WON'T HE WASH FIRST?

My husband isn't interested in hygiene. His dirty body is such a huge turnoff I don't want sex with him. I've tried hints, such as, "Honey, where's that good-smelling cologne I bought for you?" Is there something else I can do?

We suggest two approaches. The first appeals to your husband's machismo. If you have a big enough shower, invite him to play around with you while the water's going. After he lathers you up, you can lather him up with some good-smelling gel.

The second suggestion is a better long-term solution. Make a date to talk, then use a nonthreatening approach, such as, "Darling, I have a problem I can't seem to solve. I really need your help." That appeals to a guy who wants to fix things.

Then tell your husband that your sense of smell is directly connected to your sexual-response center. That makes you vulnerable to such things as male body odor, so even though you really want to make love, your brain shuts down. You can only respond when a hot shower minimizes that odor.

LYNN AND BART: PMS KILLED THEIR SEX LIFE

Lynn and Bart had a great marriage with a wonderful sex life. They waited five years to start their family while Bart finished graduate school. When Bart got a job, Lynn became pregnant. They had a little boy. A few years later, along came a baby girl.

After the second pregnancy, Lynn suffered menstrual irregularity followed by cramping pain and discomfort with intercourse. Bart suggested she see a gynecologist. The doctor diagnosed endometriosis and put Lynn on hormone therapy. That worked for a while, but Lynn didn't want to take hormones that might cause breast cancer, so she quit. The endometriosis came back.

Bart was irritated that Lynn was not following her doctor's

orders, but he also didn't want her to have breast cancer. The couple's love life stalled. Bart tried to be the same gentle, thoughtful lover that he'd always been, but his wife's constant refusals for sex were getting old. Before long he withdrew emotionally and sexually from his wife.

Lynn asked what was wrong. Bart tried to explain his frustration, but it came out sounding like an accusation against Lynn. Nothing seemed to work.

When Bart continued to stay away from Lynn, she began wondering if he was involved with another woman. She knew how strong his sex drive was and figured that if he wasn't having sex with her, he must be having it with someone else. Bart insisted he was faithful and resented her accusations.

Lynn went back to her gynecologist. He suggested surgery. After the procedure, Lynn felt better. So did Bart. Their sex life was great for a few years. Then Lynn started getting irritable a few weeks before her period. She'd be a witch half of the month and feel guilty about it the other half. She tried tranquilizers, diuretics, diet supplements, exercise, and every other cure she read about. Nothing helped.

Once again Bart felt cheated. At one point Bart asked Lynn if she wanted a divorce. That's when the couple came in for counseling.

Lynn went back on hormone replacement therapy and found some relief. She and Bart also did some much-needed work on restoring their sexual intimacy. We had them do some exercises. (See "Sensate Focusing," 161.) The marriage survived.

WHY HIS EQUIPMENT FAILS

Our culture leads us to believe all guys are ready and eager for sex at any time, but that's just not the case. At various times a man has a problem with sexual function.

For young men, the most common factors contributing to erectile dysfunction or impotence are fatigue and stress. For older men—age fifty or older—sex problems may be due to aging equipment. Most men begin to experience changes in sexual function as they get older.

There are other factors to consider. Certain medications can interfere with a guy's sexual physiology. So can alcohol or drugs. Or depression. Anxiety about sexual prowess impedes erectile function. Once a man fails to maintain an erection, fear of failure adds to the problem.

Relational issues contribute to sexual dysfunction. Unresolved conflict in a marriage makes a man or woman resistant to sex. Guilt over real or imagined sin interrupts lovemaking.

WESLEY AND JAN: WHEN ERECTIONS FAIL

Wesley, age fifty-two, was a hardworking guy with a loving wife. Jan went through menopause in her midforties. Once the threat of pregnancy was over, she had more interest in sex than ever. The couple had read that in midlife the sex drives of a man and woman would become about equal. They both celebrated.

Then one night, Wesley had trouble responding to Jan's caresses. He was tense and tired from a long, stressful day at work, but he thought sex might help him relax, so he was willing—at least in spirit. The trouble was, his body wouldn't follow.

Wesley never before had trouble getting an erection. He was embarrassed and a little fearful. He managed to stimulate Jan manually to

"I brought you the strongest pain reliever you can get without a prescription—me!"

orgasm. They hugged and went to sleep. But he lay awake for a long time, wondering, *What's wrong with me? Will this happen again? What if I am no longer able to make love?*

FIVE WAYS TO HANDLE IMPOTENCE

Talk about it. Talk to each other—but if you're the wife, be careful. A husband feels embarrassed, sad, angry, scared, or even hopeless about not being able to make love. He needs a wife's reassurance, tenderness, love, and praise to get through what may be a temporary problem.

See a doctor. This seems so simple, but it is so difficult. Most guys don't like going in for a physical, much less bringing up the subject of sexual dysfunction. Still, a simple exam plus a change in medication may be all that's needed to restore or rejuvenate sexual function.

Don't reach for a pill. Viagra gets a lot of play these days. But a man who reaches for magic in a pill may be missing out on the most effective cure—the encouragement of a loving wife who can help him work through the prob-

lem to a more satisfying long-term solution.

Work on deeper issues. Don't let the strong feelings associated with the problem of impotence keep you as husband and wife from discussing deeper issues that are contributing to the problem. Talk about what's been going on and how each of you feels about it.

Get counseling. Sex is such an important part of your relationship that you shouldn't ignore problems. Get some help. (See "Signs That You Need Therapy," 292–94.)

Q & A

WILL ANTISEIZURE MEDICATION FOREVER DIM DESIRE?

I've had a problem with my sex drive for many years. I think one reason is that I was on antiseizure medication for fourteen years. After I had brain surgery, the seizures stopped and I got off the medication. But my libido is still low. Will I ever get back a strong sexual desire for my husband?

Your anticonvulsant treatment may have contributed to the problem of low libido, although that's not a usual side effect. More often, this drug affects the ability to achieve orgasm. However, failure to reach orgasm diminishes sexual interest. After all, why get sexually involved if it only leads to frustration?

Surgery may have affected your libido. Some areas of the brain are involved in sexual function. We encourage you to discuss your medication and your surgical treatment with your neurologist.

Your question implies that you once had a more satisfying libido. In most women, libido is directly related to relationship, so we encourage you and your husband to take a look at your marriage. How are you getting along in other areas besides sex? How did your seizure disorder and its treatment affect your closeness as a couple? Do you still feel cherished by your husband? Have you developed a good sex life in spite of your lack of libido?

Finally, what do you expect of your sex drive? Perhaps your level of interest in sex is quite normal at this time of life. Anxiety about being healthy has a strong negative effect on sexuality. It would be helpful for you and your husband to talk with a marriage counselor to identify the issues more clearly.

Q & A

SHOULD I GET OFF PROZAC?

I have been on Prozac for more than four years. Before going on Prozac, I didn't have a strong sex drive, but now it is practically nonexistent. I'm happy and don't feel deprived. Of course, my husband doesn't feel that way. I want to want him but I feel like I'm faking it. I don't think I could go off my antidepression medication. My doctor has given me Wellbutrin, which is supposed to boost my libido. So far it hasn't. Any suggestions?

Depression decreases libido, as do most antidepressants. Wellbutrin may increase libido, so it is good that your doctor suggested it. It may take a few months for it to take effect. Talk to your doctor about that.

You say your sexual drive has never been very high. That may be due to several things:

You're an ordinary woman. Low libido is common in women. The most important factor affecting the level of a woman's interest in sex is emotional intimacy.

You don't think much about sex. If you aren't mentally tuned in to sex, you probably aren't in the mood for it. Thinking about positive sexual experiences several times a day has been shown to increase a woman's desire.

You have health problems. Depression may be dimming your desire. Maintaining a healthy diet and a proper exercise program are essential for helping you feel good about yourself—which, in turn, leads to increased interest in sex.

You have negative thoughts about sex. Some parents fill their children's heads with negative beliefs about sex. Overcoming the idea that sex is sinful can be hard to do, but it's possible. You may never have as high a libido as your husband, but with some adjustments, you can enjoy mutually satisfying sexual intimacy.

WHEN THE SYSTEM FAILS

The male reproductive system is intricately designed and balanced. When things aren't working smoothly, a man feels quite threatened. One of the most effective treatments for erectile dysfunction is the calm reassurance of a loving wife. A wife's attitude and assistance are crucial for healing.

When the erectile system fails, there are a number of ways to get it working again. Before trying any of these, we encourage you to see a urologist or other qualified doctor. If there is a dominant psychological cause for sexual dysfunction, you should see a therapist. A physician might suggest one of the following:

Surgery. An inflatable air bladder is implanted in the penis and pumped up to provide an erection when needed.

Medication. Prescription drugs such as Viagra, Cialis, Levitra, or Caverject increase blood flow into the penis, causing an erection.

Mechanical aids. A suction device draws blood into the penis, then a constricting band is applied to the base of the penis to keep the erection firm.

Natural remedies. Herbalists claim results from certain preparations, such as salves, oils, and pills. These should be used with caution since the U.S. Food and Drug Administration has not approved them.

HOW VIAGRA WORKS

Drugs such as Viagra, Cialis, and Caverject ease the problem of erectile dysfunction by stimulating the dilation of arteries to erectile tissue. That's enough of a boost to increase sexual desire in males and females—although it should be made clear that the effect on libido is primarily psychological.

One advantage to using Viagra and other drugs is that they allow a couple to retain spontaneity in sexual relations. The oral drugs allow normal foreplay to proceed toward intercourse without having to stop to hook up some mechanical device or to inject a substance into the penis. The side effects of these drugs can be severe, however, so use them only with a doctor's approval.

WEIGHT ISSUES

Do a little people-watching sometime, and count how many people exiting a building are overweight. If your statistics match the national average, at least 64 percent will be overweight or obese, meaning their weight is at least 20 percent above the maximum desirable for their height. According to the National Center for Health Statistics, 97 million Americans today are obese.

Obesity results from an energy imbalance. Too many calories are taken in and not enough are burned off. Over time, this imbalance accumulates around a person's midsection, thighs, and back end. Inside the body, obesity clogs the blood, the arteries, and other vital pathways, putting people at risk for health problems such as coronary artery disease, stroke, diabetes, gallstones, kidney stones, respiratory problems, and some types of cancer.

Obesity also affects relationships physiologically and emotionally. In addition to feeling less attractive, an overweight person may find sexual activity too strenuous. The sex drive may also lessen in the overweight person as well in the spouse, who finds all the layers of insulation a real put-off.

Three things usually account for unhealthy weight gain:

Lifestyle. We take the car instead of walking. We ride elevators instead of climbing stairs. We watch television instead of playing catch with the kids. We eat out more and get served bigger portions. We snack a lot. Is it any wonder, then, that we don't move enough to burn what we eat?

To get our weight under control, we have to get our lives under control. At home and work, we should spend more time moving around, building physical activity into our regular routines. We should hike, bike, throw balls, saw wood, swim, wash cars, polish furniture, paint walls—anything to get off the couch.

We should also make wise choices about food, opting for what is low in fat, calories, and sugar and cutting back on portion sizes. We should cut back on fatty, salty, and sugary snacks and make room on our plates for five servings of fruits and vegetables a day.

Genetic patterns. Sure, some forms of obesity are due to genetics, such as Bardet-Biedl syndrome and Prader-Willi syndrome. But how common is this? More often genes and behavior combine to increase one's susceptibility to weight gain. Mama and Daddy were pretty heavy, and so are the kids. A closer look reveals that the family tends to socialize around big bowls of food and an oversize TV.

We can't change our genes, but we can change our behavior. Even small victories in weight loss—10 percent—can have positive effects on health, well-being, self-concept, and sexual libido.

Emotional issues. Sexual intimacy threatens some people for various reasons: fear of conception, discomfort during intercourse, or physical closeness in an unhappy relationship. For instance, a woman may gain weight to insulate herself against sexual involvement.

Most people who gain a lot of weight know it's a problem. Many also know the problem can be overcome with the right help. Losing weight should begin with a thorough medical exam, including a metabolic evaluation. Typical treatment involves changing eating habits and getting more exercise.

Spiritual and emotional work is necessary to deal with issues such as body image, self-concept, and relational factors. Spouses help their partners through this process by being cooperative and supportive. A spouse should never act like a food cop or diet enforcer, nor should a spouse tempt a dieting partner with the wrong kinds of food.

PART 4: MAKING MARITAL ADJUSTMENTS

If a wife, for instance, has trouble accepting her husband's overweight body, she should think about him as he used to be. Expressing her appreciation for him as a loving partner—no matter what his weight—is important for strengthening the healthy aspects of the relationship. This can also help the spouse lose weight.

Q & A

AM I GAINING WEIGHT TO AVOID LOVE?

I've struggled since adolescence with my weight. Last year I got on a serious diet and lost sixty pounds. That felt so good! I actually began to like myself. My husband loved the new look too and was especially amorous. I also got a bit of attention from guys at work. I didn't quite know what to do with that. It made me feel very uncomfortable.

I began to cheat on the diet and have now started gaining the weight back. Could this weight gain have something to do with my feelings about sex?

Louis: It could indeed. And your experience is not uncommon. Many women became threatened by their sexuality during adolescence. If they were taught at that time that being playful or flirtatious—or even attractive—to boys was dangerous and bad, they may have sought some protection.

Some learned to withdraw relationally. Some hid behind spirituality. Some got rid of their seductive curves by becoming

---

Talk about It

If one or both of you is neglecting diet, exercise, and/or medical and dental checkups, ask each other why. Are you letting your health go because of underlying problems you should deal with such as anger toward each other, self-loathing, boredom, or fear of intimacy? Ask each other how you can help each other make improvements in diet and exercise.

skeletal through anorexia or by padding their bodies with fat. Fat became a safe hiding place in which to avoid sexual temptation.

Getting fat isn't usually a conscious choice. But your experience with a successful eating plan and your reaction to how your thinner body prompted sexual attention certainly suggests why you're putting on weight again. As you became more attractive to your husband and other men, old messages about becoming an evil seductress probably kicked in.

Thank the Lord you made the connection. Now tell yourself the real truth: having a healthy, attractive body is a gift from the Creator. You can enjoy being attractive without responding inappropriately to men. Set the boundaries for them, but let your husband enjoy the new you.

You might also want to look at other aspects of your marriage to see if being overweight is a way to avoid other intimacy issues such as hurt, anger, power, control, or dependence.

Melissa: Yes, gaining back the pounds you lost could be related to your feelings about sex. If a woman feels threatened by the leering looks of a man, she may abandon good nutrition, diet, and exercise so that her looks don't attract attention. She may put on weight to avoid having sex with her husband. Clearly, this is an issue that needs exploring.

Q & A

WHY WON'T SHE LOSE WEIGHT?

My wife has gained twenty-five pounds since we were married. I don't get as excited looking at her as before, and find myself not making advances. I also compare her to thinner women. My wife is aware of my feelings and is trying to lose weight, but she's not having much success. I know I don't have a perfect body and that physical attraction isn't everything. How can we improve our sex life?

You mentioned you don't have a perfect body. Has your wife lost her attraction to you?

Sex, love, and marriage go a lot deeper than a dress size and abs of steel. Focus on the things about your marriage and your sweetheart that attracted you in the first place. Rid your mind of negative thoughts. It's your choice to approach your wife sexually. Serving one another is what love is about.

It sounds like your wife has been feeling a lot of stress. We suggest the two of you seek counseling now rather than letting destructive patterns solidify. Her weight gain might be stress-related and will only increase with the pressure she's feeling from you.

When she's feeling your love and affirmation more than your criticism and disappointment, she'll be more motivated to change. Maybe you could exercise and improve your diet together.

Q & A

HOW CAN I LOVE HIM WHEN HE'S FAT?

Since my husband had major surgery about five years ago, he has gained nearly a hundred pounds. The weight gain doesn't bother him, but I'm petite, and he, at 270 pounds, is too big for me. I also don't find him sexually appealing. I want to show him more love, but he doesn't want help. What should I do?

Louis: Anyone who has experienced such a significant alteration in size or metabolism should seek medical help. Perhaps your husband's traumatic experience with surgery makes him hesitant to investigate another physical problem.

Even if he is unwilling to lose weight for the sake of his health, you can take the initiative. To describe how you feel as a petite woman faced with the prospect of sexual play with a 270-pound man, you might say: "Darling, I want to feel turned on like I did those nights we parked at the lake, remember? Now I feel so different. It's like getting into a dream car for a thrilling run and finding that it has changed. I can't see out the windows and feel dwarfed by the steering wheel. I can't reach the accelerator or gears. The whole experience makes me want to get out of there!"

Of course, your word picture composed from your own experience will be more effective.

Melissa: Approach this in terms of your own needs. Tell your husband, "I want to have the sort of satisfying sex we used to have. But I'm struggling with a lack of motivation. I need your help. What can we do?" Such a statement does not blame your husband or tell him what to do. It asks him for help.

If you haven't already suggested changing your position for sexual intercourse, make it clear now that the more traditional male-above position does not work for you. Tell your husband you feel smothered. Consider talking to your husband's doctor too. A huge weight gain is not healthy. Perhaps the doctor will offer advice.

PART FIVE:
SEX AND THE
REST OF LIFE

13

SEX AND OTHERS:

The Influence of Family and Friends on Lovemaking

Sex is not a spectator sport. Nor is it a group experience. It works best as a private expression of love between a man and a woman in marriage.

In many ways, you find this out on your own. You were created with the basic physiological package for sex and some awareness of how it works. You saw an attractive person—maybe your spouse-to-be—and something happened inside. You were driven to connect with that person on the deepest, most intimate level.

Sex sounds simple, doesn't it? It's not—because the brain controls the entire operation, and that complicates the picture. Through your brain, your sexuality is influenced by a host of spectators and critics. Some of them have been recording messages in your brain for a long time, shaping your atti-tudes and expectations about yourself as a sexual person. For example, young men often get the message that their adequacy as males depends on making sexual conquests. This tape seriously conflicts with marital vows of fidelity.

Some critics are still influencing you—if not in person, then in other, less obvious ways. You may be so influenced by messages from others that sexual interactions between you and your spouse become a kind of group event. Parents, cousins, uncles, teachers, neighborhood bullies—and other people—have been inside your head, talking to you for years. When their messages are unconscious, they have the greatest control. For example, if you have an unconscious belief that sex is evil, you'll become very anxious as sexual situations develop but will have no idea why. The way to change that idea is get at those unconscious beliefs, then test them against reality. The idea that sex is evil, for example, rarely holds out against the beauty of marital sexual intimacy. So let's work at pulling messages out of the unconscious and examine them to move you along the path toward sexual health and happiness.

BOBBIE'S PARENT TAPES

Bobbie was having trouble in her marriage. She had waited to get married until she was thirty-one, and she had held off on sex until the honeymoon.

Deep down, Bobbie realized she had some fears about being sexually intimate. She felt uneasy about her attractiveness even though she was a beautiful woman. She had some experience with dating but had always backed out of a relationship when it threatened to get serious. Somehow Mark had overcome that resistance and gently won her heart. Now Bobbie and Mark were struggling with bedroom intimacy. They even went to a counselor. In one session, Bobbie was asked to write her sexual history.

She told how she was the fourth of four daughters. After she was born, her parents decided to give up trying for the boy her father wanted. Bobbie sensed that disappointment, and she became Daddy's sidekick. Her sisters wore dresses and lace, but Bobbie wore jeans and T-shirts. The sisters had to help Mom in the kitchen, but Bobbie did farmwork with Dad. Bobbie became Daddy's favorite—the boy he had always wanted. He

---

Talk about It

Think back on the sexual attitudes and ideas you each developed as you were growing up. What did you hear about sex from older women or older men in your family? What did you learn about sex from friends or enemies? How could those ideas be affecting your marriage today?

never hugged her or was tender with her. His way of showing her affection was to poke her on the arm or conk her on the head.

As a married woman, Bobbie adapted to most of the expectations for her gender. Yet, deep inside, she still heard her mother saying, "Go help your dad. You're stronger than your sisters." That was enough to make her doubt her femininity.

Recognizing the power of her mother's tapes allowed Bobbie to reprogram her thinking about herself. With time, she became Mark's willing wife and lover.

MESSAGES IN THE WOMB

It is amazing how people perceive their parents as sexual beings. We've known intelligent people who were convinced that they were either adopted or left behind by a stork—since it's inconceivable that their parents ever had sexual intercourse.

Despite what you think, chances are very good that you were conceived during sexual intercourse between your mother and father. Your parents also taught you much of what you know about yourself as a sexual being. The parental messages began before you were born, and your waiting brain began recording them when you were still in your mother's womb.

Our youngest son and his wife recently had their first child. That little one was much anticipated and much loved, even before he was born. He greeted the outside world with a lusty protest. After he was cleaned up, weighed, and footprinted, he was given to his dad, who began speaking quietly to him—as he had been doing for the past eight months. Instantly, the baby stopped crying.

Imagine the contrast, then, to a baby who has been recording only messages of anger and rejection. Multiply the effect of love or neglect by lifetime memories of love or neglect, and you can imagine what conclusions spouses reach about sexual intimacy.

HOW PARENTS MODEL SEX

There's a huge difference in how parents exhibit sexuality. At one extreme are parents who never touch each other in front of their children. Their kids are likely to say later on, "I never saw my parents kiss or hug each other. So when I wanted affection and started petting on dates, I felt terrible. Good kids didn't do that."

At the other extreme are parents who are immodest and exhibitionistic. This kind of behavior only creates anxieties in children, especially when what was so natural at home conflicts with other people's standards of modesty. For example, changing clothes in the living room at home may have been all right, but it wasn't OK in someone else's family room when other people were present.

Between these extremes are many appropriate ways for moms and dads to show affection for one another. I never doubted my father's love for my mother, for example, because of their frequent hugs, pats, and playful nibbles. I learned a lot about enjoying sexuality from that role model.

WHAT PARENTS EXPECT

Children watch how their parents relate to each other. What they see forms deep and powerful templates for what we think marriage should be. Those expectations include things like what Mama cooked and how she fixed it (particularly favorite foods), what Daddy did in his leisure time, who

made the financial decisions, who exerted control, and how disputes were settled. Those behaviors may have been ineffective and even painful, but they became familiar, predictable, and comforting to you. You expect your mate to do things the same way.

Melissa and I discovered one such difference early in our marriage. If someone became ill in her family, that person went into seclusion. After all, why would you want a bunch of spectators to see you at your worst?

My family responded to sick people the opposite way. If you got sick, you got lots of attention. Mother would check on you frequently, put a cool washcloth on your brow, slip a thermometer under your tongue, and give you a tablespoon of Milk of Magnesia.

Imagine then how Melissa and I reacted after we were married and got sick. When Melissa caught the flu, I sprang into action. When she didn't thank me for my attentiveness, I thought she was ungrateful. Then I got sick. Melissa politely closed the door so I could have privacy. I felt abandoned.

After we talked, we realized how each of us had been hurt by each other's unconscious expectations. Today, if Melissa gets sick, I leave her alone. If I succumb to a germ, she brings me Milk of Magnesia.

Our Conflicting Values

Dan's parents thought money was evil. They lived frugally and were generous with what little money they had. By contrast, Nancy's family saw material blessings as a gift from God. They made generous contributions to their church and other charities, but they lived in upper-middle-class comfort.

These differences caused problems for Dan and Nancy. Nancy was disappointed that Dan didn't give her a wedding gift. She was devastated when he gave away presents from her family. She bounced between guilt about her materialism and anger at his asceticism. Dan was confused by Nancy's reaction. He thought she agreed with his values of thrift and generosity.

The values you got from your parents that conflict with your spouse's values are difficult to deal with. Compromise is hard where absolutes such as thrift and generosity and gift giving are involved, so it may be better to work on tolerating your differences and focusing on values you share. Years later, after you and your partner have survived other difficulties, you may find that your relationship supersedes conflicting values.

Scrambled Signals from Childhood

In a complex process, satellite communication signals are

Talk about It

List some ideas or practices you and your spouse have carried from childhood into marriage regarding gift giving, celebrating a birthday, teasing, or being sick. Compare the two lists. Which ideas or practices are similar? Which are dissimilar? How have you worked through the differences?

electronically scrambled, then unscrambled for proper reception on Earth. Many of us have a similar communication system. We have scramblers that confuse certain messages that are sent our way and filters that unscramble those messages. The problem is that these filters alter incoming signals to fit a carefully programmed system from our childhood. The distorted messages form the nucleus for our parents' continued influence in our adult lives. Here are some of those signals:

Word choice. Certain words are behavioral cues. For example, I knew that if I was addressed by my full name, Paul Louis McBurney, what followed was negative. So I reacted to the use of my full name with all the defenses I could muster. Even sweet-sounding terms can be behavior cues. Using "honey" or "sweetheart" in a super-syrupy way, for example, makes you tense up because those words usually precede a request like, "Could you take out the garbage?"

The look. The cold scowl from your father was such a powerful filter in your childhood that a similar look from your spouse—even if it

has nothing to do with you—makes you afraid or rebellious.

Implied disapproval. Some spouses who could never please their parents developed a filter that interprets nearly everything people say to them as disapproval. They automatically deflect any praise, telling themselves, "If they really knew me, they'd never say that."

Relentless control. A trigger may be something as subtle as a facial expression or tone of voice. For example, Sam's mother used to make all his decisions, so he was determined never to let a woman tell him what to do. He interpreted many of his wife's messages as attempts to dominate. His response was to explode in anger. Sam didn't realize what he was doing until a friend talked to him. Then Sam realized he was pushing away his wife because she reminded him of his mother.

Guilt and blame. Beth's father would tease her in front of family and friends. He thought it was cute to see Beth blush, then burst into tears. When Beth finally told her dad how painful teasing was for her, her dad said she was being childish and oversensitive. His response made her feel worse. While feeling compelled to apologize, she became increasingly angry.

Beth carried that tendency to link apology with anger into marriage. For example, whenever Beth's husband, Frank, responded negatively to something Beth did, Beth would respond with profuse apologies, but then she'd refuse to discuss the problem or to actually change her behavior. She was too angry for that.

Two Ways to Decode Distortions

To unscramble distorted messages from childhood, you need to take two steps.

First, identify the faulty filters. Look for patterns in your relationships that may be inappropriate. For example, some people respond defensively to anyone in authority because their filters were set by a controlling parent. They then see anyone in authority as dominating and controlling.

Second, listen to what your spouse says, then repeat what you hear. That will help clarify what is said and what it means. When Beth did this, she began to recognize how angry she was whenever she said "I'm sorry" to her husband.

She also discovered how annoyed her husband was with her profuse apologies. Beth stopped apologizing, realizing that most of her guilt was inappropriate. With further therapy, her anger melted away. And intimacy with her husband improved.

In-Law Interference

To whom are loyalties most due—one's spouse or one's parents—and who has the most control? Those seem to be the issues when either a husband or wife hasn't cut a parental tie and become fully committed to the spouse.

We often don't see the glaring flaws in our parents that our mates see because we've had a lifetime in which to practice denial and rationalization. As counselors, we've heard many in-law stories—from the wife who considered it perfectly appropriate to ask her mother for approval to take a trip with her husband to the husband who was perfectly at peace about spending every holiday fishing with his dad.

Do in-laws invade the bedroom? Before dismissing the idea as Freudian foolishness, realize that your spouse's parents had a lot to do with your mate's sexual identity.

Most of your spouse's attitudes about being your lover were conditioned by what was seen and heard at home.

Acknowledge interferance. In our experience, in-laws rarely meddle openly. But some continue to try to run a child's life. One couple we worked with had constant tension over his mother's intrusions. Actually her little boy didn't really mind all of his mother's calls. She was only trying to be helpful, he said. Most of the time, he sided with his mother rather than his wife. That made Mother's calls all the more infuriating to his wife.

Stop it. Parental meddling can often be stopped by a firm word from Mother's little boy or Daddy's little girl. Even if the attempts continue, divisiveness can be avoided if a husband and wife are totally committed to each other. The marital bond is stronger than apron or purse strings, making it possible for a couple to ignore and even chuckle at intrusive comments from a well-meaning parent.

THE MARK OF SIBLINGS

If you're familiar with family-systems theories or watch TV dramas about families, you're aware of the powerful influence that brothers and sisters have in our lives:

They help define our roles. The roles we assume in families often carry over unchanged into our marriage. Peacemakers, rescuers, scapegoats, controllers, heroes, and

rebels remain the same, regardless of context.

They affect our sex lives. The roles we assumed with siblings carry over into sexual activity. Peacemakers deny their own sexual desires to avoid conflict. Heroes ignore appropriate sexual boundaries in order to gratify their need for attention. Scapegoats do things that assure rejection.

They affect our view of a spouse. A person often projects the role of a sibling onto a spouse. A guy might say, "My wife is bossy just like my big sister!" His wife might respond, "My husband acts like my spoiled brat brother." Such perceptions hardly promote sexual intimacy.

They may introduce us to sex. It is very common for preschoolers to satisfy their curiosity about gender differences by comparing their anatomy to others. Less common is sexual abuse committed by older adolescents on younger siblings. We have heard some heartbreaking stories. Less extreme experiences can also scar a person's sexual perceptions. A single incident of one sibling fondling another may create an acute sense of guilt and the perception of being damaged goods. Those

voices are powerful influences on a person's sexual self-image.

The good news is that we've seen many examples of confession, forgiveness, and healing between brothers and sisters who wronged each other in childhood. Voices from the past lose their power when that occurs.

FRIENDS AND YOUR SEX LIFE

By now, you may be thinking about other voices from the past that could be affecting your sex life. We suspect that some sound like those of high school and college buddies who talked a lot about sex.

Those friends helped shape your perceptions of yourself as a sexual adult. If they offered positive ideas, they helped you develop healthy sexual boundaries. If not, the messages could have persuaded you to have multiple sexual partners. Those experiences may now be affecting your desire to be sexually faithful to your spouse.

Who are your current friends and what influence do they have on you? Through the years, we've worked with couples who have been crushed by infidelity. Time and again we learned that the "other woman" was the wife's best friend or that the "other man" was the husband's best friend. Two couples had gone to dinner, enjoyed picnics, or even vacationed together. The relationships slipped into adultery when the husband of one couple began meeting with the wife of the other couple. Adultery could have been avoided had the couples observed better boundaries. They could have agreed not to share confidences belonging only to their mates. They could have agreed not to meet with each other when their mates were absent. They could have nixed any behavior their own spouses would have questioned. And they could have walked away from anything that felt furtive or secretive.

Q & A

CAN GRIEF SHUT DOWN SEX?

My husband's dad died last spring, and my husband has grieved since. I've been as supportive as I can during this time. I've felt pretty close to my husband—except for one area. He seems to have shut down sexually. Is this normal for a grieving person? What can I do to help him?

Louis: While some phases of the grieving process are similar, the way a person grieves is unique. Normally, grief lasts six to twelve months and is expressed in sadness, withdrawal, tears, and various physical symptoms. The survivor can become obsessed with his own mortality. If the relationship with the person who died was conflicted, that complicates the grief process.

Since sexual function is intricately connected with our feelings, grief and its accompanying emotions certainly affects sexual interaction. Depression, which is common in mourning, often lessens interest in sex. However, some survivors who now realize life's unpredictability may want sex more after losing someone they love.

If your husband's interest in sex doesn't return after a year, something else may be going on. Consider these possibilities:

He feels guilty. Some survivors feel bad about enjoying physical pleasure during a time of loss. If your husband feels he didn't do enough for his dad during his final illness or that he never measured up to his dad's expectations, he might have trouble investing fully in life. Living with that kind of unfinished business is difficult.

He fears his own death. This worry can be exaggerated by reports of death caused by sexual exertion—even though those deaths are extremely rare.

He grieves about your relationship. Sometimes a bereaved person's focus on his own mortality intensifies his view of marital disappointments. It highlights a rift between the spouse and the deceased in-law, amplifying feelings that the spouse didn't treat the in-law kindly.

Drugs are pulling him down. Sometimes a grieving person uses alcohol, antidepressants, or tranquilizers—with or without a spouse's knowledge. These chemicals affect sexual function.

Melissa: Be patient and keep supporting your husband. Talk about these issues. Let him know how you feel—and express your desire for him. Do not withdraw physically from him. Even though he's not responding the way he usually does, he needs to feel your affection. Chances are good that your husband's time of mourning will pass soon and full sexual pleasure will return. If your sex life doesn't get back to normal in a year, seek help from a professional Christian counselor.

A GUIDE FOR WHOM TO CONFIDE IN

Marital sex is personal, private, and exclusive. Yet there are times when a couple needs help. Having someone to talk to other than your mate can save your sexual relationship. It's probably unwise to broadcast the news of your husband's erectile dysfunction or your wife's orgasmic failure, but discreet revelation to a trusted friend may be good.

There are some guidelines for whom to confide in:

They must keep what you say confidential. Your first clue about whether a person can keep things confidential is what he tells you about others. Someone who says, "I'm not supposed to tell anyone this, so promise not to breathe a word . . ." is not worthy.

Preferably, they're not in the family. You may trust a sibling or parent with most confidences, but sharing sexual concerns is more difficult. Obviously it takes a mature family member to keep your secret.

They should be nonjudgmental. A good confidant listens objectively to what you say and doesn't blame you or your mate. A helpful response is compassion coupled with sensible questions to guide your understanding of the situation. In counseling we often ask, "What do you think your spouse would say about that?" That is helpful.

They don't try to triangle. A triangle develops when you try to get your confidant to straighten out your mate. A wise person avoids being put in the middle. He or she might offer to help you and your mate talk to each other about the problem. But imagine the effect it would have if the third party did confront your mate. Let's say Melissa had a close relationship with Louis's mother, and she told her mother-in-law that Louis was treating her poorly. What if Mama did something? The effect would be worse than the original problem.

They're the same gender as you. Baring your soul to a person of the opposite gender is dangerous. Professionals are trained to hear your sexual frustrations without taking advantage of your vulnerability. If you get any sense of inappropriate advances, run!

Q & A

WHY DON'T I WANT HIM ON TOP OF ME?

When my husband begins to get on top of me during lovemaking, I go crazy inside. I've been wondering if someone abused me when I was a child. I have some vague memories of my brother getting me involved in sexual play, but I don't remember any specifics. What should I do about this?

Louis: It's quite possible that memories of experiences with your brother may now be emerging as you interact sexually with your husband. Before you accuse your brother of anything, cautiously seek evidence from other siblings or your parents. Ask them if they remember any suspicious behavior involving your brother. Often sisters have had similar experiences with an abusive brother.

It's also important to talk to your brother to find out the truth. If he has abused you, and he confesses it, try to forgive him. Working through that process should unlock the oppressive feeling you feel toward your husband during sexual play.

Talk about It

How do you and your spouse handle problems with each other? Whom do you talk to? How does confiding in someone else help your marital relationship? How does it hurt? List some ways each of you might be helped through a time of marital stress without compromising your relationship.

14

SEX AND RAISING CHILDREN:

Loving with Interruptions

⌒

Pregnancy and childbirth are joyful experiences, but they sure do complicate lovemaking. Did you ever try to make whoopee with a toddler yelling for attention or a teenager having a sleepover? Ah, blessed parenthood!

Let's look at the whole experience, from deciding to conceive to pregnancy, childbirth, the postpartum period, and the complications various-age children bring to marital sex. You may decide to skip some of these stages and move directly to the empty-nest syndrome. Take it from Melissa and me, that stage isn't bad at all!

THREE REASONS TO HAVE KIDS

Why is procreation so important? Here are some reasons:

God delights in it. "Be fruitful and multiply," said God to the first man and woman. The Creator eternally delighted in making new life. Look around you at the extravagance of nature—pollination and seeds are everywhere.

We're designed for it. God was grandiose when he designed our human reproductive systems. Think of it—every little girl is born with about two million eggs in her ovaries. Of that number, three hundred thousand eggs will be available for release in monthly cycles when she enters puberty. During a woman's childbearing years, only about five hundred eggs will actually be released. If you think this is overkill, consider the male reproductive system. From two small testicles in a man's scrotum, about two million sperm are released per ejaculation. If a guy has roughly three ejaculations per week for fifty or sixty years—well, sperm production is staggering.

It's an innate desire. Having children is a natural desire. When a woman's biological clock begins to run down, she can become desperate to get pregnant.

Any couple contemplating marriage should discuss their wishes and expectations about childbearing. Disagreements about if, how many, and when to have children can set the stage for long-term conflict.

Warning: If you have significant differences regarding having children, don't avoid the subject and assume it'll work out. Postpone or cancel wedding plans until you've resolved the issue.

Q & A

How Can We Have Kids If He Never Wants Sex?

My husband has a lower sex drive than I have. He's fine with having sex once a week; I'd like it every other day. Our involvement at church and at work keeps us busy but not stressed. He wants to have children in the future, which I'm open to, but from everything I've read, couples have sex less often after *children arrive—and I'm unsatisfied with the frequency as is. Help!*

How does your husband respond to your wish for more sex? Who initiates sexual foreplay? Is sex satisfying when it does occur? The answers may provide useful insights into your husband's infrequent desire for sex.

Since you connected the problems of frequency to having children, I'm wondering how your husband feels about pregnancy. Sometimes men feel threatened by parenthood and try to minimize the possibility of pregnancy by not having sex. If that's what your husband is thinking, reassure him that today's forms of birth control are effective. If he's still nervous about pregnancy, lay off sex during the time when you're most fertile.

It's possible that your husband has a low testosterone level. This can be determined with a simple blood test. Based on the results, he'll find whether he needs treatment. Finally, you may want to reconsider your assumption that frequency of sex will decrease after children come along. This isn't necessarily so. We've known many couples whose lovemaking increased after they had children. You may find the same thing happening in your marriage.

Q & A

WHY HASN'T HE TOUCHED ME SINCE THE MISCARRIAGE?

Shortly after my husband and I wed, I became pregnant. We ended up losing the baby, but since then our sex life hasn't been the same. Sometimes my husband doesn't make advances toward me for several weeks. He also rejects my advances. What should I do?

Losing a child is very difficult for a couple. Think about some of the complications of losing a baby:

Spiritual frustration. Anger, guilt, and blame may be a natural reaction to an inexplicable tragedy, but these emotions pull you away from God and each other. Deal with the emotions and recognize your need for God's healing and each other's love during this time.

Relational tension. One spouse may eagerly anticipate starting a family while the other has reservations. One may need to feel in control of conception and resent loss of agreement on that issue. Any of those expectations can be clouded by the loss of a baby. Those feelings may be expressed in withholding sexual intimacy.

Emotional pain. Men who are less in touch with their feelings than women are prone to minimize or deny the pain of miscarriage. A husband's get-on-with-life attitude does nothing to help his wife mourn the loss of a life she felt in her womb. In rare cases, those emotions can be reversed—a man can have grief he can't express and a mate who wants to dismiss the loss and get on with life.

Guilt. A husband or wife can feel guilty after a miscarriage, thinking that premarital or extramarital sex contributed to the loss. Or the loss is blamed on strenuous physical activity—a boisterous sexual encounter or a long bike ride.

Spiritual frustration, guilt, anger, and other emotions related to miscarriage can interfere with sexual intimacy. Talking about these issues can bring a couple through the pain to forgiveness and resolution. Counseling may be useful as you deal with the process.

THE OOPS PREGNANCY

For some couples, pregnancy isn't good news. Poor timing or

bad circumstances make the dream look like a nightmare. When that happens, a couple has more work to do besides painting the nursery. They've got to find ways to adjust to this new reality. There are no easy answers for this, but here are two crucial goals:

⋙ Both husband and wife must share responsibility for the pregnancy rather than playing a destructive blame game.
⋙ Both should consider the needs and well-being of this baby over their own.

If you are having difficulty with the pregnancy, you and your spouse should see a counselor. In addition, you should seek support and encouragement from friends. Many couples have successfully survived unplanned pregnancies. They can help you. So can community and church groups that have been created to help expectant parents. Ask your pastor or counselor for suggestions.

Q & A

WHAT SHOULD WE DO ABOUT INFERTILITY?

My husband and I have been trying to have a baby. We're going to a fertility specialist, but we have questions. Does the Bible say anything about infertility? How can a Christian couple know what medical options are acceptable for achieving conception?

Louis: The Bible is all for pregnancy and having children. But it offers few guidelines that apply to the scientific possibilities that are now available to help couples conceive.

Joe S. McIlhaney Jr., a Christian gynecologist who specializes in infertility, makes this observation in *1250 Health-Care Questions Women Ask*:

It is my personal commitment to do all I can, within my ethical and moral limits, to aid infertile couples in achieving pregnancy. In the process I remind myself and the couple that there are higher goals in life—the protection of the dignity of an individual, the preservation of the family as ordained by God, and the maintenance of healthy relationships within those families. Despite the intensity of their desire to have a child, I believe infertile couples must not and should not be coerced into using any technique they cannot whole-heartedly accept.*

Whatever is done, full agreement between husband and wife is essential. If either partner has spiritual or emotional doubts about a fertility procedure, it is unwise to proceed.

Melissa: Infertility is traumatic. Lots of prayer and lots of understanding for each other is necessary. So is listening to one another. Above all, avoid blaming and put-downs so you come through infertility into childbearing with your relationship intact. A support group for each of you would help you express and deal with your feelings.

HER CHANGING BODY: IS SHE STILL SEXY?

As pregnancy progresses, a couple must adjust to physical changes in the woman: enlarging breasts, growing belly, aches, awkwardness, and swollen ankles. She may also have unexpected mood changes. However, most pregnancies are joyful experiences. Many women say they felt better about themselves during pregnancy than ever before. Undoubtedly, part of that is related to having more attentive, protective, and adoring husbands.

Sexual relations can continue during pregnancy with little danger to the growing baby. You'll need to experiment with positions for intercourse as the baby grows. Often the lateral or rear entry positions are more comfortable than straight-on sex. Unless a woman is having problems carrying the baby, she can continue intercourse throughout pregnancy.

Q & A

CAN WE HAVE SEX DURING PREGNANCY?

I don't want to hurt our baby, so how long can we have sex during pregnancy? What's appropriate, and what do the Scriptures say?

Louis: As far as we know, the Scriptures don't mention sex during pregnancy. The simple answer medically is that if your pregnancy is normal, with no complications such as bleeding or premature opening of

---

*Joe S. McIlhaney Jr., with Susan Netherly, *1250 Health-Care Questions Women Ask* (Grand Rapids: Baker, 1985), 659–60.

the cervix, it's OK to have intercourse throughout pregnancy.

You'll discover, however, that making love as your womb expands requires creativity. Some couples find the husband-on-top position for intercourse just doesn't work. The wife above, lateral, or rear-entry approaches may be more comfortable. When nothing seems to fit, you can still enjoy mutual stimulation orally or manually to orgasm.

Your baby is well protected in your uterus and is unlikely to be affected by your husband's thrusting erection. There are other considerations, however, that can affect your mutual enjoyment of intercourse. You might experience some physical symptoms related to your pregnancy that make intercourse unpleasant. Some common complaints are ankle swelling, breast tenderness, backache, nausea, constipation, indigestion, or hemorrhoids. If these are bothersome, talk to your doctor and get appropriate treatment. Don't allow such problems to interrupt your sexual enjoyment.

If you have any questions as your delivery date approaches, talk to your doctor. Sex during pregnancy is a common concern, so don't be embarrassed to ask your doctor for advice.

AFTER THE BABY COMES: A TIME TO ADJUST

Hold off on intercourse for about six weeks after childbirth. After that time—assuming there are no complications—resume lovemaking. Remember that even if she breast-feeds, a woman will begin ovulating as early as four weeks after delivery. So contraception is important.

Another adjustment: a guy can get jealous of all the attention the baby is getting. Sometimes a new father isn't conscious of feeling jealous but just becomes irritable or demanding. Once a husband realizes that jealousy is a normal reaction to a new infant and that he doesn't have to feel guilty about it, he and his wife can work on rejuvenating their relationship.

Another possible adjustment is postpartum depression in a new mom. These bouts of moodiness are related to the hormonal changes that occur in a woman during and immediately after delivery. She feels unloved, withdrawn, and even suicidal. She may have trouble bonding with her baby or be afraid to hold or nurse it. Postpartum depression is usually transient, but it should always be taken seriously. Medication and even hospitalization may be necessary. Getting help with the new infant is essential.

Q & A

AREN'T MOMS DESIRABLE?

Since my husband and I had our son a year ago, my husband has had no interest in sex. Even when I initiate sex, he turns me down with excuses about being tired or having financial worries. I wonder what it would be like to be married to someone who made me feel wanted and beautiful. What do you suggest?

Pregnancy and delivery of a baby cause more than just abdominal stretch marks and postpartum depression for the mother. New dads get their own set of psychological "stretch marks" that can make sex less appealing:

Invasion of space. A father often reacts to no longer having his wife all to himself. There's this other little person who's always at her breast.

Less attention. The baby puts new time constraints on both husband and wife. Also, your attention and affection have shifted toward your son. Your husband knows that he's not supposed to feel jealous of the baby, but subtle resentment can develop.

Her new role. Subconsciously, a husband may not be able to see his wife as both mother and sexual playmate. A mother is supposed to be off-limits sexually. A husband may need help making this transition.

Her changing body. Men can be squeamish about earthy stuff like labor and delivery, episiotomies, and lactation. The idea of getting you pregnant again may also cool him toward intercourse.

If a husband loses interest in sex after his wife has a baby, here's what a woman can do:

- She can ease some of the pressures and financial demands on her husband.
- She can ask if he has emotional needs that have been unmet since the baby's arrival.
- She can work toward regaining her figure and her availability for sex.
- She can hire a babysitter, kidnap her husband, bring him

to some romantic spot, and seduce him.

⋈ She can let him know he's still her hero.

Q & A

HOW CAN I FEEL SEXY WITH STRETCH MARKS?

When I was pregnant with our son twenty-seven years ago, I got hideous stretch marks on my abdomen, buttocks, breasts, and backs of my arms and thighs. I have tried everything to get rid of them, but I am embarrassed about them. I won't put on sexy clothing for my husband because of how ridiculous I look. My husband doesn't understand why stretch marks are such a problem for me. We have good sex, but I don't fully enjoy it. How can I when I'm so embarrassed about my body?

Melissa: Why do you hang on to a negative self-image? Answering that question may be more important than your stretch marks. If you had no stretch marks, would you be satisfied with your body? I suspect that if you took care of the marks, some other flaw would surface.

Take a look at John 8:32, which says, "You will know the truth, and the truth will set you free." You have ugly stretch marks. The truth that sets you free is that your husband loves you, stretch marks and all.

If you can't get past the stretch marks, ask a dermatologist or plastic surgeon what to do about them. Then ask yourself, "What's more important, fully enjoying sex or holding on to negative perceptions of my body?" You have the power to control your thoughts and feelings. Give that a try.

PRESCHOOLERS, FATIGUE, AND LOVEMAKING

If you manage to get your preschooler stowed away so you finally have some quality time with your spouse, you quickly discover that a good nap looks more enticing than sex.

We suggest you work out an agreement with other parents of preschoolers. Barter for some free time: You take my kid on Friday night, and I'll take yours next Friday. Try to get some time alone with your mate at least once a month.

Remember that this time with toddlers will pass. In a few years, your preschoolers will be in school. You'll have several years to recover before the little ones become teenagers.

SURVIVING ADOLESCENCE

Toddlers become teens in no time, presenting new challenges to a couple trying to maintain a healthy sex life. The major problem is embarrassment; the kids now know what you're up to when you lock your bedroom door or sneak away for some backyard smooching. Just remember it's normal and healthy for you to express yourselves sexually. Showing affection for each other is also great modeling for your kids.

A few tips about teens and sex: First, *be totally open with them about sexuality*. They're bombarded daily with raging hormones and all kinds of talk about safe sex, breast enhancement surgery, and Viagra—all from less-than-reliable sources. They need a place to go to check out the truth of what they're hearing. Be a trusted ear for them. Even if you don't have all the answers, you can look up things together.

Second, *treat your teens with respect*. They'll respect your private lives if you show respect for who they are. This includes accepting their mood swings, fashion statements, self-consciousness, and awkwardness. It means giving them the security of reasonable limits.

Third, *remind your teens that God made their bodies beautiful and precious*. Their modesty at this time of development should be safeguarded and honored, for chastity becomes difficult without modesty. Chastity grows out of gratitude for the bodies God has given them and a sense of responsibility about how he wants those bodies to be used.

Though teens often add stress to a marital relationship, it's still possible for parents to maintain sexual intimacy. But sexual interludes take careful planning. Talk to each other about how you relate to each other in front of your teens. Talk about how you can reserve time for intimacy inside and outside the home. And talk about the time when the kids are grown and gone and all you have left is each other. Your romance will be stronger than ever if it is sustained and nourished throughout the child-rearing years.

Q & A

Should We Hide Love-making from the Kids?

My husband and I have three children under the age of ten. He and I set aside some time on Saturday mornings to have sex. Currently, my kids have no idea what we're up to, but it won't be long before they'll understand what we're doing. I don't want to give up my special Saturday times, but I'm uneasy about the kids knowing that their dad and I are in the middle of a sexual encounter. Any words of wisdom?

Most kids know more about sex than their parents suspect. Though there's no reason for you to feel embarrassed about your lovemaking sessions, be sure you lock the bedroom door first. Also, get some good material for teaching children about sex when they ask questions.

Your Saturday morning sessions are also teaching tools. When kids see how their parents take time for each other, they learn how important that is. They also feel safe and stable in this loving environment. Don't give up those special times.

Q & A

Has Being a Mom Killed My Desire?

I enjoy having sex with my husband, but ever since I became a mother eight years ago, I have been unable to have an orgasm. What used to stimulate me doesn't work now. My husband

In spite of their hectic schedules, Sue and Bob always looked forward to their weekly date night.

and I have tried various techniques, but none work. I'm so focused on pleasing my husband and mothering my kids that I can't focus on myself. How can I get the pleasure back?

Louis: Although childbirth may have caused some change in your sexual physiology, the fact that you're able to get close to achieving a climax probably rules that out. Distractibility is more likely the issue.

Reaching orgasm requires abandonment. It means giving up control. Can you put aside your concern for your husband's pleasure and your children's well-being long enough to allow yourself pleasure? That's the issue. Thankfully, there's help.

NUDITY IN THE HOME

Whether or not parents are naked in front of their children—and up to what age—seems to be a cultural thing. Japanese families traditionally bathe naked together in hot tubs. So do many Europeans. That said, the attitudes parents have about nudity and associated sexual behaviors seem to be the most important factors in determining how kids respond to nakedness in the home.

Attitudes about nakedness and sexuality develop early. A baby senses nonverbal signals that demonstrate how his or her parents feel about sexuality. Shame, embarrassment, discomfort, or delight is evident already during diaper changing or baths.

A small child discovers the pleasurable sensations of being touched when naked. Those pleasurable feelings may become confused if anxious adults bring shame into the picture. For example, if a

---

Talk about It

How has your lovemaking changed since you've had children? In what ways has sex gotten better for each of you? In what ways has your enjoyment lessened? Make a list of things you can do as a couple to enrich your lovemaking.

child touches himself and a parent slaps his hand away, crying, "Naughty!" that child will associate pleasure with wrongdoing, shame, and punishment.

In early adolescence, children may become uncomfortable about nudity because it awakens sexual arousal, especially if the family has never talked about sex. However, in a relaxed, intimate family circle, exposure to noneroticized nudity should cause no damage.

Q & A

SHOULD THE KIDS SEE US NAKED?

Recently, my nine-year-old daughter accidentally saw me naked. She got a good look at my penis. I didn't know what to do. In general, at what age should parents stop allowing their kids to see them naked?

Louis: I see no real difficulty with your nine-year-old daughter accidentally seeing your genitalia. If it seems appropriate, you might talk to your daughter about the differences between male and female anatomy. The talk could blossom into a natural discussion about reproductive physiology and

the moral and relational aspects of sexuality. Age nine might be a little late in these days of pervasive sexual awareness, but if you're comfortable with the subject, you may learn a lot about what your daughter knows.

Similarly, little boys should be instructed about a woman's body. By age nine, a boy will probably have a lot of questions about female anatomy. Those questions should be addressed well before puberty.

Melissa: Many people try to do away with modesty, believing it's based on unhealthy feelings of shame. But modesty doesn't have much to do with shame. According to the Bible, shame entered the picture when Adam and Eve disobeyed God and sin entered the world. Most passages that refer to nakedness and covering up have more to do with sin, vulnerability, and loss of dignity. Nowhere does the Bible teach that the body is something evil or shameful and needs to be hidden.

Children should be taught that God made their bodies beautiful and precious. Modesty should grow out of a sense of responsibility about how God wants us to use our bodies. The Bible teaches modesty for a good reason: Chastity becomes more difficult without modesty. Your children will need a healthy respect for modesty as they mature.

Q & A

WILL I EVER HAVE ENOUGH ENERGY FOR SEX?

My husband and I have two children—one who's seven months old. I have so little energy for sex. When we do have sex, it's great. It just seems there are so many pulls on our time. Is this just a phase? Does it get better?

Children cause significant changes in your marital relationship, including sexual intimacy. This can't be ignored. However, there are ways to minimize the erosion:

Try to reduce other demands. When work, church, or play activities erode time and energy for marital intimacy, it's time to cut back on other commitments. Time for each other must be a top priority.

Take time for each other. Plan dates or excursions away from your children on a regular basis. Even the baby won't suffer if you go away for a day or two. If Mom is breast-feeding, she can use a breast pump to provide milk for the baby during her absence.

Go with the flow. Be flexible in your lovemaking routine. Maybe you'll have more energy for sex at a time other than nighttime. After you put the kids down for their naps, lock your door and enjoy your husband for a "noonie."

Eventually this demanding time will ease up. In the meantime, you can look for creative alternatives to preserve your intimacy. It's a gift you can give your children and each other.

Q & A

HOW CAN WE MAKE LOVE WITHOUT FEELING RUSHED?

While my husband and I frequently have sex, sometimes I feel rushed. Foreplay is reduced to about two seconds. We have three kids, we both work outside the home, and we rarely have time alone as a couple. What can we do to make loving less hurried? Are there any techniques that would help?

Not having time to relax is the scourge of today's families. Failing to set boundaries in your life can prove deadly. Eventually, you'll pay the price—whether it's the loss of sexual intimacy, breakdown of your physical health, or distance in your family relationships.

Why don't you ask someone to take care of the kids and get away for a weekend? One night isn't usually enough for a stressed-out couple. The first night they hit the bed and crash. Once they've caught up on some sleep, they can start enjoying each other. Share your thoughts with your spouse about how rushed you feel. Tell him you want to slow down and have more "free time." We're sure he'll agree.

SEX AND WORK:

Making Time for Love

"All work and no play make Jack a dull boy." That was an oft-repeated proverb in my mother's family, the Kincannon clan. I totally embraced the wisdom of that proverb. The second proverb I learned was "Any job worth doing is worth doing right."

I struggle to balance work and play while doing right by both. You might have guessed that for me sex is play—and what keeps me from being a dull boy. Conveniently, much of my work as a psychiatrist also focuses on sex. And since Melissa and I work—and play—together, our combination seems about as good as it gets.

We realize most people struggle to find the right balance of work and play. Some of you find great satisfaction in work, while others endure work only as a means to play. In either case, we

see sexual intimacy and work as important to your fulfillment in marriage.

HOW WORK AFFECTS SEX

Work makes sexual play possible. When we're financially successful at work, we have more opportunities for romance: dinners out, dates without the kids, movies, concerts, nights in resort hotels.

Money isn't always necessary for sexual play. Melissa and I have enjoyed budget picnics on a nearby beach, free concerts in the park, and afternoon movies with babysitting provided by other student couples. Even a rendezvous in a hospital cafeteria was exciting—there was no sex but we could hold hands and think about what would happen after we got home.

Work promotes partnership. Your commitment to work for each other outside and inside the home is a gift to the marriage. It shows how much you care for each other. By now you've probably found unique ways to show your love at home as well. Whether it's breakfast in bed or taking turns with a fussy baby, you lighten the load for your mate. That frees up time and builds the motivation to enjoy sex.

Work allows you to share life experiences. Through work, you acquire new friendships, new stories, and new experiences. Sharing what happens at work with your spouse builds intimacy in a marriage. Failing to talk about those experiences puts up a barrier that is bound to affect sex. Asking, "How was your day?" is important to stay connected.

Work helps define who you are. When my wife, Melissa, became a mother, her identity took on a new dimension. Likewise, when I became a resident in psychiatry, my exposure to unbelievable facets of the human mind brought new information into our marriage. We believe such stimuli are designed to deepen the marital bond, not to push us apart.

HOW SEX AFFECTS WORK

Sure, work affects sex, but it can also work the other way around. In our work together as therapists, Melissa and I have learned how sex affects our work performance. Here are some ways:

Sex makes us more effective at work. Melissa often comments that I work better as a therapist after we've made love. Conversely, if we haven't been sexually active for a while, I am more easily distracted. Since sex is such an important emotional and physical need, it's not surprising that our work reflects our level of sexual fulfillment.

Sex is a stress-management tool. Whether stress is related to parenting or meeting a sales goal or a deadline, lovemaking is an effective tranquilizer. Men are often aware of the need for sexual satisfaction, but most women also enjoy the pleasure. They may sigh afterward, "Thank you, darling, I needed that!" The kids are probably thankful for the good moods of Mom and Dad—whatever the cause.

Sex helps us celebrate what happens at work. Sex is frequently the way a couple celebrate work success. "Honey, I got a raise—let's celebrate!" he says. The first stop is the bedroom. Likewise, birthdays, anniversaries, promotions, finished projects, and financial coups are worthy of celebration. What better way to celebrate than to make love with the person closest to you?

Sex reduces the temptation to stray. The workplace brings many wives and husbands in contact with attractive people of the opposite gender. Most of the individuals we've counseled who were involved in infidelity strayed with people they met at work. Feeling sexually frustrated in marriage ramps up the degree of attraction to other people.

WHEN WORK THREATENS INTIMACY

In every marriage seminar we hear a common theme: The greatest challenge to intimacy is work. So how can we find enough time for our occupations and our marriages?

Your work requirements may be set by an inflexible, demanding boss. Or you may be setting impossible commitments for yourself, thinking it's the only way to get ahead. With a demanding work schedule and parenting duties, it's no wonder you have little time or energy left for sex.

If you're also a performance junkie or a perfectionist, you probably allow little time for unwinding. Doing a job well for you means self-consuming drivenness. This pattern, which is as common in women as in men, is equally destructive for both.

Have you ever experienced a boss who had no home life and no respect for anyone who did? Ted was that kind of boss. He had no desire to go home after work, so he'd insist his staff join him for a few drinks at the club after work. Allen tried to slip out of the obligation, but Ted was insistent. Finally, Allen realized that the only way he could preserve his marriage was to look for another job.

At some time in your career, you might find yourself working for a person of the opposite gender who makes sexual overtures. You may desperately need the job, so it may be hard to walk away. But living with sexual harassment is a nightmare of unrelieved tension. If you compromise your sexual fidelity in response to the seduction, you'll soon find yourself in deep trouble. This is a no-win situation. Ditch the job.

Q & A

MUST WE ALWAYS SCHEDULE SEX?

My wife is a successful business-woman. I'm thrilled that she is fulfilled in her work, but she brings that same mind-set home. I can handle the way she manages the household but not the way she dictates the terms of our sex life. She schedules sex as an agenda item to be completed between the weather report and Nightline. *Her driven nature may work great in the business world, but it fails miserably in bed. What should I do?*

Melissa: Sex should be driven by your relationship, not a production quota. If either partner makes sex a control issue, intimacy drops off the profit chart. Your wife's controlling style has worked well for her on the job, so it's hard for her to relinquish it at home. To deal with this problem, borrow some terms and methods of relating in the business world, where your wife feels comfortable:

Speak her language. Make an appointment with your wife. Call her secretary, if necessary, to reserve the time.

Affirm her as a successful executive. Tell your wife that

"IT HELPS ME TO UNWIND."

you're proud of her success as a businesswoman and her time-management skills.

Assure her of your support. Tell her you love her and assure her that you're not staging a walkout.

Ask her to consider your view. Tell her you want to have a closer, sexual relationship with her. Tell her you feel unfulfilled, disregarded, and relegated to the status of one more agenda item. Tell her you want more say in your sex life.

Get her input. Ask her what she'd like from you. Since your wife is an assertive person who is used to taking control, she may be waiting for you to exert more leadership. Even strong women like to lean on their men.

Propose a contract. This agreement asks for more romance and warmth in your partnership. Working out the terms of this contract may require some lunches and weekend conferences.

PROBLEMS WITH WORK TRAVEL

Work sometimes requires periods of separation for a couple. Those times apart create two significant problems:

Not enough bonding. When a husband or wife travels, they don't have much time for the closeness necessary for sexual intimacy. For example, if Steve is on the road most of the week, Judy has to function as a single mom. When Steve returns, Judy has to shift back to her role as wife and parental partner. A welcome-home kiss is prelude to a backlog of problem solving. The adjustments required of the traveling spouse and the one who stays home often leave both feeling resentful.

Loneliness and temptation. Steve and Judy both became aware of the danger of loneliness when they found themselves attracted to colleagues in their companies. Once they recognized the danger of those attachments, Steve and Judy both set some boundaries. They agreed not to spend time alone with members of the opposite gender, no matter how innocent the occasion.

They also agreed to talk by telephone every day. Hearing each other's voices at a set time helped them overcome loneliness. It also built up their relationship. In these daily discussions, they were better equipped to share responsibility for decision making. That helped reduce tension over control and abandonment issues.

Q & A

WILL HIS TRAVEL KILL OUR LOVE?

My husband travels a lot. He leaves on Sunday evening and isn't home till Thursday. He can't wait to make love at night, but I have a hard time warming up to him. I'm too exhausted trying to keep up with the kids, the housework, and day-to-day crises. I don't want to dump on him when he steps in the door, but I can't instantly become a willing playmate. How can we keep up our love life under these conditions?

It's understandable that you don't feel like melting into your husband's arms when he walks through the door after he has been gone all week. Nor does he have the energy to lift your burdens of parenting. This dilemma calls for a world-class demonstration of negotiating skills.

We suggest you set time aside for undisturbed discussion. This might be a Friday night after your husband has rested up and the children are in bed, or during the day, when the kids are in school or at a babysitter's. Plan on three to four hours to talk.

This talk should begin by focusing on each of your expectations and desires. Next, you should each list your interests for your marriage and family. Negotiate these to help close the gap between you. You'll begin to see things from a new perspective. You'll also find that you have more interests in common than you realized. For example, you're probably both interested in sexual intimacy, healthy children, and financial security. As you compare your lists of interests, consider how you can work together to achieve your goals.

Next, brainstorm solutions. Write out various ways of fulfilling these expectations, regardless of their practicality. For example, you might list leaving the children with friends and flying off to meet your husband for a romantic sexual interlude.

OK, we said it didn't have to be practical. Have fun sorting through the ideas; you may be surprised at the creative solutions that emerge. Finally, agree on making some changes that will help you fulfill your expectations. Then celebrate your agreement. Make a date for a Friday night. Relax and enjoy each other.

We suggest that you declare a truce zone on Thursday evening—or any other evening that your husband returns from a road trip. Dedicate that time to readjustment and rest. Recognize that neither of you has the emotional or physical energy to make that evening a sexual homecoming. Save lovemaking for a time when you both can look forward to it.

THE FATIGUE FACTOR

Work-induced fatigue is a detriment to lovemaking. For example, Bob, who is a carpenter, acquiesced to his crew's wishes for long weekends. Instead of working five days a week, the crew worked four ten-hour days. The three-day weekends were nice, but the other four days Bob came home so exhausted he had no energy left for his wife and family. On Fridays he was so busy playing catch-up that he was worn out.

His wife, Shirley, was totally frustrated. She wanted more companionship from her husband. She also needed more sexual play than what she was getting on Saturday night.

Mothers of small children struggle with fatigue. From time to time, Melissa asked me to take care of our three kids for a day just to remind me of how draining that is. I never had the opportunity to

"Maybe a quickie before breakfast is just too much for you, Roger?"

let her take one of my thirty-six-hour shifts in the hospital, but when I'd go to sleep while eating supper, she got the message.

THREE WAYS TO BALANCE WORK AND PLAY

Most people can't quit working to allow more time for their mates. However, neither can they deny their need for sexual intimacy. Here are some ways to maintain the balance between work and play:

Set priorities. When we hear couples talk about all the activities they're involved in, we stare in amazement. How can they possibly have time for all of that and sexual intimacy too?

Correcting a priority problem is difficult because it may mean saying no to some great opportunities for you or your children. In considering which activities to maintain, first ask whether your marriage relationship is at the top of the list. If it isn't, put it there. Then sit down with your spouse between soccer, dance lessons, and Bible study—or on your cell phones en route—and list your activities. Decide which ones have the most eternal spiritual and relational importance. Try dropping just one activity and spend that time together.

Get help. Your load may be heavy because you're trying to do everything yourself. Ask some friends for help. Barter for exchanging times in babysitting, carpooling, or homeschooling. Get your kids to help at home. It eases your burdens and teaches them valuable life skills.

Talk about It

When has the relationship between work and play been most balanced in your marriage? When not? What was the effect on your sex life? What practical steps can you each take to make sure that work supports rather than competes with your marital relationship?

Give up stuff. If you've maxed out your credit cards, your appetite is too big for your budget. Even those pay-nothing-till-2010 deals eventually come due—plus interest. All those toys you buy to keep up with your neighbors aren't worth anything if they take time away from your marriage. You wouldn't have to work so much if you said no to some of your desires. Just turning off the television can help, since 30 percent of what you see on TV convinces you to buy something.

Q & A

IS HER DESIRE LINKED TO MONEY?

My wife's sexual desire seems to be tied to my income. When I make more money, sex is good and frequent. When my income is down, she has no sex drive or desire. We are both Christians, but I fear this problem is leading us toward divorce.

Identifying how your wife's sexual behavior relates to your income is crucial to effecting change. It's equally important to recognize that sexual intimacy is what happens between two people and is rarely the problem of just one partner. So while you work together on understanding your wife's behavior, take a hard look at what you may be contributing to the problem besides a variable income.

Start with money as a symbol. Ask yourselves what money means to you and your wife. In our culture, money is associated with power, competence, and prestige. When a person's sense of personal worth is linked to wealth, his or her relationship with others is affected by increases or decreases in finances. Wealth—and what it can buy—becomes the basis of self-worth. Ups and downs in finances in turn affect a person's feelings about sexual attractiveness or desire.

Similarly, if money is equated with power, the person who is financially successful feels more attractive and the person who fails financially feels ugly and worthless.

The presence or absence of wealth can also be linked with feelings of safety and security. Depending on a person's childhood experience, a person may become anxious if assets are threatened. That fear prompts withdrawal from others, just as a sense of security prompts interaction with others. Sexual desire is very sensitive to underlying anxiety—whatever the cause.

If a husband's primary way to show love has been in material gifts, the level of income and the goodies that he provides may be an important indication to his wife that she is loved. When money is tight and the husband fails to provide good things, his wife feels unloved.

Finally, if a husband's income decreases, he may be less loving toward his wife. By contrast, when a man's income goes up, his mood may improve and he may be more loving toward his wife. In addition, when a couple doesn't have much money, they may have to forfeit such pleasures as eating out, going to movies, or hiring a babysitter so they can have a date night.

Whatever the factors are, it is vital to talk with your wife and perhaps with a counselor about your concerns.

Q & A

Is She Stuck on Her Boss?

My wife started working about six months ago. She has a wonderful boss—too wonderful, I think. She's always talking about him, saying how warm and affirming he is. Lately they've had quite a few lunches together. My wife swears this is all business, but I'm not so sure. Am I right to worry? What should I say to her?

We're with you. The relationship your wife is developing with her new boss is potentially dangerous. Since she's either unaware of those problems or purposefully ignoring them, you and she need to have a serious talk. However, be very careful. We suggest four ways to make this session work:

Schedule time for a serious talk. Ask your wife for a date, then take her to a favorite getaway. Leave the kids with a babysitter. Leave the cell phone home, too. You don't need interruptions.

Set the stage for discussion. Let her know your position and agenda, using first-person statements. You might say, "Honey, I'm having some feelings I need to express. Our relationship is the most important part of my life, and if I don't talk about my feelings, it won't be healthy."

Tell her how you feel. Don't accuse her of anything; just let her know you feel uneasy or worried about losing her. Tell her you feel inadequate and left out of this very important relationship. Avoid blaming her or arguing with her if she gets defensive. Stick with "I'm not accusing you. I know my own feelings and want you to understand them."

Do not attack your wife's boss. He is your wife's hero right now. If your wife feels she has to defend her boss, that will only push her toward him. As much as possible, ignore the boss. There may be a time for more aggressive intervention, but this is not that time. If hearing your feelings brings her around, that's much more effective.

Q & A

MUST I VACUUM TO EARN SEX?

My wife and I are no longer having sex, even though when we married four years ago we were very passionate. Believe it or not, she claims her aversion to sex stems from my not doing a fair share of the housework. How can I find out what's really wrong?

Louis: Your refusal to help with the housework is precisely what may be wrong. Most relationships glide along smoothly on the oil of trade-offs, as in "You do the wash; I'll fix supper." It's hard to be joyful in a relationship when one person has to do all the work.

Maybe your wife feels like you've stopped appreciating her. Maybe you were more attentive and helpful when you were courting her than you are now. When a wife feels unappreciated and overworked, it's difficult for her to give sexually. This works both ways. Many husbands complain that their wives fail to appreciate the hard work they do to support the family. Thus they don't have much enthusiasm for helping around the house.

For you—and most men—the desire for sex is a compelling physiological drive. For most women, sexual commitment grows out of an emotional awareness of being treasured and pursued relationally. When that sense of being cherished fades or dies, the desire to connect also falters.

You could work through this issue with a counselor, but before doing that, you might try helping out more at home. Do the dishes, pick up dirty clothes, clean the toilets. See what happens.

Melissa: Maybe your dad never helped around the house. That taught you that real men don't vacuum or dust or clean. If that's true, work on overcoming this prejudice.

Consider how your father's actions (or inactions) affected your mom and their relationship. Was Mom so burdened with caring for the house and family that she rarely had time for fun? Understanding your parents' relationship may make it easier for you to change.

Deal with your emotions about doing housework. Then get practical. Ask your wife what she has in mind for you to do around the house. You might be surprised to find that her expectations aren't difficult to meet—and are worth the effort to boost your sex life.

AGING AND SEX:

Loving through Life's Phases

Sure, bodies age. Things droop that once were firm. Uninvited pounds and inches creep on. Muscles and bones once taken for granted lose strength and grow brittle. Illness threatens. Trips to the doctor increase. Prescription bottles take up more room in bathroom cabinets. Your sweetheart's hair thins or turns gray. Neither one of you sleeps through the night.

Your sexual equipment slows like the rest of you. But that does not mean you have to be done with sex. According to Ed and Gaye Wheat, authors of *Intended for Pleasure*, "Sex after sixty can be better than ever! This is not propaganda to encourage the faltering, but a frank statement of fact."* This is especially encouraging, since married couples generally live ten to fifteen years longer than singles.

Stay married and stay interested. You won't live as long as Methuselah, but you can still enjoy a rich and varied love life.

WHY THE MAGIC FADES

Recently, Melissa and I were going through our wedding album. As we sat in front of the fireplace and looked at photos of ourselves as twenty-three-year-olds, we caught our breath. *Who are those kids?* we wondered. *What on earth were they doing?*

We spent the next hour sharing memories and lots of laughs. When we were done, we rejoiced that after forty-plus years we are still together. We're keenly aware of how unusual that's getting to be. Many of the

---

*Ed Wheat and Gaye Wheat, *Intended for Pleasure* (Old Tappan, N.J.: Revell, 1981), 203.

couples we work with in counseling have trouble remembering what brought them together and how they once were happy.

When did the good times stop happening for them? When did their feelings for one another drain away? When did romance slip out the door? When did sex begin to look like more effort than it was worth?

How Life Phases Affect Us

Considering the phases that marriages go through, it's not surprising that couples drift apart over the years. These phases call for continual reassessment and renegotiating in marriage. Here are some of those stages:

The establishment phase. This is the stage of life when couples focus on what will make them competent members of culture. They're busy proving their worth in a chosen career, setting up a house, and beginning the lifelong job of parenting. While these are all worthwhile pursuits, they can be barriers to intimacy.

The midlife phase. Not all couples experience crisis in this stage, but it is a time of emotional and physical transition. This is when we recognize that time is moving swiftly. Our bodies are changing. We tire more easily. We occasionally think about death.

Family life shifts: the kids leave and aged parents need help. All of these things force couples to closely interact with each other. Unhappily, that is when many discover that they hardly know each other.

During this phase, some men realize they need something other than financial success to complete their deepest longings. Unfortunately, they may have been so busy with their careers that their wives have emotionally disconnected from them. So it's not uncommon for these men to look elsewhere for affirmation and support.

The retirement phase. Poet Robert Browning wrote to his wife, Elizabeth: "Come grow old with me, the best is yet to be." He was right; a couple that reaches this stage of life together often cares for each other more deeply than ever before. But some elderly couples feel unspeakable loneliness.

Why Couples Drift Apart

As some couples move through different phases of life, intimacy suffers. Some reasons for that:

A dependency shift. When a couple dates, one person is attracted to the strengths of the other. The weaker one longs for a protector or surrogate parent who will forever provide loving care. The marriage contract becomes a you-be-the-strong-one-and-I'll-be-the-weak-one agreement. In time, dependency is burdensome to everyone. The strong partner gets tired of carrying the load, and the dependent mate feels controlled or squelched.

When Melissa and I married, I saw myself as the rescuer who was saving her from the burden of singleness. She seemed to need and appreciate my strength and wisdom. But after several years, we arrived at a crisis point. We had to reassess the dynamics of our dependency to account for her competence and my need for her strength.

A pile of hurt. Another reason spouses drift apart is that they allow hurts to build. As Christians, we know and probably hear at weddings the verse from 1 Corinthians 13:5 that says, "[Love] keeps no record of wrongs." Hearing this at a candlelight service is a lot easier than applying it to the wounds we receive from each other. Gashes of disappointment from those wounds cut deep into our romantic expectations.

For example, Melissa expected me to call if I'd be late for dinner. She also expected I would always take the lead in our family's spiritual life. In turn, I expected her sexual passion to be undaunted by motherhood. Learning otherwise caused superficial abrasions, which could be forgiven quietly.

Deeper hurts are harder to keep off a marriage scorecard. If a husband and wife aren't careful, they'll drag out that tally at every opportunity.

Tough stuff. When couples promise at their wedding to love each other "for better or for worse," no one thinks about the "worse" part. When something really awful hits a marriage—as is inevitable— a couple falters.

For example, how do you cope with the loss of a child? There are few satisfactory explanations for that kind of crisis. How do you deal with economic loss or catastrophe? That wasn't part of the dream for marriage. What about chronic illness? That can be more difficult to handle than death. We have a friend whose wife was in an accident. Her mind has been deteriorating ever since. For seven years he's been dealing with a wife who offers none of the expected benefits of a marriage partner.

Tough stuff. It's no wonder many couples begin running from each other rather than dealing with the pain.

Q & A

IS INFREQUENT SEX OK?

Although my wife and I rarely have sex, neither of us minds much. For a long time we were preoccupied with our kids, our business, and some family illness. Not having sex became a habit, and we don't really miss it. But I have to believe a sexless marriage isn't what God intended. If neither of us wants sex, how can we both get more interested?

Louis: This is well-worn advice, but "if it ain't broke, don't fix it!" From what you say, you and your wife have a comfortable and meaningful relationship. If you feel satisfied that your relational needs are being met, I wouldn't worry much about your sexual frequency.

However, you should talk about this. Honestly express how you feel about the situation. Talk about times that you have made love, and what made it good. Brainstorm things you can do that will draw you closer.

God wants us to become one. Our culture defines oneness primarily as sexual. Because of that, other aspects of intimacy go unnoticed. It's not uncommon for sexual drive in a long-term marriage to diminish and to be replaced by

Talk about It

⌒

If you're having problems in your marriage, don't stifle your disappointment, figuring it's too late to do anything. Talk to your spouse about your hurts. Ask each other what might be done to restore your relationship. See a counselor if necessary. Your marriage is a gift that's meant to be enjoyed for a lifetime.

other acts of affection. For example, Melissa and I love taking a walk on a beach or holding hands during a movie. If that closeness leads to something else, that's OK. If it doesn't, that's OK too.

Melissa: Are you certain you're speaking for both of you? Your wife may have some unspoken wishes or longings. Have a good, long talk about it. That could lead to a more fulfilling marriage.

SEVEN WAYS TO CHANGE A DESTRUCTIVE DANCE

In our work, Melissa and I see aging couples who know their relationships are in jeopardy. Each can describe in detail the destructive dance they're engaged in.

For example, she asks, "Why are you late this time?" (It's not a question.)

He replies, "What does it matter to you?" (Again, not a question.) This dance is well rehearsed and the outcome sadly predictable. The partners have long ago emotionally separated.

This old dance doesn't have to continue. Either partner can change it by learning a new step. Here are seven ways to change the dance:

Commit to change. This is hard when you're tired, discouraged, and ready to bail. That's precisely when you need to step back and look at the consequences of your actions. While separation and divorce could provide you with initial relief, the single life also brings complications. Furthermore, walking out of a marriage sets you up for other problems. By contrast, committing to change because of what you've already invested in each other's lives will bring rewards to your marriage.

Talk about the pain. Without casting blame, list events that were hurtful for you in the past and how you feel about them. For example, one husband told how his bride cried when she left her mother on the wedding day. The groom thought his bride was so enmeshed with her mother that she'd never adjust to marriage. The bride didn't remember wanting to go back home to Mom. She only remembered being physically and emotionally exhausted after the wedding. Yet her tears had created such resentment in her husband that he burned about them years later.

We're all guilty of feeling hurt because we've interpreted an event the worst possible way. A husband and wife must clear the air of such hurts. When they share these thoughts to work toward understanding, everything looks different. Forgiveness and intimacy follow.

Trace the roots. Think of how each of your parents worked out disagreements, made decisions, celebrated holidays, and disciplined children. When you quit being defensive, you'll probably laugh at some of the peculiar things they did—which you assumed were the only ways to do things because that's what was done at home.

Melissa and I began to discover those patterns early in our marriage. I rearranged her kitchen the first week of marriage because she didn't have things in the "right places." Boy, did I learn quickly how unhelpful that was. Then Christmas came, and she expected to open presents on Christmas morning instead of Christmas Eve. Can you imagine such a thing?

Family patterns are deeply engrained, yet they don't matter much—if we don't let them. It's better to give them up than to let them rob you and your mate of enjoyment.

Decide what's important. What's important for couples in their golden years? It's the need for feeling accepted and loved, having enough space, being listened to without put-downs, and achieving sexual satisfaction. The bottom line is that we all want to feel safe, cherished, and respected. When those needs are met, more goodwill is available to allow for differences about little things like up-or-down toilet seats or kitchen cabinet organization.

Choose a new response. Discuss some behaviors you'd like to see changed in each other, then pick one or two to work on. This might be as simple as putting the milk back in the refrigerator, clearing the table of dirty dishes, or dumping a negative attitude. No one wants to be around a whiner or complainer. Talk about the good things in your life. Try to see humor in a minor upset. Start small; you don't have to solve all the world's problems the first week. Victories in small things will encourage you to tackle bigger problems.

Be accountable. Praise each other each time you master a new step. Reinforcing new behaviors with frequent encouragement is far more effective than pointing out failures. If you're really brave, ask your mate to remind you if you slip. That can be risky if firing criticism at each other has been a favored war strategy. Declare a truce and discuss how you're feeling about these changes. That helps to reaffirm your commitment. So does calling in outside help such as a trusted friend or professional counselor.

Celebrate success. As you see improvements in your relationship, give each other some rewards. Take each other out for dinner or see a new musical. Plan a trip. You've done a great thing.

Q & A

WHAT CAN WE DO ABOUT A DULL SEX LIFE?

After thirty years of marriage, my wife tells me our sex life is dull. Now I'm afraid to initiate sex for fear she'll get bored. What can we do to make things more exciting?

After thirty years of marriage, sex can lose its zip. It can sink into a routine that saps the excitement out of everything. The secret is to acknowledge the problem and to accept the challenge to woo back your wife. We could give you a formula, but what works for us probably wouldn't work for you. So let's consider what most women find appealing:

Relationship. Rather than thinking about improving sex, concentrate on improving your relationship. Your wife needs to hear you talk about your feelings, thoughts, and opinions. She'd probably love to hear your memories of great times with her.

Maleness. Most women love a delicate mix of strength and tenderness in a guy. Try talking to her about the feelings you just described to us. Listen when she talks about her feelings. This will help you feel emotionally close, which will naturally lead to more physical affection and sex. Don't make sex your goal, though. Let oneness be the goal, and sex will follow.

Leadership. Your fears about a dull sex life should dissipate as you deal with this problem. Focus then on your wife's needs. Otherwise, she'll sense intuitively that you're afraid—and that isn't attractive to most women. Want another tip? Ask her what you can do to make things more exciting in the bedroom. We bet she'd love to tell you.

Q & A

IS A SLOWDOWN IN SEX NORMAL?

My husband and I have a good marriage. But since my husband turned age fifty, his lovemaking has slowed down. Is that normal?

When young, a man becomes quickly aroused and has a firm erection. But with age come problems: it takes a guy longer to become erect, his erection isn't as firm, and ejaculation is delayed. Regardless of the cause, when a man fails to respond sexually, he becomes fearful of repeated failure. He loses self-confidence and begins to avoid sex.

The most common causes of sexual slowdown—fatigue, stress, medication, physical illness, relational conflict, and alcohol use—can be easily remedied. So the first step is to see whether any of those are contributing to your husband's condition and to make adjustments. Another step is to have him see a doctor to rule out thyroid dis-order, diabetes, or other cardiovascular and neurological conditions that can cause sexual problems.

If nothing much is found, your husband may benefit from counseling. You can be a great support by encouraging him.

Q & A

WHY ARE HIS ERECTIONS LESS FIRM?

My husband and I have hit middle age, and suddenly his erections are less firm. He says this is normal, but intercourse just isn't the same for me. Is there something we can do about this problem?

Louis: When changes in erectile function create tension in a marriage, it's time to see a urologist or sex therapist—or both. There are ways to enhance a man's erections. Suction devices can draw more blood into the corpus cavernosum and the corpus spongiosum, creating an erection. The use of such a device, combined with a stricture applied to the base of the penis to keep the blood in place, creates a firm erection.

A wife can enhance her husband's erection by putting pressure on the upper side of the base of the penis, where the major venous drainage flows. This can be done comfortably during penetration.

Medical compounds can be injected to stimulate erections. These are quite effective and relatively painless. Drugs such as Viagra, Cialis, or Caverject will also produce erections. (See "How Viagra Works," 178.) Check with a physician for suggestions.

Melissa: Your husband seems most anxious about your reaction to his problem. He's also probably very sensitive about it. Assure him of your love, admiration, and respect. A problem like this calls for teamwork. You might find yourselves more satisfied with your emotional intimacy as you work together to tackle the physical problem.

MENOPAUSE

Sometime after age forty and for the next ten years, women begin to notice body changes due to the waning production of estrogen. Along with mood changes, sleep problems, and hot flashes, a woman notices difficulties in intercourse. She experiences some discomfort, even pain, during lovemaking. That's primarily due to the thinning and dryness of her vagina. Estrogens taken orally or as vaginal creams can restore lubrication to ease lovemaking.

If a woman is in good health generally, age may actually help her enjoy sex more. With child rearing and work behind her, she may actually experience an increase in libido and response to sexual stimulation.

PART SIX:
SEXUAL SINS
AND SECRETS

Bedroom Toys:

Fantasies, Spicy Videos, and Other Additions

Some of us drag outside influences into our private moments of intimacy. We experiment with devices to enhance the pleasure of sex. Vibrators to stimulate sexual organs. A sexy negligee or a provocative movie for visual stimulation. Spicy videos to learn new techniques. Internet search engines for erotic fantasy.

Let's take a look at these additions to the bedroom and consider how they affect our relationship.

WHEN FANTASY STARTS

"Play like I'm a big, strong man and you're my little friend and I rescue you from a dragon and you love me forever . . ."

Does that sound familiar? Children have active imaginations that express themselves in play. Sometimes their fantasies get acted out with real playmates and some-times with make-believe play-mates. Either way, fantasy is a way to act out inner desires, feelings, or conflicts. It is a world that can be safer and more satisfying than the real one.

Those flights into an imaginary world continue to provide relief from anxiety in adulthood. They can be fleeting, elusive thoughts or elaborate, well-organized fantasies, but all deal with a person's self-concept and wish fulfillment.

WHAT A MAN FANTASIZES ABOUT

Various sexual behaviors with his wife. These fantasies have an element of wish fulfillment. They put the guy into a role that makes him look desirable to women. Fantasies about sex with his wife may replay real encounters. Or fantasy may play out a sex technique, such as oral sex, that isn't part of the marriage.

Sexual relations with another woman—or a group of women. These fantasies may feature a female friend or a sex goddess in Hollywood. They may show the guy being seduced by several women. These fantasies are dangerous because they erode the healthy boundaries that preserve marital faithfulness. That's why Jesus expanded the definition of adultery to include lusting after a woman. Enjoying a woman's beauty and focusing on her as a sexual object are two different things.

WHAT A WOMAN FANTASIZES ABOUT

She and her husband in an unusual sexual situation. He is a handsome Marine who swoops her into his arms as he rescues her from enemy soldiers. This kind of fantasy prompts sexual readiness toward an unromantic spouse.

She and another guy having sex. These are prompted by novels, conversations, movies, or Internet chats. Internet chat rooms are dangerous because predators tend to get into those rooms to prey on lonely women.

Having the kind of sex that she would ordinarily refuse. Danger or adventure enhances eroticism. A woman who is very restricted sexually fantasizes that she is an expensive call girl performing sex acts that she would never try with her husband.

Q & A

WHY DOES HE TALK ABOUT GROUP SEX?

My husband and I are both Christians. We have a great sex life as well as a good relationship outside the bedroom. My husband enjoys talking to me during sex, but what he talks about concerns me. He talks as if other people are doing things to us. He once told me he would never actually bring in other people for group sex, but he enjoys fantasizing about it. I don't know how to talk with him about this. What should I do?

Not knowing all the details, we may not correctly address your concerns, but we'll try. Here are some suggestions:

Find out why he talks that way. Although sex play is primarily visual and tactile, vocalizing can be stimulating for some people. That may relate to how they learned about sexuality. Adolescent boys usually hear about sex from other boys. The vulgar vocabulary of middle school locker rooms provided the foundation for sexual arousal and enjoyment. The titillating images and ideas that contributed to those early fantasies were often derived from smutty magazines or dirty talk. If you haven't done so already, you might ask your husband what sex talk means to him.

Ask what he wants of you. Your husband may be stimulating himself through talking. For some people, saying words or describing sexual activities is quite exciting. Your husband may not be expecting anything of you other than to

listen. However, it does sound like you'd like to know exactly what he expects of you when he talks about others. Ask him!

Tell him how you feel. Since you describe your relationship with your husband as healthy, we assume that his talk about group sex hasn't created serious barriers to your sexual enjoyment. If it does, you should explore that with your husband, telling him how his talk minimizes your sexual enjoyment.

Determine how real the fantasies are. If your husband's verbal fantasies include real people, that crosses the line into adultery. Although it's practically impossible never to think sexually about someone other than your mate, it isn't

---

Talk about It

Talk to each other about fantasies. Begin by recalling some of the fantasies you had when you were a child. What fed into those fantasies? How much time did you spend daydreaming? How much time imagining what might happen to you? Did parents and other adults encourage fantasy or try to squelch it? What are some images and events that slip into your mind while lovemaking? Do they help you love each other more? In what way might they be harmful to your relationship?

healthy to nurture such images. They lower one's resistance to infidelity. If your husband shows interest in pursuing group sex, insist on immediate intervention.

Q & A

CAN WE SPICE THINGS UP?

My wife and I have sex regularly, but it's always the same. When I try to spice things up, my wife becomes shy or embarrassed. Then I feel like a big jerk, forcing changes where she doesn't want them. I've heard that sex between married people gets better, but that's not true for us. What can I do?

Louis: For some men, fantasies about sexual variety can be more exciting than the actual experience. For some women, new techniques or positions may be threatening because they're uncertain about how to perform. They worry that these variations will be uncomfortable, painful, or demeaning.

I'm convinced that sexual experience can become better throughout marriage. What's key is that you communicate and listen to each other's desires. While stating your wish for more variety in lovemaking, you must be sensitive to your wife's need for security, trust, and fulfillment.

PROBLEMS WITH FANTASY

Sexual fantasies become dangerous when they become preferable to sexual intimacy with one's spouse. Pornography is particularly seductive in leading a person into a world of fantasy that replaces reality. The visual or verbal stimuli of pornographic material tend to create an increasing need for more intense, more explicit, or more bizarre images. In time, images can become more alluring than marital intimacy.

The content of fantasy is crucial. Do you fantasize that you and your spouse are on a romantic cruise? Does she imagine you as some gorgeous hunk who is about to seduce her? If you fantasize about each other, that's harmless. If the fantasy is about someone else—someone you met on the Internet or someone you work with, or even someone you've read about—that is dangerous. Those fantasies are unfaithful to the partner with whom you are in a committed relationship. They might lead eventually to adultery in the flesh.

Given the power of sexuality, it's unlikely that anyone is free of sexual fantasies. However, we can control the script of make-believe scenarios. Wish fulfillment is made real in marital relationship. Rather than getting hooked by the imagery of pornography, create your own script. Make your spouse the star of your fantasy. Work together to build experiences that dreams are made of. These experiences can protect you from drifting into extramarital sex. They can also make your fantasies contribute to marital excitement, health, and satisfaction.

Q & A

How Can I Stop Self-Protective Fantasy?

For fifteen years I was married to a very abusive man. The only way I could get through sex with him was to fantasize. I would pretend that I wasn't even there. Now I'm married to a great Christian man, but I can't break that habit of mentally disengaging. I can't even tell my husband because it would hurt him so much. What can I do?

Louis: Retreating into fantasy, or disassociation, is a common way of dealing with painful situations. It provides psychological protection when physical escape is impossible. As the pattern for escape becomes set, certain signals or stimuli tap into the thought routines. For instance, if your abusive ex-husband signaled his demand for sex in certain ways, those signals probably still trip you into fantasy.

Become conscious of what those stimuli are. Recognize that your husband's touch, looks, or words don't mean that abuse will follow. You might ask him to change some of the trigger behaviors. I don't think he'd be hurt if you explained that something he does gives you flashbacks of painful experiences.

It might also help to take more initiative in sexual play with your husband. Your intentional actions may help remove that sense of impending danger that made fantasy necessary.

Melissa: Many women fantasize during intercourse. The problem comes when fantasies interfere with expressing love for your husband. Here are steps to help you change your fantasies:

Take your thoughts captive. Second Corinthians 10:5 tells us to "take captive every thought to make it obedient to Christ." Take control of your fantasies by the power of God. Start by replacing fantasies with thoughts about your new husband. Eventually the fantasies will disappear.

See how false fantasies are. You have a wonderful husband who will not abuse you. That is the truth. Believe it. The fears that trigger fantasies are unfounded and untrue.

Use love to drive out fear (1 John 4:18). As you focus on loving your new husband, God's perfect love will help you drive out fears of your former husband.

Absolve yourself. You are not guilty—your abuser was. So quit beating up on yourself. Give this up to God.

Talk to your husband. He needs to know what you're dealing with so he won't blame himself for the problem. As you and your husband work through this situation, your relationship will grow stronger.

SPICY VIDEOS: A TEACHING TOOL?

Sure, pornography is bad, but what about using instructional sex videotapes or books? Can they improve a couple's sex life?

For many individuals, particularly males, seeing videos or photos of sexual acts is erotic. Even looking at drawings can produce arousal. Some sex manuals depict unusual positions for intercourse. They introduce a whole new level of sexual play that take unusual strength or acrobatics to achieve.

We see two problems associated with using spicy videos:

They make us doubt ourselves. Spicy videos feature models with exceptional bodies. When watching such models at work, you become intimidated because your body is far less attractive. Your spouse doesn't compare well, either. Sure, you might learn some exciting techniques, but you also might lose interest in trying them out with each other.

Instructional manuals about sex usually have drawings rather than photographs. That reduces the risk of unpleasant comparisons. The figures are not designed for arousal as much as for instruction.

They open the door to pornography. Getting turned on by sexually explicit material builds a hunger for more. As the addiction builds, increasing amounts of the stimulus are necessary to produce the same high. Like a heroin addict who has to keep increasing the dose, a pornography addict needs more tantalizing pictures to produce the desired excitement.

Q & A

SHOULD WE VIDEOTAPE OUR LOVEMAKING?

Being very visual (as most men are), I'd find it exciting to watch my wife and me making love on video. Our lovemaking in itself is memorable, but why not preserve some of the memories for future enjoyment? If my wife agrees, do you think videotaping our lovemaking sessions for later viewing together would be appropriate?

Louis: My basic instinct says don't do it. But being the mature, broad-minded shrink that I am, I'll consider your question more carefully.

Filming your lovemaking is OK as long as you both agree to it, neither forces the other to do it, and it doesn't take the place of genital union. Still, our hunch is that a woman who allows lovemaking to be videotaped would eventually feel guilt, embarrassment, and ultimately resentment—particularly if she gave in to your pressure but wasn't fully honest with her feelings.

We're also concerned about the voyeuristic nature of videotaping. Is there something about watching yourselves on film that's more stimulating to you than real-time enjoyment of each other? Like pornography, videotape could become a substitute for the intimacy God intended for you to share.

Finally, it's amazing how personal property such as journals, diaries, emails, and photos have a way of showing up in unexpected places. If your children, parents, or neighbors saw your tape, you would have some serious problems.

The bottom line? Don't do it. Enjoy each other in privacy.

SEX TOYS: FIVE DANGERS

Sex toys come in all shapes and sizes. Vibrators increase the intensity of genital stimulation. Videos or movies produce arousal. Rings over the penis enhance its size. Artificial penises (dildos) substitute for the real thing. Bondage equipment comes in leather or chains. Asphyxiation devices intensify orgasm.

We see potential problems with sex toys. Here are a few:

They focus on individual pleasure. That minimizes or ignores the relational aspect of sexual play. It takes marital intimacy out of the picture. We don't think a vibrator or dildo should ever replace a spouse.

They're addictive. Their effect tends to max out—which means you'll have to keep increasing the stimuli for the same degree of pleasure. So what may begin with an R-rated movie can easily progress to X-rated videos.

They cause pain, physical harm—even death. Some deaths ruled as suicide were due to games of sexual enhancement through asphyxiation and bondage. Aids that mix pain with pleasure are dangerous and should be avoided.

They're conceived in sin. The producers and marketers for these products are part of the dark world of pornography, prostitution, kidnapping, child abuse, drug trafficking, and murder. Don't put any of your money into that world. Like other questionable or frankly criminal activities in our culture, the outlets for these sexual devices are not necessarily dingy, windowless adult bookstores. You can find sexually explicit videos in brightly lit stores in neighborhood shopping areas.

They're a form of idolatry. Unlike relational marital sex that celebrates God's love and creativity, sex toys separate us from God. These temptations are the latest version of the kind of Baal worship that plagued Israel. Don't be deceived.

Q & A

CAN WE ENJOY SEX WITHOUT PORNOGRAPHY?

For years, my wife and I enjoyed watching pornography together because it enhanced our sexual excitement. As we've come to know God, we've tried to give him control over every area of our lives. We've rejected pornography. The trouble is, now we're having problems with sex. We miss the stimulation we used to get from pornography. Are we doomed?

Louis: I sense that you're wondering if your Christian convictions will be a permanent barrier to sexual enjoyment. Here's the good news: While it's true that it's difficult to break the hold of pornography, it's far from impossible.

Pornography leaves powerful and lasting visual impressions. Fascination with those images is enhanced because they are forbidden. The combination of strong visual and auditory stimuli, the high risk-taking quality of naughty behavior, and our own sexual response system creates strong patterns. Break those patterns by substituting new mental images for the old through the power of the Holy Spirit.

When pornographic images come to mind, think about something else. Each time you refuse to replay pornographic tapes in your mind, the associations get weaker. Then substitute new images for the old ones. Real live experiences with your wife will have a powerful long-term effect. They will protect you from the destructive effects of pornography.

You have a powerful ally in fighting evil. God wants you to fully delight in each other without the intrusion of unhealthy images. Pray for the Holy Spirit's help in replacing pornography with honest, healthy sexual encounters.

Q & A

MUST I INSIST HE GIVE UP THE TOYS?

I've recently become a Christian. Now I'm praying that my husband will become a believer. We've had a rocky marriage, but the most stable part of it has been our sex life. That sex was pretty adventurous, involving toys and some porn. Now I'm trying to get up the nerve to tell my husband I don't want to do those things. I'm afraid it will make him resent my faith and take away the one point of connection that's been good for us. What should I do?

Louis: Many Christian wives have to put up with all sorts of pre-Christian behaviors in their relationships. It's hard to balance obedience to God with Paul's admonition for a wife to act in such a way that she attracts her husband to Jesus (1 Corinthians 7:12–14). So make it your goal to love both God and your husband as completely as you can.

At the same time, let me affirm your instinct that sex toys and porn have no place in a believer's sex life. Using sex toys and porn to enhance eroticism is dangerous. In our counseling practice, Melissa and I see increasing numbers of men and women who are seriously addicted to pornography.

The side effects of pornography are emotionally and relationally destructive. They erode self-respect, trust, and marital pleasure. They are also physically destructive when they result in extramarital affairs. But you are married to an unbeliever and long to see him come to Christ. So let your loving submissiveness in other areas besides sex convince your husband that your Christianity is a reflection of God's grace. I suspect he already knows that toys and porn are not compatible with your faith. As he becomes convinced of your willingness to honor him, he will be more likely to consider your God.

Melissa: Now would be a great time for you to do a Bible study on marriage to discover how important marriage is to God. You'll discover that fidelity is crucial in God's plan.

You'll also realize you have God's Spirit in you, which gives you the love and power to make your marriage what God intends it to be. Your concern about sexual practices is an important one, but it is only part of the bigger marriage picture. Learn to love God and your husband—and everything else will fall into place.

Q & A

CAN WE USE A DILDO TO AVOID INFECTION?

My pre-Christian experiences left me with an incurable sexually transmitted disease. It isn't deadly but something my wife and I now have to live with. We've been using a dildo to avoid infecting each other. Are we sinning by using a sexual aid?

As far as we can tell, using a dildo isn't sinful if both the husband and wife agree to use one—and neither coerces the other to do so. That said, there are problems with using a sex toy. Outside of an intimate love relationship, sex becomes a mechanical release of tension. It also becomes self-focused.

Relying on toys to enhance orgasmic response can develop into a desire for new, different, and more stimulating devices. This pattern can destroy a marriage. We suggest you find other ways to protect yourselves from passing disease to one another. Ask your doctor for suggestions.

LEATHER AND OTHER STUFF

A friend told me that black leather underwear and vibrators have turned his sex life around. I wonder if he is seeking more out of sex than God intends for us. Within reason, outside props, such as sexy lingerie or soft music, can make a positive contribution to sex. But we have real concerns about relying on sex toys to enhance sex.

One problem is that sex toys must be upgraded over time to provide the same level of excitement. For many couples, sex toys are only a short step away from sadomasochistic practices. Sadomasochistic sex or bondage fantasies move sex out of the arena of selfless love into that of power or domination. Sex becomes an invasive, controlling behavior, which perverts the act and creates shame, humiliation, and ultimate devaluation of one or both of the partners. When domination becomes a necessary ingredient for sexual pleasure, increasing levels of excitement are required to achieve gratification. In its extreme, bondage sex leads to pornography, rape, and even murder. Obviously this is not what God intends for sex.

Sexual pleasure should draw a husband and wife together in such a powerful bond that they become one flesh. We don't think there is any way to get more out of sex than what God intends. The intense, joyous release of orgasm, which is based on two people being truly vulnerable to each other, should be free of fear and fantasy.

If the magic has gone out of your sexual romance, try the following:

Take a look at your relationship. Are there better ways to build your passion for one another, such as spending a quiet evening together away from the kids and the television?

Decide whether you're angry or disappointed with each other. You may be losing interest in sex because you have unresolved difficulties. Clearing up those problems will release energy for sexual enjoyment.

Think about how you prepare for sex. If you come to bed exhausted and settle for a quickie night after night, it may be time to invest more energy in lovemaking. Leather undies aren't going to make up for physical exhaustion.

Decide what's important. Whatever you do to enhance sexual enjoyment, be sure it draws you more deeply into oneness with your mate and with God.

SEX AND INFIDELITY:

Threats to Marital Intimacy

Keith called. He and his wife were interested in coming to Marble Retreat as soon as we had an opening. We asked why they wanted to come. Keith calmly said, "I've been involved in a brief affair, and Lisa just found out. The affair wasn't more than a one-night stand, but Lisa is pretty upset and thinks we need counseling."

We asked: "Do you both want to work on your marriage?"

"I'm willing to come if Lisa wants to," Keith said.

Keith was right; Lisa was "pretty upset." Homicidal is more like it. When the couple came in for counseling, we learned that their marriage was great—but only for Keith. He was so totally self-centered that he couldn't understand why his liaison bothered her so much.

Keith's attitude is common. Men, in particular, think having sex outside of marriage is no big deal. According to some surveys, 70 percent of married men and 50 percent of married women have had affairs.

Does that make adultery OK? We don't think so. We've heard too much heartbreak to pass off adultery with a shrug. Let's take a look at infidelity from various angles, such as what it is, why it happens, what leads up to it, whom it affects, what to do about it, and how a damaged relationship can survive.

ADULTERY: A BROADER DEFINITION

The simple definition of adultery is sexual intercourse between a married person and someone other than the lawful spouse. If the other person is unmarried, he or she is a fornicator, not an adulterer. Neither adultery nor fornication is worse than the other, because both are destructive to marriage. Each time you share your body with someone other than your spouse, you erode the bond of intimacy.

Jesus said adultery is an affair of the heart and mind. That means that having sex is the physical expression of what has already happened in your heart. The breaking of trust and commitment began when you let someone other than your marriage partner move into your soul.

Derek, Nancy, Bill, and Ellen: Adultery among Friends

Derek and Bill became friends at work. Soon their wives became friends. Bill and Ellen would join Derek and Nancy to play cards, go out to dinner, attend sporting events.

One time when Bill and Nancy weren't around, Derek started telling Ellen some of the problems he was having with Nancy. He was just looking for a bit of friendly support.

Ellen listened. Initially she wanted to help Derek and Nancy find a way to fix their damaged relationship. As Derek began calling more often and began meeting her for coffee or lunch, the friendship intensified. Ellen ignored some internal warning signals as well as cautions from friends, reasoning that she could keep things from going too far. After all, it was just friendship. They weren't doing anything wrong.

By the time Ellen finally admitted to herself that Derek wanted more than just friendship, she was emotionally out of control. Refusing to consider the effects of her behavior on Bill or their children, she stepped into an affair.

The affair led to three divorces. Derek and Nancy divorced first, then Bill and Ellen. The marriage between Derek and Ellen ended in divorce as well. Six children and four sets of parents were also hurt in the process.

Infidelity is the ultimate selfish act.

The Real Reasons for Adultery

He's on the road. She's gained too much weight. The kids are exhausting. The in-laws are intrusive. There's not enough money.

Excuses for adultery abound. But what really makes a person step over the line into infidelity? Here are some setups for adultery:

We're naturally attracted to it. Ever since the Garden of Eden, we have not wanted anyone—not even God—to tell us what to do. We've wanted to live life on our own terms. We feel entitled to receive pleasure, regardless of how that might affect others. Sex is one of the strongest, most potent pleasures in life. Tests have shown that laboratory rats would rather starve than give up stimulation of their pleasure centers. We've seen humans do the same thing.

It promises so much. Sex promises power, love, excitement, happiness, security, and relationship. A person is most attracted to adultery if he or she feels impotent, rejected, fearful, unsafe, unloved, lonely—even bored—in a marriage.

It fills a spiritual hole. Most people we know who have walked through the darkness of adultery could identify a time when their connection with God's Spirit began to erode until his voice gradually became silent. It's possible the spiritual distancing came first and the adultery followed, but it's also clear that sin separates us from God. Seeking solace in a relationship outside of marriage only deepens the divide between a person and God.

We want it. We live in a culture that has abandoned marital fidelity. In addition, individual freedom has superseded responsibility to family or society. If we personally want something, we go for it, reasoning, "What I do in my private life is my own business."

STEPS TO INFIDELITY

If you feel lonely in marriage or distant from God, you are vulnerable to adultery. But hold on— there are more enticements. Here are some:

Flirting. Some people are flirts. They may not consciously try to lure you into bed, but they dress in provocative ways, ignore usual personal space considerations, and often lace their talk with suggestive comments. Although they may not be seeking sexual intimacy, their come-ons lead others into compromising situations.

Anonymity. A situation that allows a man and woman to be together in secret is a setup for trouble. When people think no one knows who they are or what they're doing, they are more open to infidelity. Getting away with a secret sin is enticing. Anonymity is one element of cybersex that makes it particularly dangerous.

Feeling deprived. Many people today think it's OK to flit from one lover to another. Someone who was abstinent before marriage and has been faithful since may feel out of the swing of things. Adultery may seem like the thing to do.

Attraction. Someone who offers attention, affirmation, and affection is attractive, no matter what. If a person is feeling lonely, inadequate, or rejected, the three A's of adultery become irresistible.

Q & A

Why Does He Keep Looking at Other Women?

My husband says he loves me, and I believe him. But he can't seem to stop checking out other women— even when I'm with him! When I confront him, he says it's just a habit, and it doesn't mean anything. But it makes me feel insecure. I admit I'm also miserable about being fifteen pounds overweight. How can I get him to stop?

Melissa: Girl watching is natural for a guy. Louis used to do it. He'd even joke about it, saying, "Just because I'm on a diet doesn't mean I can't read the menu."

Talk about It

⌒

Talk about some marriages that have been torn apart by infidelity. What were some indications that the marriage was in trouble before one partner strayed? How might you build up your relationship to keep each of you faithful to the other? What are some safeguards to keep each of you from getting sexually or emotionally involved with another person?

It wasn't so funny to me. Finally I said to him, "I don't think you really want another woman, and I trust you to be faithful, but when you look at other women I feel like I'm not good enough for you. I'd rather feel like I'm the only woman who lights up your life."

Louis: When Melissa put it that way, she got right through my defenses. I sensed her hurt and understood that what I saw as a harmless habit was eroding her self-confidence. I knew that whatever thrill I was getting out of checking out another woman wasn't worth causing my sweetheart pain.

Sometimes girl watching indicates other problems. A man looks at other women because his wife is cold, unaffirming, and unconcerned about his needs. Those are problems that need to be addressed. But in our case—and I think in yours—looking at other women was a habit. It was an indulgence that had nothing to do with my feelings.

Melissa: You might try sharing your feelings with your husband like I did with Louis. Can he make a conscious choice to forgo a brief snack for his eyes so that he can hang on to a gourmet feast for a lifetime? That's a no-brainer.

You might also consider making some changes in diet and exercise so that you can lose fifteen pounds. You'll feel better about yourself when you do—and sexier toward your husband.

Q & A

IS IT WRONG TO LOOK?

Sometimes when I look at a woman I become aroused. I'm happily married, and I don't intentionally set out to get turned on. It just happens. Is that wrong? How long is too long to look at a woman—especially if it's at the movies or on television? I know the Bible talks about lusting in your heart, but that leaves a lot of gray area.

It's certainly a normal male physiological response to be aroused by seeing an attractive woman. Short of having some serious, disfiguring surgery to rid you of sight, that tendency may continue into old age. But here's the real issue: What does a guy do in response to visual arousal?

As we see it, there's a continuum of acting out on sexual

impulses. At the most aggressive end of the spectrum would be a sexual assault, such as rape. A less aggressive response would be to masturbate while fantasizing about a woman. Farther down the continuum, a guy might use the fantasy-induced arousal to have intercourse with his mate. Note, all of these acts involve stimulation from a visual image. That's where lust begins.

With God's help, you can overcome lust. You come to the point where you look at an attractive woman and, instead of lusting, you acknowledge, "Wow, didn't God do well when he designed women?" You then remember that your spouse is God's gift to you and look away. That may include changing channels or simply walking away.

Seven Signs of Marital Erosion

The sense of unity and fulfillment that is so essential to a successful marriage isn't destroyed by a single, cataclysmic event. It erodes gradually in small, barely discernible ways. Only after months or years do you realize how far you have drifted apart.

To get a feel for where your marriage is, take a look at these seven signs of erosion:

You find it difficult to be with your spouse. Busyness is always a barrier to intimacy, but when your marriage slips to a lower priority than the children, work, church, or community activities, watch out. A marriage that provides minimal rewards will get minimal attention. Conversely, a marriage that gets minimal attention will provide minimal rewards.

You are irked by your spouse's behavior. Normally we adjust to quirks in our mates that we find annoying. However, when things aren't going well between us, those habits grate at us. We may react with put-downs, patronizing, sarcasm, or avoidance, but the effect is the same—wider distance between us.

You depend less on your spouse. A healthy marriage includes a comfortable balance of dependency. This is not codependency—an unhealthy dynamic that squelches individuality. Rather, it's two partners leaning on each other for support. When one or both partners are dissatisfied with the marriage, dependency creates guilt or anxiety. It becomes easier to regress to independence than to ask your mate to meet your needs.

You quit sharing details of your life. In the daily routines of life, spouses share bits and pieces of information. When the marriage is slipping, sharing even minor experiences and ordinary schedules feels threatening.

You're less interested in sex. A man's drive for sex and a woman's need for closeness aren't enough—when the magic between them is gone, so is sexual desire. Spouses purposefully avoid each other. Or they subtly increase the emotional distance between them by voicing physical complaints, arguing prior to bedtime, or going to bed at different times.

You want to spend more time with someone other than your spouse. Remember that adrenaline surge you felt when you first saw your mate? Whatever that was— hormones, unresolved needs, the competitive urge, or heavenly touch—lovers light up when their beloved appears. When you find yourself lighting up for someone else, look out.

You get secretive about money. When marriages begin to fail, partners start looking out for themselves rather than each other. They open separate bank accounts and stop giving full disclosure about their finances. Money, like sex, is a powerful barometer of marital health. Withholding money signals problems.

ARE YOU PRIME FOR AN AFFAIR?

If you are wondering what it would be like to be married to someone who makes you feel wanted and beautiful—rather than the inattentive, unresponsive person you're stuck with—you are vulnerable to an affair. Please be careful!

Someone doesn't just wake up one morning and decide to have an affair. Infidelity is a gradual process. It begins innocently enough. We gradually ignore moral warning signs that speak to us softly through our consciences, more urgently from our mates, and loudly from God's Word. Rationalization joins forces with temptation, dulling those warnings. We tell ourselves: "I can control this. I'm just having fun. I'm not doing anything bad."

We keep going, justifying along the way: "One little hug is all right. Why shouldn't we go to lunch together once in a while? God brought us together; we seem made for each other. How can something that seems so right be wrong?"

Don't make the mistake of thinking you can listen to someone tell you how beautiful or intelligent you are and not be lured into trouble. Read Proverbs 5 and 6; its advice to young men about prostitutes goes for young women, too. Decide that you will not let vulnerability trap you into a compromising situation.

Get some help for your marriage, too. You and your spouse should look into professional Christian counseling or attend a marriage-enrichment seminar. Propose that after confessing to your spouse how unhappy you've been and how much you want things to improve.

Q & A

I Slipped Once; Will It Happen Again?

About two years ago I had sex with someone. It was only a one-night stand, and I confessed everything to my husband. I know I hurt his sense of self-worth, but my husband is still unable to forgive me. To be honest, I'm not sure why I allowed the affair to happen—which is the worst thing about it. We're both afraid something like that will happen again. What should we do?

When you say the affair was a one-night thing and you're not sure how it happened, we're not surprised you and your husband worry that it won't happen again. We're also not surprised your husband hasn't forgiven you. In our experience of working with couples, we've found the betrayed spouse often has a hard time forgiving adultery. Healing is possible, but it takes commitment and change. Here are some steps to take toward recovery:

Tell your spouse how sorry you are. Many adulterers minimize the significance of betraying their vows. Our secular culture reinforces the notion that a one-night stand or a simple affair is no big deal. That type of thinking is deceitful and dangerous. Adultery causes incredible hurt. It destroys self-worth and erodes trust. It raises a barrier against ever trusting again. Not only did you jeopardize your marriage, but your casual attitude toward it jeopardizes relationships with your family and God. While you can find repentance, grace, and forgiveness, they come with a price. Genuine remorse is the first step.

Confess your sin without justifying it. Honest confession makes you aware of your vulnerability. You have a will and the power to make choices. As a Christian, you also have the Holy Spirit to help you avoid giving in to temptation. Think of what 1 Corinthians 10:13 says: "God is faithful; he will not let you be tempted beyond what you can bear. But when you are tempted, he will also provide a way out so that you can stand up under it."

Try to understand why you had the affair. If you honestly explore the underlying causes of your adulterous relationship, you'll find answers. Maybe you had doubts about feeling attractive or desired. Maybe you were bored and wanted some excitement. Maybe you were challenged and felt like taking a risk. Maybe you were impulsive.

Those feelings, plus many others, can contribute to adultery, but they're only excuses. None will stand up to the scrutiny of almighty God. Contrast those excuses with what King David expressed in Psalm 51:4 after his adultery with Bathsheba. Realizing his sin was an affront to God, he cried out, "Against you, you only, have I sinned and done what is evil in your sight." This kind of conviction is essential for restoration.

Set boundaries on your behavior. As a man, I know when a woman is coming on to me. I know how flattered I am by such attention. I could flirt with the woman, reasoning it's just harmless fun. But in doing so, I risk exposing myself to the excitement of her sensuality. This, in turn, can lead me to respond with inappropriate touch or talk. You know what follows. Steer clear of that. Set boundaries on your behavior that will keep you from falling.

A final warning: If a wife has had sex with another partner, she should be checked for possible infections. Her husband should also be examined.

WHO IS HURT BY ADULTERY?

To understand how infidelity hurts people, look at all those it affects:

The spouse. Trust is the foundation of a marital relationship. When one partner is unfaithful, the spouse becomes suspicious. When he or she questions the partner, the usual reaction is denial. Rarely does the offender admit infidelity. Instead, the truth comes out another way: it is exposed by the adulterer's partner, a sexually transmitted disease (STD), pregnancy, or some other circumstance.

The immediate response of the spouse who is betrayed is to question his or her adequacy—even to the point of feeling responsible for the adultery. An inner voice may whisper, "If I were good enough, my mate wouldn't have found someone else. What's wrong with me?"

The lover. The effect of adultery on the lover (the person the spouse commits adultery with) depends a lot on the lover's situation. If married, the lover may suffer the consequences of a broken relationship, including divorce and disgrace. If single, the lover may be brought down in shame. The lover may be angry at having been exposed. That anger can be directed at the betrayed spouse who demands that the affair end. Or it can be against the partner in adultery who is forced to break off the relationship. The lover can respond by foot dragging, put-offs, or outright rejection.

The adulterer. As for the person who strayed, what began as an exciting romance turns ugly. The adulterer struggles with guilt and anger at being found out. The adulterer loses self-esteem, reputation, romance, finances, and relationships with family and friends. He or she becomes anxious about the future, ambivalent about all the choices that must be made, and protective of the wounded lover. That is a devastating load.

Relationally, choosing between spouse and lover is a huge dilemma. Should the wedding vows taken before God and witnesses, years of investment with a spouse, and responsibilities toward children, family, and society be honored? Or should the adulterer honor the lover? Both the adulterer and lover have invested much in their relationship. Can that be abandoned without a backward glance? What about all those whispered promises made in passionate embrace?

Family and society. Playing around with someone other than your spouse may sound fun, but in time it's not. The spouse, the lover, and the adulterer all lose. So does everyone around them. Think about what infidelity and divorce do to children, the extended family, the church, and culture.

We all pay the price of broken marriages. Melissa and I see it as we counsel adults who struggle with the pain of their parents' divorce. One thing we've concluded is that an individual's pleasure should never be placed above the welfare of others. Freedom without responsibility is narcissism at its worse.

We recognize what pushes some people into infidelity. Empty, cold marriages produce hurting people—we hurt for them too—but we're more tired of hearing about the pain of infidelity. It's no wonder the punishment for adultery was once death, since the results of it are the emotional deaths of so many.

WHAT SHOULD WE DO?

Many couples who struggle in the wake of infidelity feel trapped. They don't know whether to bail out of their existing marriage or grit it out. Let's consider some of the choices:

You apologize and move on. You, the wayward one, murmur, "I'm sorry." Your spouse says, "I forgive you." Then you both slide right back into your old ways of relating. Those are the same patterns that led to the adultery. This alternative doesn't seem very productive for a couple in crisis.

You split. Many Christians do not believe divorce is an option. I, too, am firmly committed to marriage and work hard to support it. In counseling troubled couples, however, I've found that beating people over the head with Scripture only causes resistance. It makes couples feel trapped and less willing to work on necessary changes.

I've had better results sorting through the messy details of divorce. We talk about divorce as a quick fix, then discuss the long-term negative effects of it. I make it clear that after the initial relief of getting out of a painful marriage, most people grieve for a year or more. The sense of loss can be severe, depending on the circumstances.

My wife and I have been walking with a friend through divorce. After two years, Jane is only beginning to come out of depression. Even now, tears flow when certain things remind her of her ex-husband. Jane's former husband, Bob, had developed a romantic attachment with another woman. He continued to say he loved Jane and was committed to their family. So his sudden announcement that he wanted a divorce shocked her. Bob's relationship with his lover initially prevented him from feeling the grief of divorce. Sadness came later as he discovered what he had lost with his sons.

Loss of self-esteem is another effect of divorce. After a marriage breaks up, people wonder: *What's wrong with me that I couldn't make our marriage work?* Damage to their self-concept persists into future relationships, making self-disclosure and trust difficult.

My pastor-friend Ken counsels many couples considering divorce. One devastating aspect of divorce, he always points out to them, is its financial toll. He asks the man, "Do you really think you can afford to divorce? It may bankrupt you."

That gets the guy's attention. Ken then offers details. Aside from legal fees, there's the expense of maintaining separate houses. Add more as children's needs skyrocket or a second mate and stepchildren factor into the budget. Money alone may not be an adequate reason to stay married, but the debits of divorce can be good incentive to reconsider the decision.

One other long-range consideration is the dissolution of the nuclear family. The problems of children of divorce remain long after the breakup. Their initial confusion, sense of abandonment, and grief get acted out in school problems, drug and alcohol abuse, depression and withdrawal, delinquent behavior, and even suicide. Another effect is that children of divorce tend to divorce more easily, revealing a long-term deficiency in forming committed relationships.

Remarriage isn't easy, either. When a parent remarries, children experience a further sense of loss and rejection. Discipline complicates the picture. Children quickly learn which parent to manipulate, and both parents are vulnerable. Let's face it: nobody wants to be the bad guy—especially when the good guy is the former mate.

Even as adults, most children of broken homes say they wish their parents had not divorced. Their lives are burdened with logistical problems at graduations, weddings, holidays, children's births, and even funerals.

Staying together for the sake of the children has its merits. Our culture places such inflated value on personal pleasure and fulfillment that the legitimate needs of others, including children, are often ignored. I've known couples who have stayed together for the children and bequeathed stability rather than strife, continuity rather than confusion. I have seen such marriages return to close, mutually satisfying relationships as life goes on. Even after infidelity has shattered trust, couples need to consider the costs before divorcing.

You work through it. Realizing that divorce is too costly can be a practical motivation to recommit to the marriage. Add that to the biblical position on the permanence of marriage, and there's little question of the need for reconciliation.

SIX BARRIERS TO RECONCILIATION

Most Christians are remarkably willing to attempt to rebuild a marriage—even after it has been torn by infidelity. Some common barriers may complicate the process, however:

Anger. The injured spouse has every right to be angry. But the offending mate may be just as angry about having been discovered, about struggling with ongoing disappointments in the marriage that were evident long before the affair, and at himself or herself for being so stupid in having an affair. Some adulterers become hostile because the spouse won't let the matter drop. The anger may progress to unforgiving attitudes and bitterness—two most formidable walls to reconciliation.

Pride. Both husband and wife must take some responsibility in repairing a marriage damaged by infidelity. If either is too proud to accept a share of the guilt and the need for change, reconciliation is impossible. The task is too heavy to bear alone.

Fear. The injured spouse is afraid to trust the wayward spouse. The adulterer fears that the spouse will use the sin for leverage. Both fear having the incident exposed. Any of these fears threaten reconciliation.

The third person. What the lover chooses to do is unpredictable. One thing is certain, though. His or her continued presence creates significant tension. The adulterer feels responsible for the lover, but any impulses to help the former lover must be squelched. All contact must be eliminated.

Old patterns of relating. Ineffective ways of doing things in the marital relationship hinder reconciliation. For instance, if a couple related to each other as parent and child before the affair, that pattern must change to allow a more mature style of relating.

The cost of the affair. Affairs commonly accrue major financial or social costs, causing proportionate resentment in the injured spouse. Since many couples are on a tight budget and have to watch their spending, finding out a spouse has dropped a lot of money on gifts, travel, meals, and motels to keep an affair going is bound to infuriate his or her mate.

Ways to Heal a Broken Marriage

Redemption and restoration in a marriage torn by infidelity are not only possible but usually happen when given a chance. The process of reconciliation is painful, however. It requires intense self-examination, communication, remorse, confession, forgiveness, and change. C. S. Lewis once wrote that permanent marriage is impossible without Christ. That is true because marital faithfulness is essentially a spiritual issue. As Michael Mason says in *The Mystery of Marriage*, "Paul, a confirmed old bachelor, compared the one flesh of marriage to the spiritual union of us with God. Maybe without that spiritual dynamic, maintaining marriage is just too hard."[*]

We believe marriage is worth preserving, even if it has been shattered by infidelity. Here are some steps toward rebuilding a relationship:

Begin with spiritual commitment. Creation teaches us that there is order in the world. In this order, God speaks to the needs and desires of our hearts.

---

[*]Michael Mason, *The Mystery of Marriage* (Portland, Ore.: Multnomah, 1985), 377.

His pronouncement is that a man and woman should become one flesh. If you're in a miserable marriage, you may think God doesn't know what you're going through. He does know, and he shares your sadness. Above all, he wants you to feel whole. Only as you lose yourself in God will you begin to have the understanding, motivation, and empowerment to work through recovery from adultery.

Talk about what you've done. To restore the damage you've done in adultery, be open and honest in communicating with your spouse. The unresolved conflicts in your relationship must be addressed. What were the problems and disappointments that contributed to your infidelity? What were your unmet needs? Those are hard questions to address, but talking through them is essential.

Repent, confess, and ask for forgiveness. Both partners in the marriage must acknowledge ways they've hurt each other. They should confess those wrongs, express true remorse, and ask forgiveness of each other. Most marriage partners realize they don't want to go back to the way things were. With more open communi-

cation and deeper understanding of each other's true feelings and desires, they are better equipped to change.

Work toward change. Change involves a new understanding of old patterns and where they came from. That includes sexual attitudes and responses. You may need professional help to put your desire for renewal into daily practice. We encourage you to work through this. It's worth it. We know this from decades of experience as counselors, forty-two years of marriage, and most of all, the assurance that when you're going in God's direction, you have his power behind you. Through that, you can do all things—even make a broken marriage better than it was before.

DON'T FORGIVE TOO SOON

Jan discovered that Peter was involved with another woman. She confronted him, and he confessed. Wanting to move past the pain, Peter asked Jan's forgiveness and promised he'd never see the other woman again. Jan readily agreed. They kissed and made up.

Months later, Peter and Jan were still having problems. Both were confused by why they weren't getting along. Jan kept telling Peter she forgave him, and Peter kept telling Jan the affair was over. Somehow neither felt that it was.

The couple had completed only one part of the difficult process of reconciliation. There is more to rebuilding a relationship than forgiving.

FOUR AREAS
FOR RESTORATION

When you promised to stay with your spouse "for better or for worse," you thought "worse" meant illness, problems with children, or financial difficulties. You never imagined it meant facing betrayal by your spouse.

Barb realized this heartbreaking truth after twenty-one years of marriage when her husband, James, confessed he had been unfaithful. What's more, James had been involved sexually with Barb's best friend, so Barb felt doubly betrayed. She had sensed a growing distance with James, but she had never suspected adultery.

In decades of marital counseling, Melissa and I have seen pain caused by all kinds of betrayal: financial mismanagement, gambling, embezzlement, drug or alcohol abuse, pornography, cybersex, emotional affairs, and infidelity. In all of these, the dynamic is the same: habitual hidden behavior that destroys trust in a marriage.

It's devastating to find that your spouse has kept a part of his or her life a secret. Initially, the sense of betrayal is so strong that reestablishing trust seems impossible. But as Barb and James found, it is possible to rebuild a relationship. The process demands much and involves every part of you. Here are some steps that will help restore faith in your mate:

Start with the emotions. When secrets in a marriage are exposed, they leave a trail of pain. Healing begins with honest communication and a growing understanding of the emotions both partners are dealing with. It's essential that the offending spouse acknowledge the hurt that he or she has caused. I'm not talking here about a casual "I'm sorry" followed by an implied "Get over it." I'm talking true remorse.

Andy and Becky came to counseling soon after Becky found an X-rated video hidden in her husband's closet. When confronted with the evidence, Andy reluctantly confessed he'd been looking at porn since age twelve. To his surprise, the confession relieved some of the guilt he'd been carrying. Once he apologized, he felt the whole thing was over. He couldn't figure out why his wife wouldn't let it go.

Becky was devastated. She couldn't believe Andy didn't understand how terrible she felt. She doubted her sexual attractiveness. She wondered where Andy's mind went when they were making love. She wondered if there had been physical infidelities as well as fantasy affairs. Most difficult was realizing Andy had kept a part of himself hidden from her.

Andy tried to avoid Becky's emotional struggles. But soon he realized his eagerness to move on with life was short-circuiting his wife's need for him to acknowledge the hurt his addiction had caused her. Healing began when Andy truly started listening to Becky. In time, his loving attention helped her to begin risking intimacy. As she started to lower her protective barriers, she began to sense what it must have been like for Andy to struggle with his secret addiction for twenty years.

Free the mind. Most people think forgiveness is a feeling. It's not. Fundamentally, forgiveness is a choice, an act of the will. That's why God commands us to forgive. Forgiving involves acknowledging your hurt, releasing your thoughts about being wronged, and giving up the urge to exact revenge on the offender. If you are the spouse who has been wronged, it may seem strange that the burden of this stage of healing falls on you. But forgiving has more to do with the health of your spiritual and mental life than it does with your spouse's. Forgiving releases your spouse from your anger, but—more important—it frees you from the destructive bondage of unforgiveness.

For a time, Becky got stuck in recycling Andy's betrayal, complete with vivid replays of the initial shock she felt and possible scenarios of revenge. She got rid of those negative thoughts by choosing, again and again, to shut them out. She leaned on God, begging him to keep those ideas from dominating her thinking. She also learned to substitute good memories of their relationship for the negative thoughts. In time, she found that easier to do, especially as Andy showed more awareness of the hurt he had caused. Forgiveness is tougher if the offending spouse doesn't acknowledge sin and the pain it causes, but it's still necessary.

Change the behavior. Becky wanted to forgive her husband, but she found herself doubting Andy any time he was late coming home or not available when she called him at work. For years she had not questioned him about what he did away from her, but learning about his addiction with pornography changed that. She had a hard time believing his explanations.

To rebuild trust, Andy worked on changing his pattern; he tried to let Becky know if he was going to be later than usual or away from the office. In time Becky trusted Andy enough and didn't check on him so much.

Becky and Andy changed other behaviors. Andy told Becky the times of day when he typically felt tempted. They made a pact that he could call her for support anytime his mind turned toward improper fantasies. Eventually, those calls became opportunities to express their love for each other instead of updates on his struggle to overcome addiction.

At home, the couple became more open in their sexual relationship. Andy was surprised to find that Becky was sexually more adventuresome than he. She began to initiate sex, which made Andy feel more desirable. The new behaviors didn't produce an instant fix, but they were necessary steps in learning new skills.

Give it time. Time is necessary to rebuild trust in a relationship. Happily, that process is made possible by God's grace. However, along with grace, you need tough love. And this love must set clearly defined limits—especially if you're facing the disastrous consequences of infidelity, such as sexually transmitted disease, physical abuse, or financial ruin.

While rebuilding your relationship, you both have to deal with new revelations of past failures, admissions of ongoing temptations, and expressions of anger. Expect those setbacks, and keep accepting one another with grace. Don't let difficulties prevent you from achieving your goal.

As you invest time in the healing process, make sure you celebrate victories. Rejoice over a day when you no longer feel angry or guilty, a time of tenderness and intimacy, a month free of an addictive behavior. Check in periodically with a counselor or accountability group. Celebrate together the progress you make. In time, you may realize the incredible truth that what once seemed an irreparable wound has been transformed into a stimulus for growth.

I Can Forgive, But Can I Forget?

In the wake of an affair, a marriage may be so shaky that both partners avoid expressing anger for fear of forever driving each other away. But anger remains. An injured spouse is angry over the invasion of special places, music, and memories by a spouse's lover. Anger smolders over the dulling of sexual play, the death of hopes for the future, the erosion of respect for a mate, and the sense of abandonment. That anger should be explored during the rebuilding of a marriage.

The next step is forgiveness, which, yes, means forgetting. When we have been hurt, the event and its associated feelings are stored in our brain. We can review this memory, rehearsing it until it is etched in our brain, or we can choose not to replay it, thereby relegating it to the unconscious. That mental choice is called forgiveness. The painful memories are still there, but when life circumstances bring them to mind, we choose to extinguish them rather than reinforce them.

Forgiveness is not a single act that removes all memory and pain; it's a repetitive choice. It's an act of volition rather than a feeling. It is a process rather than an instant cure. It's not pretending there was no hurt. It acknowledges the pain but refuses to be captive to it.

Shouldn't I Know Everything That Happened?

You may want to find out exactly what happened in your mate's affair. Squelch it! The details can only hurt you. The more you know, the more images you'll have of your mate with another person. Those images may destroy any positive associations of your marriage that remain. For example, if you have enjoyed romantic evenings at a certain restaurant, discovering that "they" went there together may shatter those memories.

Your persistence in asking for details makes you look obsessive and morbid. It also keeps bringing the lover to your spouse's mind instead of relegating that person to the past.

JACK AND JUDY: CLIMBING BACK TO TRUST

Sometime after marriage, Jack discovered that Judy had gotten sexually involved with an old boyfriend. She met the boyfriend when she went home for a visit. Judy confessed the infidelity after Jack confronted her with the evidence.

Jack forgave Judy. However, every time Jack and Judy began to make love, he couldn't help picturing Judy with the other guy. Jack remembered Joe from high school. He had always envied Joe, who had been a star athlete. Now Judy's infidelity raised doubts in Jack's mind about being enough of a man for his wife.

It took hard work in marriage counseling for Jack to trust Judy enough to risk sexual intimacy. Eventually, regaining confidence in her exclusive commitment to him conquered his fear.

19

SEX ADDICTIONS:
Passions That Erode Lovemaking

When I was in medical school, I did a research study on appetite control. I concentrated on a specific area of the hypothalamus in mice called the ventromedial nucleus. Our work eventually showed that mice overate and became obese if that V-M cell cluster was destroyed or was genetically smaller than normal. The mice got fat because their V-M nucleus wasn't releasing enough of the kind of neurochemical signal that made them feel full. Without that signal, they just kept eating.

Our brains also contain control centers for various feelings and behaviors. Some of these centers prompt feelings of pleasure in response to certain behaviors. When you see a sunset or listen to the "Hallelujah Chorus" or have a sexual climax, your pleasure centers are secreting endorphins.

These are morphine-like chemicals that create feelings of well-being, joy, and relaxation. Other cell clusters release adrenaline-like molecules that make us feel excited and full of energy.

Some people become addicted to the feelings that those pleasure centers produce. The chemical high becomes so important that a person goes after it even when the consequences are destructive. Alcohol, marijuana, and cocaine produce the kind of high that can lead to addiction, regardless of the consequences. So does sex. If a person becomes obsessed with a need for a sexual high, for example, he or she resorts to abnormal, compulsive behavior to get it.

A current example of sexual addiction is cybersex addiction. People who are caught up in the high that Internet pornography produces become so desperate for it that they spend hours on the computer. Pornographic indulgence is just as unhealthy for them as overeating is for the mice I studied, because as the addiction progresses, more stimulation is needed to get the same response. It becomes an all-consuming obsession.

The good news is that, with God's grace and a lot of therapy, those centers in the human brain can be reprogrammed and healthy patterns restored.

Let's take a look at some behaviors that can become addictions.

ADDICTED TO ADULTERY

Hank was one long drink o' water, as they said out in ranch country where he grew up. Hank was herding cattle, branding calves, and breaking broncs by age ten. He learned all about being a cowboy—which was a must to survive in that hot, dusty place.

Part of his initiation into manhood, besides drinking and brawling, was womanizing. Hank's dad broke Hank in at the local brothel when Hank was thirteen. Scoring with women became part of Hank's sexual identity. Getting saved and marrying didn't change that pattern of adulterous sex. Hank would spot a vulnerable female and move in for the conquest. He continued to proclaim his love for his wife, insisting that extramarital sex was just part of being a cowboy.

Hank's problem was not his wife; it was how he felt about himself as a man. He had been taught that promiscuity was proof of his masculinity.

CAUSES OF SEXUAL ADDICTION

Hank's pattern of sexual addiction is unusual. Most heterosexual men become addicted to sexual stimulation through pornography and masturbation, not sexual relationships with women. Sex addiction is not limited to men; women can also be obsessed with having multiple lovers. In both males and females, sexual addiction has several features:

Sexual abuse in childhood. In a way, that was Hank's experience, although the abuse would not have been recognized as such in a cowboy culture. Early abuse blurs sexual boundaries, making promiscuity likely.

Narcissism. A narcissist has little regard for anyone's feelings other than self. He or she requires lots of attention and acclaim. Anyone of the opposite gender who responds to this need is seen as an available and appropriate sexual partner, usually for a one-night stand.

Risk taking. People addicted to sex love to live on the edge of danger. The thrill of an adrenaline rush is more appealing than sexual gratification. A sex addict may become involved in several extramarital affairs at once, just to see if he or she can get away with them. Individual relationships are unimportant.

People pleasing. A compliant, passive, people-pleasing person becomes involved with anyone who comes on to him or her. The underlying reason for this is lack of self-confidence, vulnerability to being loved, or the inability to establish behavioral boundaries. For example, Joan was clearly taught that she should never say no to someone who needed her. No one bothered to differentiate sexual lust from any other need. So whenever a man came on to Joan, saying he needed her, she'd readily comply.

Mental illness and addictions. People with schizophrenia, borderline personality, bipolar mood disorder, drug addiction, or alcohol addiction are often promiscuous because they have difficulty defining relational boundaries.

Recovery from sexual addiction is possible, though it requires dealing with the underlying disorder. A redemptive relationship with Jesus is the first step, followed by individual and marital counseling to overcome the destructive lifestyle. Hank has experienced this kind of life transformation. His marriage survived. Today he's a one-woman man, and still one tough cowboy.

Q & A

WHY DO I WANT SEX WITH STRANGERS?

Before I got saved and married, I slept with numerous women—some of them nearly strangers. Today, sex with my wife, whom I love very much, is OK, but it's nothing like what I had before I was married. I still have strong desires to have sex with other women. It's a constant temptation that I don't want to give in to. What can I do?

Louis: Stop dwelling on past memories of hot sex. The more you choose to replay those tapes, the more intense they will become. When I'm struggling with fantasies or sexual images, I mentally turn to a different channel. I try to tap into a great memory of the super sex Melissa and I have enjoyed.

This is a good time for you to work on improving marital sex. Look for ways to add a little more intrigue, romance, variety, and surprise to keep you and your wife passionate for each other.

Melissa: In a way, you're like a person who uses pornography. Images of past sex are interfering with your marital intimacy. When you step off the path God puts you on, you become involved in all kinds of wrong thinking. Turn back to God and you'll be amazed at how he provides the incentive, energy, and expertise you'll need to focus on loving your wife.

Q & A

HOW CAN I LOVE A SEX ADDICT?

My husband and I have been married seven years. During that time he's been involved with pornography and voyeurism. He has been through therapy and counseling again and again, but nothing changes. It's impossible for me to feel like having sex with him, since I know how much time he spends lusting after images of other women. I find his behavior intolerable, but don't know what to do. Do I have to live with this problem?

Louis: There are times when a spouse must show tough love. If you honestly feel there is no sign that your husband intends to break his addiction, it is necessary to draw some lines. Setting sensible boundaries and sticking with them is the only course of action that works.

Reasonable limits in marriage are sexual fidelity, honesty, financial responsibility, and meeting each other's needs. Clearly spelling out such limits and the consequences of a mate's refusal to meet them is well within your rights. Such boundaries should be communicated in first-person statements. For instance, you might say, "I realize you have a serious addiction. I'd like to have a relationship with you, but I can't change your behavior. I also can't continue to live with you as long as the addiction remains. So here is my decision: I will stay with you until I have reason to believe you have failed to let go of your addictive behavior. If at any point I see you looking at pornography, I will ask you to move out. We will pursue and enforce legal separation until I can be assured of your recovery."

Whatever boundaries you set will likely be challenged, so don't make any statements you're not willing to follow through on.

This clearly places responsibility for change on your husband. That's important because most addictive personalities blame others for their problems. If you've been shouldering some blame for your husband's problem, dump it. You are his wife—not his parent, cop, or enforcer.

Q & A

AM I A SEX ADDICT?

After having a ho-hum sex life for the first four years of marriage, my husband and I finally talked things out. Now we have wonderful, incredible sex. My problem is I feel like I'm addicted. It doesn't seem right for me to want sex as much as I do. This can't be godly behavior—even if my urges are directed toward my husband. How can I get control of this?

Louis: Sexual pleasure is part of God's creative design. The problem comes when a person's sexual feelings and fantasies go outside the marital boundary. It's important for you and your husband to keep on talking to protect your faithfulness in marriage.

You have a problem if sexual thoughts or behavior interfere with other responsibilities. If you withdraw from other relationships, become negligent in caring for your children, or abandon your spiritual life, control is necessary. Here are some ways to control compulsive behavior:

Try a spiritual approach. When sexual thoughts enter your mind, substitute prayer or devotional reading for the obsessive thoughts. The frequency of your sexual thoughts will decrease.

Work it off. Go for a walk or do a physically challenging job. Reducing excess energy diminishes the intensity of the sex drive.

Find an accountability partner. Call a trusted woman friend when your sexual drive is overwhelming. Your husband could be that accountability partner, unless your sexual desire is too distracting for him.

See a professional counselor. Find an experienced, female Christian therapist. Explore the reasons for your intense turn-on and establish better control.

You didn't mention how long this current heightened sexual desire has been going on. If it's still pretty new, take advantage of the added enjoyment you are experiencing with your husband and rejoice in God's gift.

Melissa: Your level of desire may seem extreme compared to what you experienced before, but perhaps you're simply blessed with a drive to match or exceed your husband's. Don't worry—God doesn't frown on the marital pleasure he created.

Is Masturbation OK?

Masturbation means stimulating your or someone else's genitals, usually to orgasm. It usually involves fondling, caressing, or stroking the penis or the clitoris. There is no scriptural command against masturbation, although

there are cautions against its associated behaviors:

- If self-stimulation is accompanied by lustful fantasies of someone other than your mate, it becomes adultery, according to Jesus (Matthew 5:28).
- If self-stimulation becomes compulsive, it becomes idolatrous. Obsession with orgasm becomes more important than worshiping God (Romans 1).
- If masturbation is used to avoid marital sex, that puts selfish desire over sexual intimacy with your mate (1 Corinthians 7:4).

When a husband and wife are separated by distance, sickness, disability, or pregnancy, masturbation is an option. Some would say that a man who is deprived of sex would have a nocturnal emission anyway to relieve the pelvic discomfort of a seminal buildup. That's one way of looking at it. You must decide what God requires of you. To our way of thinking, the Bible is silent on the rightness or wrongness of individual masturbation.

There seems to be no problem with mutual masturbation or masturbating one's mate as a part of lovemaking. Masturbation is a loving way to provide sexual release for your husband or wife when intercourse isn't possible. Like intercourse, masturbation is more effective with good lubrication and with guidance from the person being masturbated.

Q & A

WILL MASTURBATION HURT OUR MARRIAGE?

I've been married for several years, and our sex life is pretty good. But occasionally I masturbate. Is this something that will damage my relationship with my wife?

Louis: Masturbation does pose some threats to marriage. Here are some:

✁ Masturbatory fantasies can be adulterous. If you think about having sex with another woman while you are masturbating, it erodes your erotic feelings toward your wife.

✁ Self-stimulation could become so addictive that it replaces marital sex. Some men find masturbation a convenient way to avoid marital intimacy.

✁ Masturbation can make your wife feel inadequate or unappealing. Many women have no inkling of how common masturbation is for men. They are astonished when they discover their husband doing it.

Masturbation offers some positive effects. It relieves sexual tension when a man and his wife have very different sex drives. It is an alternate way to pleasure each other when intercourse isn't desirable due to advanced pregnancy, recent childbirth, or illness. It is a hedge against unfaithfulness when a man's wife is unavailable and temptation presents itself.

Since you have doubts about the effect masturbation may have on your marriage, it would be good to ask your wife how she feels about it. Her response will tell you a lot.

Q & A

WHY CAN'T HE CLIMAX WITHOUT MASTURBATION?

My husband can't climax while having sex—though he can by masturbating. I've never heard of such a thing. I've tried to keep him from seeing that this really bothers me, but it does. I think he'd be appalled at the idea of seeing a sex therapist. What else could we try?

Louis: Is your husband concerned about pregnancy and is practicing coitus interruptus as a birth control technique? If so, he will be happy to learn that other forms of contraception are more effective. Coitus interruptus is not reliable because sperm are often released before ejaculation occurs.

Is he a fastidious individual who doesn't want to leave you with a mess to clean up after his ejaculation? Somehow he may have gotten the idea that mess bothers you.

What gives your husband sexual pleasure? Most men first experienced sexual climax through masturbation. The rhythm of stimulation, the amount of pressure applied, the excitement of seeing his erection, or of watching the ejaculate shoot out become an important part of sexual reflex. These aren't as evident during vaginal stimulation.

Understanding what your husband's ideas are about masturbation or intercourse may help you come to a mutually satisfying solution. While you're getting a clearer picture of what your husband thinks and feels, you can explain how important it is for you to have him climax in you.

Q & A

WHY DOES HE WANT HIMSELF MORE THAN HE WANTS ME?

My husband of seven years recently stopped approaching me sexually. When I ask him about that, he says we're just out of sync. But I don't buy it. When changing the sheets, I've seen evidence that he masturbates while I'm sleeping next to him. What gives? I don't know what to think or how to approach him anymore.

Louis: Sex is often a barometer of the overall marital climate. Take a look and see if you find any of these causes of a man's loss of sexual interest:

Fear of failure. Men derive much of their sense of well-being and identity from being sexually proficient. If this proficiency is threatened, a man's fears can trip him into premature ejaculation, erectile failure, or diminished sex drive.

Most men have a hard time admitting these fears. Your husband may prefer masturbation because it's safer and physiologically easier than worrying about satisfying your sexual needs. His lack of interest may be caused by fatigue, loss of confidence on the job, or from medication or drugs or alcohol abuse. Once a man experiences a sexual failure, he may lose interest in sex to avoid failing again.

Fear of rejection. A man can become so fearful of being turned down that he decides initiating sex is too risky. His wife may be on another track altogether. She may remember having occasionally said, "Not tonight, honey," while her husband is sure that twenty-seven out of his last thirty invitations were unsuccessful.

Unresolved anger. Anger is a powerful libido inhibitor. Who wants to cuddle up to someone who seems like an enemy? A man may be turned off to sex if he senses anger in his wife.

Melissa: When fear or anger dampens a husband's enthusiasm for sex, it's normal for him to rationalize the change by saying you two are "out of sync." Talk with your husband about what's really happening, not in an accusing way but with compassion. Be sure to express your desire to be connected with him sexually.

If you haven't already tried bridging the distance between you by initiating sex, go for it. Seduce him. If that doesn't work, see a counselor. If your husband isn't interested in counseling, go by yourself.

THE LURE OF PORNOGRAPHY

You'd probably never shoot heroin into your vein to see what it's like. You wouldn't smoke marijuana or sniff cocaine, either. Those chemicals are so powerfully addicting that dabbling with them isn't worth the risk.

Yet thousands of people willingly expose themselves to another chemical without thinking twice about the danger. The chemical high produced by sexual orgasm in response to pornography carries a high risk for addiction. Yet according to the *New York Times*, one in four regular users of the Internet visit a sex site at last once a month. Some get high on pornography, then proceed to masturbation till they reach orgasmic relief.

We've watched men who are Christians weep tears of guilt and shame as they beg for forgiveness for this kind of addiction—only to return the following week to the computer in search of more sexual images. We've seen women do the same kind of thing with romance novels or chat rooms or email relationships.

Someone with any kind of sexual addiction eventually pays harsh penalties. Lost jobs, broken marriages, and alienation from families are no different for sex addicts than they are for an alcoholic or heroin addict.

Q & A

Is Cybersex Cheating?

Since our daughter was born fourteen months ago, sexual intimacy between my husband and me has declined. This week I found out that my husband has been having cybersex with other women. I'm having difficulty forgiving him. People tell me it's no big deal; cybersex isn't really cheating. But it goes against everything I've been taught as a Christian. Am I making too much of this?

We think it is a big deal. We've seen Internet pornography, chat rooms, and sex phone calls become an obsession with men and women of all ages and places in life.

It would appear that this behavior is related to the birth of your baby. Often during late pregnancy and early postpartum months, a husband feels sexually and emotionally abandoned. Cybersex meets those needs at the click of a finger. Wives and babies require much more time and energy.

We wonder if this behavior is new for your husband. Many people struggle from adolescence

---

Talk about It

Take a look at what occupies most of your time and attention. Is it work, the kids, books, the Internet? Do you spend so much time with something that others are beginning to question the activity? Do you find yourself covering up or lying about what you're doing? You may have an addiction. Talk to each other about this activity and examine how it is affecting your relationship.

with sexual temptation, specifically pornography. Insist that your husband see a counselor. He also needs to get into an accountability group. He could sign up with www.netac countability.com or www.covenant eyes.com. But it would be better for him to meet with godly men who ask him weekly how things are going.

Don't see this as the end of your love relationship. Pray about this matter, but also talk to your husband. Affirm your love for him as well as your concern about his behavior. Tell him how it makes you feel. Then go to your Internet provider and set up some controls so your husband can't go to porn sites. If that doesn't work, cancel your Internet service. You can't control what your husband does away from the house, but you can set limits on what he does at home. Ultimately this addiction is his responsibility.

Q & A

WHAT'S WRONG WITH CYBERSEX?

Our marriage reached the crisis point after my wife started having relationships with guys on the Internet. She says she would never have *an actual affair with these men, but she refuses to stop flirting or talking about sex with these men. She spends so many hours at the computer that there's nothing left for us. She refuses to go to a counselor. She says she's only staying in our marriage because of our kids. What can I do?*

Louis: Your wife has a serious sexual addiction. Since she is unwilling to seek professional help, you have two options. One is to express your love for her and declare your commitment to win her back but to do nothing about her behavior. This approach would work if your wife became convicted by God and turned her life around. But that might not happen.

The second option could lead to such conflict that it could fracture your relationship. Reaffirm your love and commitment to your wife but use a tough-love approach. Disconnect the modem and get rid of the computer. Tell your wife, "I love you, but I can't watch you destroy yourself and our marriage."

This sex addiction will get worse if it's not stopped. Chances are that people your wife is playing around with in cybersex have similar addictions and love having multiple sex partners. In time, your wife's Internet sex will become real-time sex.

Your wife's problem won't be resolved quickly or easily. She will require professional help once she admits her need to change. Ultimately, her healing means accepting God's grace and recognizing the fulfilling nature of mature marital sex.

Melissa: If I could talk with your wife, I'd tell her: "You're fooling yourself when you say you are staying in your marriage for your kids. What's best for them is a strong, intimate relationship between their mom and dad. If you are really serious about doing what's best for them, get into counseling and straighten out your act.

"Your kids know more than you think. What lessons about intimacy and commitment are you modeling when you prefer a computer fantasy to your God-given husband? You were designed to be a good wife and mom. That requires hard work and commitment. But the rewards far outweigh any fun you might miss on the Internet."

SEXUAL CONFUSION:

Homosexuality, Paraphilias, and Other Issues

We have worked with only a few homosexual individuals, all of whom were in heterosexual marriages and were struggling with homosexual attractions. They had rarely acted on those feelings. And they all wanted to change.

Investigating the origins and causes of homosexuality is challenging because the subject has become such a political hot button. We find two books particularly helpful for understanding homosexuality: *Kaplan and Sadock's Comprehensive Textbook of Psychiatry, Seventh Edition* and *Homosexuality and the Politics of Truth.** These books offer a balanced approach to scientific data on genetic and environmental factors relating to homosexuality.

The genetic or biological research on homosexuality includes brain dissections, twin studies, and hormonal assessments. For example, Simon LeVay, a neuroanatomist, studied the brains of homosexuals and heterosexuals in San Francisco. He reported that one difference between them was a localized cluster of cells. Evaluations of the report questioned the reliability of the data. Critics also pointed out that such brain differences are known to occur as a response to behavior.

Another method of identifying genetic factors has been through the study of twins. Since identical twins have the same genetic material, the assumption is that homosexuality in one should be present in the other. Yet studies of twins

---

*Benjamin J. Sadock, M.D., and Virginia A. Sadock, M.D., eds., *Kaplan and Sadock's Comprehensive Textbook of Psychiatry, Seventh Edition* (Baltimore: Lippincott Williams &Wilkins, 2000); Jeffrey Satinover, M.D., *Homosexuality and the Politics of Truth* (Grand Rapids: Baker, 1996).

have found that to be true in only 50 percent of the cases. Satinover's comments on this finding are interesting. He writes, "The press has taken these ... articles as further 'proof' that 'homosexuality is genetic.' But as we will see, the results of this research by activists with an acknowledged political agenda actually demonstrate no such thing. Indeed, the researchers themselves admit disappointedly—even apart from methodological problems that tend to weaken their findings altogether—that taken at face value their work demonstrated a far smaller genetic contribution to both male and female homosexuality than they sought."[*] According to our resources, many influences—biological, psychological, and sociocultural—factor into homosexuality. Furthermore, sexual object choice in homosexuals can be successfully changed. However, gay activists are exerting pressure to ban such treatment (reparative therapy). A colleague of ours had to move his family and practice when he came under a barrage of harassment for using reparative therapy.

Such political pressure has obscured the health and relational problems that are part of the homosexual lifestyle. Suppressing that data compromises attempts to prevent the spread of sexually transmitted disease through unprotected anal intercourse—the preference of most male homosexuals, according to Centers for Disease Control's Lynda S. Doll in "Homosexual Men Who Engage in High-Risk Sexual Behavior."[†]

Other problems associated with the homosexual lifestyle include reduced life expectancy, a high rate of suicide, increased incidence of rectal cancer, higher incidence of infectious hepatitis, and associated liver cancer. That's not a pretty picture. Yet it should motivate Christians to compassion and involvement in preventive sexual education. The truth needs to be a part of any program so that ambivalent adolescents may make an informed decision about their sexual choices.

---

[*]Satinover, *Homosexuality and the Politics of Truth,* 421.
[†]Lynda S. Doll et al., "Homosexual Men Who Engage in High-Risk Sexual Behavior: A Multicenter Comparison," *International Journal of Sexually Transmitted Disease* 18:3 (1991): 170–75.

Q & A

HOW CAN I LIVE WITH HIS ATTRACTION TO MEN?

My husband of sixteen years recently confessed he had a homosexual encounter with a stranger he met at the YMCA. I was devastated. He says he loves me and finds me sexually attractive, but he also feels attracted to men. He has been in weekly counseling and wants to stay faithful, but I feel insecure and betrayed. Is there any hope for us?

There is hope for your marriage—especially since your husband has confessed his homosexual encounter and desire to you. Many men with such issues keep them secret. That only gives the behavior power. His confession and vulnerability allow you to provide support and encouragement as he works through this.

There are three concerns that must be addressed:

Sexually transmitted disease. Your husband might have contracted HIV or another sexually transmitted disease in this chance encounter. There is no such thing as safe sex, since condoms provide only limited protection. You and your husband should see a doctor and have physical exams and tests for HIV and other STDs. It can take up to six months after sex for the HIV virus to be detected. If you and your husband get tested before six months, you should both be retested after six months.

Don't rely on the word of a stranger that he was disease free. Research indicates that most infected individuals do not reveal an infection to their sexual partners. The risk is too great to ignore.

Your pain. Most spouses in your circumstance struggle with ambivalence. They know they love their husbands—and their husbands love them—yet they are devastated by their husbands' attraction to men. The question "What's wrong with me?" becomes a haunting obsession.

These emotional extremes are difficult to cope with. Yet it's important to remember that a husband's homosexuality has nothing to do with his wife's personality, behavior, appearance, or success as a sexual partner. That may be hard for a betrayed wife to believe. Talking through such feelings with a marriage therapist will help.

Understanding homosexuality. The desire to be close to men can reflect a deficit in male bonding in childhood. That leaves a guy hungry to be held and loved by a man. Unfortunately, in adolescence and beyond, many men who seek to fulfill that need become involved in homosexuality.

We recently heard from a couple that started where you are. After going through counseling, they said their level of intimacy and marital satisfaction had never been deeper. His struggles with homosexual desires and fantasies have ceased.

For more information, check out these resources: Harvest, USA at 215-342-7114; CrossOver Ministries at 859-277-4941; Exodus International at info@exodusnorthamerica.org.

HOMOSEXUAL AFFAIRS

Some people in a heterosexual marriage may act out their sexual confusion through having a homosexual affair. Such an affair always has painful consequences. It can cause job loss, social ostracism, or even criminal charges. In addition, the mate is usually deeply hurt and confused by such revelations. Does her husband's homosexual encounter mean that she is inadequate as a wife and lover? Can he stay in this marriage, knowing that she is attracted to women?

There are many treatment approaches for such couples. Individual psychotherapy, spiritual healing of memories, support groups, and behavioral therapies are helpful. Regardless of the approach, recovery works best when both partners are involved in treatment.

Warning: If a partner has acted on homosexual impulses and had sex with another partner, he or she should be checked for

---

Talk about It

Do you or your spouse struggle with attractions toward members of the same gender? Have either of you had problems with your sexual identity? How might those issues be affecting your marital relationship? What might you do about them?

infections. The spouse should also be examined. This caution also applies to any extramarital heterosexual involvement.

SEXUAL PARAPHILIAS

Paraphilias are defined by the *Diagnostic and Statistical Manual of Mental Disorders* as "recurrent, intense, sexually arousing fantasies, sexual urges, or behaviors generally involving nonhuman objects; the suffering or humiliation of oneself or one's partner; or sexual fantasies, urges, or behaviors involving children or other nonconsenting persons that occur over a period of at least six months."[*]

Essentially, people with paraphilias never grew up sexually. They got stuck somewhere in development. For example, a little child's interest in someone else's genitalia is natural, but this interest becomes inappropriate in an adult who peeks into a neighbor's window to watch someone disrobe.

Paraphilias are deeply rooted and should be treated by a competent therapist. We recommend a Christian professional because of the spiritual aspects of healing.

Experiencing loving concern with well-defined boundaries is critical.

Paraphilias include:

Exhibitionism. Exposing one's genitals to a stranger.

Voyeurism. Observing the sexual activity or nudity of strangers.

Frotteurism. Touching or rubbing against a nonconsenting person.

Fetishism. Getting sexual stimulation from a nonliving object, such as lingerie or shoes.

Pedophilia. Using children as sexual objects.

Masochism. Receiving humiliation or suffering for sexual stimulation.

Sadism. Causing humiliation and suffering in a victim for sexual excitement.

Transvestism. Dressing and acting in a style traditionally associated with the opposite gender.

Bestiality. Having sex with an animal.

Q & A

HOW CAN WE LIVE WITH GRANDPA'S EXHIBITIONISM?

After thirty-five years of marriage, my husband was caught at a mall

---

[*]*Diagnostic and Statistical Manual of Mental Disorders* (Washington, D.C.: American Psychiatric Association, 1994), 522–32.

exposing himself to a minor in a bathroom. The last time that happened was more than ten years ago. He begged for forgiveness and went into counseling. I thought the problem was taken care of. Now this happens again. I'm so confused. Why does he do this? Is it too late to expect change? What do I tell our children and grandchildren who were with us the day Grandpa got arrested?

Exhibitionism is a sexual identity issue. This disorder usually begins in childhood or adolescence. The behavior is often accompanied by masturbation and fantasies of sex with another person. In general, the behavior reassures the person about his maleness.

Paraphiliac behavior frequently decreases with age. However, it may be absent for extended periods, then reoccur suddenly in response to a stressful situation. I wonder if that is true of your husband.

Your choices of dealing with this situation vary, depending on the legal consequences of this behavior, your husband's attitude, the availability of professional help, and the family's response. In general, open communication offers the best hope for your husband and family. It would be wise for him to confess his sinful behavior and ask forgiveness of his children and grandchildren rather than your doing that for him. Depending on the grandchildren's ages, explanations about the details of his behavior will vary. Still, since even young children are being taught that their genitals are to be kept private, a frank apology would reinforce that instruction.

Your husband should get back into personal therapy. We also recommend marital counseling for the two of you. That would help you cope with the crisis you're facing.

Q & A

DOES SHE LIKE DOLLS MORE THAN SHE LIKES ME?

My wife is a doll collector. We have dolls all over the house—in cabinets, on shelves, on dressers, all over the bedroom. I've never objected to what I regarded as her hobby. However, I am getting uneasy about having to share our bed with these dolls. Each night my wife makes a big deal out of picking out a favorite and sleeping with it. Would I be unreasonable to ask her to give that up?

We are fascinated by your story and wonder what the attachment to her dolls means to your wife. We're also curious about how her attachment to the dolls affects her sexual response to you. Does she use them to avoid sexual intimacy with you? Does she use them as toys to enhance her arousal? Do they represent some blocked expression of her maternal instinct?

Just curious. Those questions may never need to be answered. Your question does, however. We believe it's completely appropriate for you to express your feelings and concerns about the dolls to your wife. Set some limits about where they're displayed and how she uses them. If she won't hear your concerns, get a counselor to facilitate the communication.

PART SEVEN:
GETTING HELP AND FINDING HEALING

MARITAL THERAPY:
When It's Time to Get Help

Are you afraid to talk to your spouse?

"Of course not!" you respond. But take a look at the way you and your spouse communicate. You might be surprised at how fears keep you apart.

At times, all of us feel like we're walking a tightrope between being true to ourselves and true to another person. We want to be independent, but we don't want to be lonely. We long to be close to our spouse—yet we don't want to be swallowed up by him or her. The dilemma is, how can we be individuals yet not be left alone?

Sometimes attempts at communication are awkward, if not downright painful. We retreat into silence because it seems safer. What prevents us from pursuing the intimacy and oneness that we all desire in marriage? Where can we get help dealing with that problem?

FIVE FEARS THAT STIFLE COMMUNICATION

Fear of failure. Fear of failure is the number one barrier to communication. Husbands hesitate to share feelings with their wives, mostly because they don't have much experience in this. When the level of conversation feels uncomfortably close, a man clams up. A woman who needs emotional closeness may knock herself out trying to get her husband to talk. After she is repeatedly frustrated with the effort, she stops trying.

Fear of rejection. Fear of rejection keeps many spouses from expressing negative or painful things. Sometimes we respond to each other in ways that imply rejection—even though that's not what we mean. In a recent counseling session, a woman told her husband, "I always feel inadequate." His response was, "I never see you as inadequate—it's dumb for you to think that way!" This husband thought he was helping his wife. It had never occurred to him that his response only reinforced her negative thoughts about herself. She had quit sharing her feelings.

Fear of conflict. Marriage inevitably spawns conflict. Both Melissa and I have rough edges that must be polished. Marriage is one of the instruments God uses to do that. When the process gets too painful and one of us withdraws into a shell, we both feel isolated. But if Melissa and I face our conflicts by talking them out, we end up with a stronger connection.

Fear of losing control. The give-and-take of becoming one in marriage is tricky. There is always the danger that one spouse will dominate the relationship. One couple told me, "Of course we want to become one. We just can't decide which one."

Persistent, honest communication can break down this barrier. As trust grows between a husband and wife, fear of losing control can be put to rest.

Fear of intimacy. Nowhere is intimacy more complicated than in sexual relations. It's so gratifying when we can please each other and so disappointing when we can't. In times of physical intimacy, each partner is exposed and easily wounded. Learning to talk to each other is essential if we're to be happy in lovemaking.

Q & A

WHY ISN'T HE HAPPY WITH ME?

My husband and I plodded along for years in our marriage. Then, two years ago, he had to work out of state for an extended period. Since he has come back home, he has been unhappy with the way we communicate, especially with how much we fight. Plus, he won't have sex with me. It's like his bargaining chip—no sex until I change. This really ticks me off, since he's blaming me for all our problems. Any suggestions?

Louis: Be glad that your husband wants your life together to change. He has said in so many words, "Let's stop the old dance and learn to tango." The old dance included unproductive ways of communicating and unfulfilling behavior patterns. He wants more from your relationship. That's good.

Ideally, you should try marriage counseling. Counseling would help you replace old patterns with more effective communication skills, understand your expectations, and learn how to meet each other's needs. It would also help you connect better sexually.

Melissa: Whether or not you get into counseling, we can offer a few new steps for you:

Take responsibility for yourself. Neither you nor anybody else can control another person, especially a husband. So change your part in the old dance.

Find out what your husband's love language is, and try responding to it. Whether your new dance turns out to be a tango or a polka, you're going to thank your husband someday for wanting to replace the old steps.

TIPS ON TALKING TO YOUR MATE

Ideally a married couple should have no secrets; anything you share—even sexual frustration—should be graciously accepted. In the real world, we need some pointers about how to communicate:

Stick with "I statements." Speak about your own experiences, feelings, and needs rather than making accusations about your mate's behavior. "I feel lonely and would like to have more time together" gets a better reception than "You're never home. You just expect sex—then you're gone."

Be clear about your motivation. Confessions about wrongdoing—even inappropriate relationships with others—are helpful only if the motive is to improve your sexual intimacy, not to clear your guilty conscience. This can be tricky. If blowing up at your mother-in-law or maxing out a credit card or lunching with a coworker has caused such guilt or fear that it blocks your responsiveness to your mate and you feel compelled to confess, prepare your husband by saying something like, "Darling, I really love you and want our sex life to be better for both of us. I realize I've often rejected your approaches. I'm beginning to realize what that's all about. I need your understanding and forgiveness for something I'm about to tell you."

Take care with confession. A soft approach should get your mate's attention. Depending on his reaction, you proceed with your confession: "I've been spending too much time with Jerry after work, and I've been paralyzed by guilt ever since. Whenever we start making love, I feel guilty all over again. It's not you I'm rejecting; it's my deceit and sin."

Such disclosure could pave the way for serious healing. Or it might make things worse. If you think confession will have a destructive effect, talk over this issue with a counselor before saying anything to your spouse. What you want to say may be better left unsaid.

WHEN THERAPY ISN'T A MUST

You're not happy with the way things are going with your spouse. Before making an appointment with a marriage counselor, consider:

This may be a phase. Most marriages go through cycles. At times a couple feels intimate and close, at other times, alienated and lonely. These phases may be due to outside stresses such as illness, aging parents, problems with children, career pressures, or financial crises.

This is due to a life stage. Childbirth, the death of a family member or friend, midlife adjustments, emptying the nest, and menopause drain energy from a marriage. If you're in one of these stages, talk to your spouse about your concerns. You may need patience more than psychology.

Try something else. If both you and your spouse want to improve your marriage, consider some alternatives to therapy. Marriage-enrichment seminars can help you learn better skills in communication, conflict resolution, mutual understanding, and sexuality. Even reading a good book on marriage together can be beneficial.

Wait. If you are pushing for marriage counseling but your spouse thinks it's a waste of time, it probably would be. It would be better for you to seek counseling alone and explore what you need to do to deal with the situation. Later, you and your spouse could go in for counseling.

SIGNS THAT YOU NEED THERAPY

How can you tell when professional help is needed to work

through problems in a marriage? Here are some key indicators:

Intense pain. Many couples come to us as a last resort. They have experienced so much hurt in their relationship that they simply can't take any more pain. For them, the choice is drastic—divorce or professional help.

Unresolved conflict. When a relationship is so severely eroded that a couple no longer is able to resolve conflict, outside help is essential.

Infidelity. When one partner has broken trust in the relationship, both spouses are suffering from significant unmet needs. The disruptive effect of an outside relationship makes work on underlying issues nearly impossible without counseling.

For example, Jane, whose husband, Jack, has just been caught in an affair, is not likely to say, "Darling, how can I be a better wife?" It is equally unlikely that Jack will say, "Honey, I've had a lifelong problem with my maleness. There—I'm glad I settled that!" Counseling can help couples deal with buried issues that are too painful to cope with on their own.

Crippling symptoms. Therapy is needed when tension in a marriage produces disabling secondary effects. A couple may deny their problems, even to each other, but the frustration literally makes them sick. One partner may have severe back pain or debilitating headaches—yet medical tests may reveal no organic cause for the symptoms.

Addictive disorders. Drug or alcohol abuse, eating disorders, explosive abusive behavior, gambling, and sexual perversions require professional counseling. Often the entire family is entangled in these problems. The earlier the intervention, the better the chance for healing.

Deep resentment. While many couples haven't pushed the panic button yet, they are wrestling with growing discomfort or resentment. We hear it expressed in different ways:

"I don't doubt her love for me, but I don't think she likes me."

"We never talk about anything important. If we do, we just end up fighting. He'll just withdraw or leave."

"I can never please him, no matter what I do."

"We don't have fun anymore. It's been a long time since we've laughed."

"Our sex life is dead. If we make love at all, it's just going through the motions."

DECIDE WHAT YOU WANT

Before meeting with someone to discuss your marital problems, decide what you want from this encounter. Here are some scenarios:

You want to vent. If you only want to unload some anger and frustration, say that. A good way to begin: "I've had it with my wife. If I don't let off some steam I may explode. I don't need any solutions, just a safe place to vent! OK?"

You want advice. You're looking for guidance in dealing with a sticky situation. You might lead with, "I'm struggling with some-thing in our sex life. I don't under-stand why it happens, and I don't have anyone else I feel comfortable talking to about it. I'd like your take on this."

You need help. You need more than advice. Your spouse is physi-cally abusive and you're afraid for yourself and your children. You don't want to vent; you need some-one who will help you find safe shel-ter. You need to express this clearly, saying, "My husband is beating me, and the violence is getting worse. I'm afraid I or the kids will be killed. Please help me get away!"

FINDING THE RIGHT THERAPIST

If you decide to get help from a marriage counselor, here are some things to look at before com-mitting to long-term therapy:

Talk about It

If you find yourself withdrawing from each other sexually, talk to each other. Ask each other when you think you stopped enjoy-ing sex and what might have brought that on. Listen carefully to each other's responses. Propose some ways you might improve the situation.

The counselor's track record. Is this person honest, reliable, and reasonably priced? Ask your pastor or doctor for recommendations. Better yet, talk to some couples who have gone through marriage counseling and get their advice.

Your reaction. See if you feel comfortable with a counselor at the first session. If you start out with negative feelings, it may be difficult for you to continue. Don't feel bad about that. Not every therapist clicks with every client. Shop around.

Certification. Some states allow almost anyone to do marriage counseling. Check for credentials granted by a recognized professional organization, such as the American Association of Marriage and Family Counseling, the Association of Pastoral Counselors, the American Psychological Association, or the American Board of Neurology and Psychiatry. That certification tells you the individual has had supervised training. Combine certification with a good reputation and you're on pretty firm footing.

Spiritual commitment. Look for a Christian counselor. However, Christian commitment doesn't guarantee professional competence. The person's reputation and credentials may be as important as his religion.

WHAT TO EXPECT IN COUNSELING

Once you have selected a reliable, fully credentialed counselor, you can expect the following:

Some testing. Personality profiles like the Myers-Briggs or Taylor Johnson can help you better understand yourself and your mate. You'll likely have some "aha" moments as you realize, "So that's why we get on each other's nerves!" Other tests help define your marital expectations or your conflict-resolution styles. These tests give you significant insights into each other and a framework for change.

Communication exercises. A counselor asks you to do exercises to help you learn how to listen to each other. Exercises show you how to become more effective at saying what you mean.

These exercises aren't always fun. A friend recently told me, "If I hear one more word about giving 'I-messages,' I think I'll throw up."

I responded, "I hear your frustration. I feel a deep concern for your hurt and just want to understand you on a deeper level."

Sure enough, she threw up.

Writing exercises. As a counselor identifies problem areas in your marriage, he or she will give you assignments to work on together. Having to do something together coupled with the accountability of reporting is a great help toward mutual understanding and change.

Whatever techniques are used, I must warn you about one relatively short consequence of therapy. As you begin to work on conflicts, hurts, and disappointments in your marriage, you will experience pain. That's because the denial, repression, and rationalization that have helped you deal with anxiety in the past are being removed so you can work on deeply rooted problems. Once the barriers are down, you must face the pain.

Still, you learn. As one man in counseling told us, "I didn't realize how much my wife was hurting or how much pain I was denying. It was hard to face all of that, but I'm glad we went through counseling. I feel close to Joan for the first time in years."

What It Means to Forgive

If anger, hurt, and frustration are keeping you and your spouse apart, you've got to work at forgiveness. Even if the hurt goes way back in your relationship, it must be dealt with. Understand that:

- Forgiveness is an act of will; it is not based on feelings.
- It is a voluntary act on the part of one person, not based on someone else's acknowledgment of wrongdoing or remorse.
- It is a gift, not an attempt to control another person's behavior.
- It does not condone the other person's hurtful acts.
- It is something that God commands to keep us receptive to his grace.
- It frees us from the costly bondage of unforgiveness.

Q & A

WHY DID SHE FAKE IT SO LONG?

During a recent argument, my wife confessed that for the entire time of our marriage she's been faking her orgasms. I still can't believe it—I feel so angry and betrayed. I thought I was doing everything possible for her during sex. Now I don't even want to make love with her because of her deception. She seems so cold. Is there any hope for our sex life?

Louis: A recent survey reported that more than 50 percent of women have problems achieving orgasm, and 10 percent never have had one.* So a wife's faking an orgasm is hardly uncommon.

Think of it—in one sense, your wife chose to give you many exciting nights of sexual pleasure. However, I can understand your disappointment in learning that she fell short of fully enjoying it. That must make you wonder about how adequate a lover you were.

I wonder whether your ego is so fragile that you won't be able to change your focus from your own feelings to your wife's years of frus-tration and distress. If you can make that shift and show genuine concern for her, there may be hope for your sex life.

The second issue is learning to deal more effectively with conflict. Your wife's confession during an argument wasn't fighting fair. She was lashing out in an attempt to hurt you. If you want to work toward a better sex life, you'll have to address other areas of your marriage, such as talking about and working through problems as they happen rather than letting them fester.

Melissa: We're concerned about your wife's inability to reach orgasm. I'm glad you tried to do everything possible to help her; that indicates a willingness to try to please your wife. That said, there are many possible reasons for her problem. Sometimes a woman's inability to achieve orgasm is due to a physiological problem. She should have a gynecologist evaluate that possibility. More commonly, though, a woman fails to reach orgasm because of some aspect of lovemaking such as timing, lubrication, or foreplay. Some adjustments usually are all that are needed to help her reach her full potential.

---

*Archibald D. Hart, Catherine Hart Weber, and Debra Taylor, *Secrets of Eve* (Nashville: W, 1998), 94.

Most often, what holds women back from orgasm is emotional: a history of sexual abuse, unresolved guilt over premarital sexual experiences, fears about losing control as sexual intensity increases, or disappointment in other areas of marriage. She may feel inadequate as a lover, which is only reinforced by her failure to reach orgasm.

I strongly recommend professional counseling, since this has been a long-standing problem. Be patient as you make needed changes. And ask for grace as you deal with your hurts and disappointments. Here's the good news: the better you and your wife get at connecting personally and sexually, the more exciting and fulfilling your marriage will become.

Q & A

WHY DO I HATE SEX?

I absolutely hate sex. Sometimes my body shows signs of arousal, but my mind doesn't follow. I'm much more comfortable with friendship than sex, but I know sex is essential to a healthy marriage. How can I get my mind and body in sync?

If your body can get sexually aroused, your mind can come around. When it does, your sexual relationship will contribute much to marital fulfillment.

We advise you to do some exploring of what may have caused this attitude about sex. There are many developmental problems that can block sexual pleasure. Probably the most common is a negative attitude about sex in your family of origin. Mothers who have had unpleasant experiences with sex often teach their daughters that sex is a necessary evil or an unpleasant duty women must endure.

A slightly different message is that a girl should approach sex with great caution and restraint. That may help a girl keep herself pure before marriage, but if it is carried over into marriage, it can cause real problems. "Good girls don't enjoy sex" is a powerful message.

More destructive is a history of sexual abuse. The memories of that trauma are often repressed and unconscious, but they have lasting impact on the emotional response to sexual intimacy. Avoiding the emotional pain that's been repressed requires the kind of resistance that effectively shuts down sexual intimacy.

We recommend counseling to explore your feelings about sex.

The effort necessary to pursue the solution can be richly rewarded as your mind and body become fully engaged.

SIX THINGS THERAPY TEACHES

We'd like to let you in on key goals of successful therapy. These are keys not just to therapy but to satisfying sex, marriage, and life in general. They're not complicated, but they are very hard to keep in focus. Whenever our sex or marriage hits the skids, we soon realize we've been overlooking one of these principles:

The importance of trust. Since we're imperfect, we often hurt and disappoint each other. Sometimes we fail each other in relatively insignificant things, like forgetting to pick up milk at the supermarket before driving twenty miles home. Sometimes we commit major offenses, such as infidelity. Rebuilding trust takes lots of work from both partners in a marriage.

Trust is essential for sexual play. Getting naked with each other makes us feel vulnerable. If we can't trust each other to be thoughtful, gentle, kind, and playful, sex is too risky. So confess your fears about trusting each other. Remember that you honor God by enjoying each other sexually.

The need to forgive. In a perfect world, grace and forgiveness wouldn't be necessary. But in our imperfect world, partners in the best marriages hurt each other. The choice, then, is for the injured partner to react with bitterness—or forgiveness.

Bitterness slams the door on sexual intimacy. Many couples have told us how something hurtful has shut down their sexual openness. Dealing with the problem rather than ignoring the problem finally released them to approach each other again. Forgiveness may have been difficult, but the intimacy that followed was worth the discomfort.

For us what works best is acknowledging what we've done wrong and verbally asking for forgiveness. A reluctant "sorry" isn't enough; what's necessary is to actually say, "I was wrong. Please forgive me."

The response is critical as well. What won't cut it is a flimsy "Oh, no problem. It's OK." Instead, what's needed is a definite "I forgive you." That kind of exchange can begin the process of releasing blame and the rehearsal of painful memories.

The need to relax. Finding a quiet place for conflict resolution may be tough in a chaotic world, but begin by eliminating needless interruptions. Turn off the television, unplug the telephone, and log off the computer. If you can't shut off the noise at home, go to a park, take a ride in the country, or go for a long walk. Leave the cell phone off.

Get rid of distractions in your mind, too. If you've brought along anxieties from work or home, admit that. Decide to work on those problems later.

Now affirm each other. Tell each other how happy you are to be together. Gently touch each other—hand-holding or a hug or a gentle massage of the neck or back is helpful for easing away tension. Once you've learned to relax together, greater intimacy will follow.

The key to listening. Attentive listening is hard work. More common is persuasive or directive listening. Both of these come with an agenda to control dialogue. Neither is genuinely focused on understanding what the other person says.

Each person has strong, compelling desires. You each are so focused on getting your needs met that you fail to listen to what your spouse wants. If neither listens to the other, both of you will be frustrated. Each of you must switch from self-focus to what the other is saying.

The importance of real talk. Real communication can do wonders. What can be most satisfying is expressing individual likes, feelings, and ideas in first-person terms. For example, you might say, "I feel sort of scattered right now. I'd like to just talk awhile before we start getting sexy." Or you might say, "I think you want to make love. Am I right?" This works better than using "you" statements that put the other person on the defensive, such as: "All you ever think about is sex! Can't you ever just talk to me like a normal human being?"

The need to laugh. Sex is pretty funny. The idea of two people getting naked, sweating, hyperventilating, and moving all over the place as they get themselves connected is quite a picture. When sex becomes a command performance, however, lightheartedness goes right out the window. It's much too serious when your sense of worth gets into the act. Lighten up and enjoy each other.

DO YOU NEED A SEX THERAPIST?

If sex therapy seems to be what you need to get your marriage back on track, look for a person who has training in that area. There are several certifying groups you can look for in identifying a sex therapist:

∞ American Association of Sex Educators, Counselors, and Therapists
∞ American Board of Sexology
∞ American Academy of Clinical Sexologists
∞ American Association of Marriage and Family Therapists

After investigating a counselor's credentials and reputation, meet with that person. If you don't feel comfortable in a face-to-face interview, look elsewhere. You will be working with this person on very intimate stuff. Don't make it harder by starting with someone who seems threatening or lacks self-confidence.

Ask specific questions about counseling, such as: How often will we meet? Will we have individual as well as couple time with you? What, exactly, will we do in these sessions? What is the cost?

Check the therapist's method. We recommend a man-woman team for sex therapy. They will

"If she's not the woman you married, what is she doing here?"

work with you individually and together. The treatment program begins with a thorough assessment of your current problems as well as sexual histories. This allows the team to design a program for you.

The team meets with you on a regular basis. The therapists help you with relationship issues such as trust, forgiveness, listening, and communicating. They'll also offer help with specific sexual problems.

Q & A

WHY CAN'T I TALK TO A COUNSELOR ABOUT OUR SEXUAL PROBLEMS?

My husband and I have had problems with sex for several years, yet he refuses to see a counselor. He says our problems are our own business and no one else's. Can talking about sex to a counselor cause problems?

Melissa and I recently gave a talk about sex to a group of young moms. We were totally unprepared for their unashamed self-disclosures and frank questions. They openly talked about orgasms, their husbands' erectile failures, and oral sex. Neither Melissa nor I have ever found that kind of openness in a group of men.

Men are threatened by such confidences because males are supposed to have an incredibly high sex drive and the natural ability to perform great sexual magic. A guy lives with the pressure to perform, and the idea that others may be discussing the truth about his sexual shortcomings is unsettling. Similarly, a woman might be uneasy at the thought of her husband telling his buddies about the way she performs in bed.

You and your husband should set some ground rules for sharing details about your private sex life. You should also decide what to do about your sex problems. He may agree to your seeing a counselor outside your circle of friends and acquaintances. In time, he might also go himself.

22

ULTIMATE SEX:

The Essence of Love That Lasts

Do you dream of a marriage that overflows with romantic words, adoring private glances, and erotic caresses? We hope you do, because that's what this book is all about. We've tried to help you take off the fig leaves of shame and fear that so often inhibit satisfying sex. We've done that by:

❧ examining the amazing way your body is created;

❧ exploring how your ideas and feelings about yourself as a sexual being came to be;

❧ exposing things that can block your sexual fulfillment;

❧ explaining some ways to overcome those barriers so you can begin experiencing sexual fulfillment; and

❧ equipping you with practical tools for maintaining the thrill of sex for a lifetime.

Melissa and I are incurably romantic. Give us love songs, moonlight, flowers, and candlelit dinners whenever possible. You may prefer a walk on the beach, a shopping spree, or a backpacking trip in the Klondike. Whatever you love doing together will do. We encourage you to include seduction as a regular part of your marriage.

We can't imagine why any couple would ever give up that fiery fun. Yet we're well aware of how the chemistry that swept us into passionate embrace can dissolve. A bond based on chemistry must be sustained by something deeper. Let's review some of the things that first attracted you to each other, then how your relationship can be strengthened with more lasting attractions.

LOVE AT FIRST SIGHT: WHAT'S GOING ON?

Have you ever wondered what you and your spouse first saw in each other? Chances are some unconscious factors were at work. A guy will marry a girl who looks a lot like his mom, and a girl will marry a boy who acts like her dad. The attraction may be based on positive qualities, but it may also include some negative but familiar ones such as control, emotional distance, or even abuse.

Whatever they are, those attributes are familiar and comfortable to you. You experienced them in your childhood, and you unconsciously want to keep them going in your marriage.

Here are some obvious elements of the chemistry that first attracts us to one another:

Physical appearance. This is usually a number one priority for a man or woman.

Personality traits. Do you like someone who is outgoing or quiet? Philosophical or a prankster?

Economic status. How about that car? Those clothes? Career prospects? Did your folks have money? Or are you both above all that?

Cultural background. Do you both come from the same kind of families—or are they so different that wooing each other is a challenge?

Social network. Did you meet his musician friends, her running partners? Do you feel at ease with her family's ski trips, his family's political aspirations?

Intellect. Do you hang out in bookstores, dissect movies, discuss football?

Education. Were you both working on graduate degrees when you met? Were you impressed that she was in culinary school, that he was a master electrician?

Spiritual commitment. She gave her life to the Lord when she was a teen and has been active in youth work ever since. He is studying to be a pastor.

Availability. Are you unattached and looking? Or are you so happy being single that you're a challenge to win?

Some not-so-obvious attributes might include:

Voice tone. Is that mellow baritone irresistible? What about her chirpy brightness?

Mannerisms. Is she confident and commanding? Is he quiet and patient?

Body type. Is he built like a football player or a dancer? Is she curvy or lean?

Dependence. Is she independent or needy? Does he lead or support her leadership?

Hair color. Do you prefer blonde, red, or beautifully bald?

Eyes. Color is important, sure, but how about expressiveness, sparkle, intensity? Do glasses add to the mystique?

Personal space. Do you refuel in quiet isolation? Or do you get energized in a roomful of friends? Do you like a lot of touching, or do you prefer physical space?

A MORE LASTING ATTRACTION

If your hopes for lasting romance are pinned on luscious looks, emotional highs, or financial hopes, hang on! You can fall out of love as quickly as you fell in. Build a more solid foundation for your marriage. Good sex must be fortified with other essentials of love. The description of love that the apostle Paul gives in 1 Corinthians 13 is a great place to start.

Let's discuss some characteristics of a lasting attraction based on three attributes of love: mutual submission, trust, and grace.

MUTUAL SUBMISSION

Couples in the most effective marriages consider each other equal partners. This is reflected in such dynamics as mutual respect, caring, and submission.

Respect involves more than allowing each other personal space. It also builds up the other person's worth. Many couples who come to us in crisis say they hurt because a spouse doesn't value them. Their sense of self-respect is next to nothing. Instead of supporting each other, each partner feels deprived and becomes centered on personal wants, rights, pleasures, and preferences. At times one may value a person outside the relationship more than the spouse.

Couples draw together as each spouse becomes aware of the needs of the other and makes efforts to meet them. For that to happen, each must keep the other informed about what those needs are. Guessing is risky and often wrong.

Mutual care and consideration also affect sexual intimacy. A wife's need for orgasmic release becomes as important as her husband's, since it requires each partner to grow in the skills of lovemaking. When both husband and wife are sexually fulfilled, both will enjoy and respect each other more.

Another facet of mutuality is submission. This is not subjugation, in which submission is gained by demand or force. Rather, each partner willingly gives up power to the other. In the bedroom, mutual submission is being willing to wait for your spouse's readiness to make love. It's openness to your spouse's preferences for foreplay. It's sensitivity to the signs of arousal. And it's willingness to take turns getting to orgasm.

TRUST

Trust is a critical component of a marriage that lasts. Yet today trust has been severely compromised by a me-first attitude. Trust in a marriage grows as spouses look out for each other, demonstrate a protective and caring attitude, and make each other feel safe.

Trust within marriage involves everything from paying bills to keeping something confidential to staying loyal to each other. In sexual relations, trust is critical because there's so much risk taking. Getting naked can be uncomfortable, especially if you've put on a few extra pounds or have lost a bit of firmness in erection. Vulnerability can become paralyzing if trust is compromised.

GRACE

Grace is necessary between a husband and wife in a fallen world. If we don't learn to cut others—including our spouse—some slack, we'll never find true intimacy. While we're at it, consider extending grace toward yourself. It's hard to be a channel of grace to your mate if you don't find it first in your own heart.

The alternative to grace is condemning others for the wrongs they have done. The hurts they have created are heavy to bear, but they're nothing compared to the weight of unforgiveness. The bitterness of unforgiveness can break you.

AN EXERCISE TO UNLOAD BITTERNESS

One way to unload bitterness is to work on a timeline with your spouse. Each of you should first take a sheet of paper and make headings for three columns titled:

"Dates I Was Hurt by You," "What Hurt Me," and "My Reaction to the Event." See an example for what you might write at the bottom of this page.

After each of you has finished your timeline, take turns reading them aloud to each other. The goal of this exercise is not to determine who is right or who has been most wronged. It is to hear both of your perceptions of and responses to what you did together.

When you listen to and accept each other's feelings about what happened, you should have a deeper understanding of each other. You can then proceed in grace to forgive each other.

In conducting this assignment, we have been astonished at the misunderstandings that couples have carried through the years. They have interpreted certain events as malicious or purposeful hurts given to them by their mates—without ever once checking it out with the offenders. By the time they did get around to discussing the matter, their mates often couldn't even remember the event that caused the hurt, much less understand why it was held against them so many years.

Unloading such garbage can be a great relief. So can having the grace to forgive. It will free you from the stranglehold of bitterness and do wonders for your sex life.

Dates I Was Hurt by You	What Hurt Me	My Reaction to the Event
May 1986: Senior prom	You danced with your old boyfriend.	I felt rejected.
August 1990: Honeymoon	You only wanted sex and forgot my birthday.	I felt like an object.
December 1995: Christmas	I upgraded your diamond. You said I spent too much money.	I felt foolish— and totally rejected.

HOW CAN I POSSIBLY FORGIVE?

Forgiveness and grace are costly. For God, forgiving us meant losing his one and only Son. For us, forgiveness means giving up pride, a sense of entitlement, and a sense of safety. As the Lord's Prayer reminds us, we must "forgive our debtors."

As you review some of the hurts your spouse has caused you, look at some reasons why you may be holding on to unforgiveness:

Pride. You are right in feeling indignant if your spouse has hurt you. Still, that may be pride talking. I know this is true of me. I don't like being told I'm wrong. I also don't like others interpreting something I do as immature, mistaken, or downright mean. That resistance helps me maintain the myth of my moral superiority. From that lofty position, bestowing forgiveness is not easy.

Power. Hanging on to your wounds gives you leverage against the perpetrator. Your occasional reminders of the misdemeanor keep your spouse in line—or at least feeling guilty. You think that if you forgive the offense, you will somehow condone the misbehavior.

The whole idea of letting someone off the hook may appear stupid, but think for a minute about the alternative. What sort of relationship is possible if one person keeps the other dangling?

STEPS TO FORGIVENESS

Forgiveness is a choice. It involves the following steps:

Letting go. All of our experiences are recorded in our brain cells and can be retrieved at will. Each time a tape is played, it becomes more powerful. So if you choose to constantly replay a memory of the time you were hurt, the pain will only get worse. When you choose not to replay that tape, it will become less distinct and harder to retrieve. It's like memorizing lines for a play. When you're done with the role, the part begins to fade. If you choose to read the script again, the lines will come back. Let go of the hurt as well as the offense that caused it and choose not to replay it.

Not waiting until you feel like it. One summer during college, I sold books door-to-door. I rang one doorbell, even though the house looked vacant. To my surprise, a middle-aged woman opened the door. Beyond her, I could see a dozen cats in a dark room. She invited me in and began spilling a tale of woe. Her husband had deserted her for another woman fifteen years before. She poured out her anger and hurt as though he'd abandoned her the week before.

I didn't sell her a book, but I did escape with the distinct impression that holding on to anger was no way to live.

Not waiting for the other person to change. It's great if the person who hurt you is repentant and begs your forgiveness, but that may not happen. So, rather than being held hostage by that person's failure to respond, remember that God forgave you even when you were in rebellion. Jesus said from the cross, "Father, forgive them, for they do not know what they are doing" (Luke 23:34).

Seeing forgiveness as a process. Scripture says that God "remembers your sins no more" (Isaiah 43:25). Likewise, you may have to recall over and over again your decision to forgive. It may take you countless times—seventy times seven—to get it right.

SHOWING GRACE IN FORGIVENESS

There may be times that you and your spouse don't seem to be in sync. He rushes things. You are distracted and slow to respond. So cut each other some slack. Remember, your relationship is a work in progress. Extend a little grace for your future's sake.

Try a little grace, too, when you're in the mood for love and your mate fails to pick up on the cues. A simple kiss or hug doesn't

Talk about It

⌒

If something happened to one of you, what would the other most miss? Talk about ways that each of you have grown to appreciate each other. What kinds of issues have you each learned to ease off on? Where has it improved your relationship and where not? In what ways have you each learned to show grace to each other?

always have to lead to intercourse. View this time as an opportunity for showing love rather than making an unwelcome demand.

Grace is necessary as we age. You may not have noticed it yet, but one day you'll realize you're living with an old person. Her hair is white; his is almost gone. She goes up the stairs with pain; he isn't quite so eager in bed. Through eyes of grace, we can see beauty beyond exterior signs.

SEX: THE JOURNEY KEEPS GETTING BETTER

Sexual intimacy is a unique event that best symbolizes the Creator's intent for you and your mate to become one flesh. When you join your bodies in intercourse, you are celebrating God's love. The journey to orgasm is along that scenic route.

We enjoy sex every time. Sometimes we sprint through it, but usually we take our time so we don't miss a single thrilling moment. Planning the venture is a lot of fun. We make a date with each other, then look forward to it. We might plan a blanket party in the moun-

tains or search the Web for a romantic country inn. Returning to a site where we formerly made love awakens erotic memories and gets things ready for a rerun.

At other times, we're swept into spontaneous lovemaking. A special glance or touch sets us off. Since we know each other's love language, we surge right up the arousal curve.

Sex may be frantic if the trip is going fast, but it's also fun to meander along. A peck and a stolen caress offer a taste of the delights to come. Along the way, we leave a trail of shoes, socks, shirts, and other articles of clothing. We settle into naked intimacy and intense sensual experience. From head to toe, we awaken each other's body until we reach climax.

Then we're totally exhausted. We put our arms around each other and relax. Later, we tell each other how much we love the loving. We playfully ask when we can do this again.

In the beginning, God created us male and female. He said it was very good. And it is.

Recommended Reading List

Arterburn, Stephen, and Fred Stoeker, with Mike Yorkey. *Every Man's Battle*. Colorado Springs: WaterBrook, 2000.

Butler, Robert N., and Myrna I. Lewis. *The New Love and Sex After Sixty*. New York: Ballantine, 2002.

Carder, Dave, with Duncan Jaenicke. *Torn Asunder*. Chicago: Northfield, 1999.

Carnes, Patrick. *Don't Call It Love*. New York: Bantam Doubleday Dell, 1991.

Chapman, Gary. *The Five Love Languages*. Chicago: Northfield, 1992.

Cutrer, William, and Sandra Glahn. *The Contraception Guidebook: Options, Risks, and Answers for Christian Couples*. Grand Rapids, Zondervan, 2005.

Evans, Jimmy, and Tom Lane. *Escaping the Porn Trap*. Chesterfield, Mich.: Majestic Media, 1999.

Fisher, Roger, William Ury, and Bruce Patton, eds. *Getting to Yes*. New York: Penguin, 1991.

Hall, Laurie Sharlene. *An Affair of the Mind*. Colorado Springs: Focus on the Family, 1998.

Hart, Archibald D. *The Sexual Man*. Waco, Tex.: Word, 1994.

Hart, Archibald D., Catherine Hart Weber, and Debra Taylor. *Secrets of Eve*. Nashville: W, 1998.

Laaser, Mark R. *Healing the Wounds of Sexual Addiction.* Grand Rapids: Zondervan, 2004.

Laaser, Mark, and Ralph Earle. *The Pornography Trap.* Kansas City: Beacon Hill Press, 2002.

Mason, Michael. *The Mystery of Marriage.* Sisters, Ore.: Multnomah, 2001.

McGee, Dan and Sandra. *Celebrating Sex in Your Marriage.* Nashville: Family Touch, 1993.

McIlhaney, Joe S. Jr. *Sexuality and STDs.* Grand Rapids: Baker, 1990.

McIlhaney, Joe S. Jr. with Susan Netherly. *1250 Health-Care Questions Women Ask.* Grand Rapids: Baker, 1985.

Miller, Sherod, Daniel Wackman, Elam Nunnally, and Phyllis Miller. *Connecting with Self and Others.* Evergreen, Colo.: Interpersonal Communication, 1992.

Nicolosi, Joseph. *Healing Homosexuality.* Northvale, N.J.: Jason Aronson, 1997.

Penner, Clifford and Joyce. *The Gift of Sex.* Waco, Tex.: Word, 1981.

Satinover, Jeffrey. *Homosexuality and the Politics of Truth.* Grand Rapids: Baker, 1996.

Schaumberg, Harry. *False Intimacy.* Colorado Springs: NavPress, 1996.

Swenson, Richard A. *Margin: The Overload Syndrome.* Colorado Springs: NavPress, 2002.

Thomson PDR Staff. *Physicians' Desk Reference.* Montvale, N.J.: Thomson Healthcare, 2004.

Warren, Neil Clark. *The Triumphant Marriage.* Colorado Springs: Focus on the Family, 1998.

Wheat, Ed and Gaye. *Intended for Pleasure.* Old Tappan, N.J.: Revell, 1981.

Wright, H. Norman. *What Men Want.* Ventura, Calif.: Regal, 1997.

INDEX

Iarriage the Way God Intended

Imagine having a resource that continually strengthens your marriage and centers it on God. *Marriage Partnership* does that with biblically-based counsel and relevant stories that take your relationship with your spouse to the next level.

With *Marriage Partnership*, you and your spouse can actively seek the marriage that God intends for you—a marriage focused on shared faith, lifelong commitment, sacrificial love, and mutual respect.

Don't miss this special opportunity to get a risk-free issue of *Marriage Partnership*! Call **1-800-627-4942** and mention offer code E4FRS4 or visit: **ChristianityToday.com/go/mpmag_ad**.

Where Do You Want to Grow?

If you love to learn and grow in your faith, you'll love *Christian-BibleStudies.com*. Dozens of downloadable Bible studies are available—just choose the Bible studies that fit your current interests, download them, and use them for your devotion time or in your small group or Sunday school class.

- Develop a **healthier marriage**.
- Gain a **better relationship** with your kids.
- Understand **current issues** and learn how to respond.
- Interact biblically with **pop culture**.
- Study **Christian history**.
- Grow toward **spiritual maturity**.

Do all of this and more with:

ChristianBibleStudies.com

> *A breakthrough discovery in communication*
> *for transforming love relationships.*

Love Talk
Speak Each Other's Language Like You Never Have Before

Drs. Les and Leslie Parrott

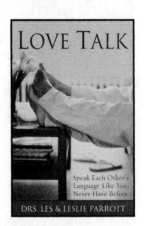

Over and over couples consistently name "improved communication" as the greatest need in their relationships. *Love Talk*—by acclaimed relationship experts Drs. Les and Leslie Parrott-is a deep yet simple plan, full of new insights that will revolutionize communication in love relationships.

The first steps to improving this single most important factor in any marriage or love relationship are to identify your fear factors and determine your personal communication styles, and then learn how the two of you can best interact. In this no-nonsense book, "psychobabble" is translated into easy-to-understand language that clearly teaches you what you need to do—and not do—to speak each other's language like you never have before.

Love Talk includes:
- The Love Talk Indicator, a free personalized online assessment (a $19.95 value) to help you determine your unique talk style
- The secret to emotional connection
- Charts and sample conversations
- The most important conversation you'll ever have
- A short course on Communication 101
- An appendix on practical help for the "silent partner"

Two softcover "his and hers" workbooks are full of lively exercises and enlightening self-tests that help couples apply what they are learning about communication directly to their relationships.

Hardcover: 0-310-24596-6
Abridged Audio Pages® CD: 0-310-26214-3
Workbook for Men: 0-310-26212-7
Workbook for Women: 0-310-26213-5

The Contraception Guidebook
Options, Risks, and Answers for Christian Couples

Available May 2005

William Cutrer, M.D.,
and Sandra Glahn, Th.M.

When it comes to birth control and family planning, how do Christian couples sort through the newest and not-so-new options, the medical implications, and the ethical and moral considerations to make wise, God-honoring decisions that are right for them?

This comprehensive guide, with its conversational, first-person style, anecdotes from real-life couples, and solid medical information, equips Christian couples to make fully informed decisions about the deeply personal questions of family planning.

For those couples who elect to use birth control, the book will educate about available methods—cutting-edge research, success rates, risks, moral and ethical issues—and provide guidance into which methods can be used without violating the sanctity of human life. Using key biblical passages, the authors reveal how the Bible can guide us by giving solid underlying principles.

This book is a thorough, engagingly written handbook ideal for every Christian couple as they consider their many options for family planning.

Softcover: 0-310-25407-8

Pick up a copy today at your favorite bookstore!

ZONDERVAN™

GRAND RAPIDS, MICHIGAN 49530 USA
WWW.ZONDERVAN.COM

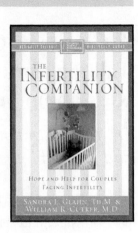

The Infertility Companion
Hope and Help for Couples Facing Infertility

Sandra L. Glahn, Th.M., and William R. Cutrer, M.D.

Infertility changes everything, shattering dreams and breaking hearts. But hope is available—today more than ever. *The Infertility Companion* draws on the Bible and on current medical knowledge, including the latest research, to shed light on such questions as:

- Can people of faith ethically use high-tech infertility treatments?
- How do we make moral, biblical decisions about medical treatment, third-party reproduction, stem cell research, and embryo adoption?
- Is God punishing me?
- Does God even care?
- Will adoption increase our chances of getting pregnant?
- How can we reduce the stress of infertility on our marriage relationship?
- How can we keep sex from becoming a chore?

These theologically trained authors have taught at a variety of conferences on infertility, pregnancy loss, and adoption, and they have helped thousands of couples to face the future through their message of encouragement.

The Infertility Companion includes discussion questions and a workbook suitable for individuals, couples, or small groups. Full of practical tips and true stories, this book will guide couples past the ethical pitfalls of assisted reproductive technologies as they travel the difficult road ahead.

Softcover: 0-310-24961-9

Pick up a copy today at your favorite bookstore!

ZONDERVAN™

GRAND RAPIDS, MICHIGAN 49530 USA

WWW.ZONDERVAN.COM

A Chicken's Guide to Talking Turkey with Your Kids about Sex

Dr. Kevin Leman
and Kathy Flores Bell

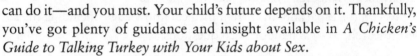

As difficult as talking with your child about sex, peer pressure, and self-image may seem, you can do it—and you must. Your child's future depends on it. Thankfully, you've got plenty of guidance and insight available in *A Chicken's Guide to Talking Turkey with Your Kids about Sex*.

Family psychologist Dr. Kevin Leman and sexuality educator Kathy Flores Bell guide you safely along the sometimes rocky road of pubescence as your child heads toward adolescence. This practical and engaging book covers his or her development not just from the waist down but also from the neck up, where the important decisions about sex are made.

Leman and Bell take you beyond sex education and frank conversations to cultivating a relationship with your child. You'll create the trust, support, and security he or she needs, and in turn you'll gain a credible voice on such intimate topics as what sexual intercourse is and why to abstain from sex until marriage.

You'll find here the tools you need to help your kids not only understand their growing bodies but also cope with the temptations and social pressures that go with them.

Hardcover: 0-310-25096-X

Abridged Audio Pages® CD: 0-310-25865-1

Pick up a copy today at your favorite bookstore!

ZONDERVAN™

GRAND RAPIDS, MICHIGAN 49530 USA

WWW.ZONDERVAN.COM

We want to hear from you. Please send your comments about this book to us in care of zreview@zondervan.com. Thank you.

GRAND RAPIDS, MICHIGAN 49530 USA

WWW.ZONDERVAN.COM